Race, Housing & Community

Race, Housing & Community

Perspectives on Policy & Practice

Harris Beider

Professor in Community Cohesion
Coventry University

 **WILEY-BLACKWELL**

A John Wiley & Sons, Ltd., Publication

This edition first published 2012
© 2012 Harris Beider

Blackwell Publishing was acquired by John Wiley & Sons in February 2007. Blackwell's publishing programme has been merged with Wiley's global Scientific, Technical, and Medical business to form Wiley-Blackwell.

Registered Office
John Wiley & Sons, Ltd, The Atrium, Southern Gate, Chichester, West Sussex, PO19 8SQ, UK

Editorial Offices
9600 Garsington Road, Oxford, OX4 2DQ, UK
The Atrium, Southern Gate, Chichester, West Sussex, PO19 8SQ, UK
2121 State Avenue, Ames, Iowa 50014-8300, USA

For details of our global editorial offices, for customer services and for information about how to apply for permission to reuse the copyright material in this book please see our website at www.wiley.com/wiley-blackwell.

The right of the author to be identified as the author of this work has been asserted in accordance with the UK Copyright, Designs and Patents Act 1988.

Library of Congress Cataloging-in-Publication Data

Beider, Harris.
Race, Housing & Community: Perspectives on Policy & Practice / Harris Beider.
    p.   cm. – (Real estate issues)
  Includes bibliographical references and index.
  ISBN 978-1-4051-9696-3
1. Housing policy–Great Britain.   2. Community development–Great Britain.   3. Race discrimination–Great Britain.   4. Racism–Great Britain.   I. Title.   II. Title: Housing, 'race' and community cohesion.
  HD7333.A3.B435 2012
  305.800941–dc23
                                           2011035189

A catalogue record for this book is available from the British Library.

Wiley also publishes its books in a variety of electronic formats. Some content that appears in print may not be available in electronic books.

Set in 10/13pt Trump Mediaeval by SPi Publisher Services, Pondicherry, India
Printed and bound in Malaysia by Vivar Printing Sdn Bhd

1   2012

Dedicated, with unconditional love, to
Jemima, Alys, Jess and Thom

Contents

Glossary

BME housing associations

Black and minority ethnic housing associations are defined as those that have 80% or more of their board or management committee drawn from black and minority ethnic communities. Black and minority ethnic housing associations were established from the 1970s onwards to meet the specific housing needs of black and minority ethnic communities. The Housing Corporation sponsored the development of BME housing associations in various policies commencing in 1986 with a view to meeting housing needs but also developing black and minority leadership and capacity in the housing sector. However, recent policy interventions and focus on financial viability has reduced the number of BME housing associations from a peak of over 50 during the 1990s and the future is uncertain.

CIH

The Chartered Institute of Housing is the professional body for people who work in the housing sector in the UK and was founded in 1938 as the Institute of Housing but changed its name in 1994 after receiving a Royal Charter. More than 19 000 people are members of the CIH. Each year the CIH organises its Annual Conference and Exhibition, which is the largest housing event in Europe.

CRE

The Commission for Racial Equality is a national organisation that works in 'both the public and private sectors to encourage fair treatment and to promote equal opportunities for everyone, regardless of their race, colour, nationality, or national or ethnic origin'. It has statutory powers under the 1976 Race Relations Act which include helping people who have suffered discrimination, harassment and abuse; conducting formal investigations into organisations who may be operating in a discriminatory way and oblige them to change; taking action against organisations or adverts that are discriminatory and helping individuals with judicial review action against the decisions by public funded organisations such as local authorities. In 2007 a new Commission for Equalities and Human Rights will be established to provide a single point of access for equalities matters. For the time being, the CRE has decided that it will not be part of this new body believing that amongst other issues that race equality will be diluted.

Council housing

Council housing was built and managed by local authorities in the UK during the twentieth century to meet the needs of local people. After the World War II there was a major boom in council housing given that one out every three houses was destroyed. In addition, slum clearance in cities was a key policy priority. Many developments during this period were characterised by generous standards of space and layout together with gardens and inside toilets. Council housing from the 1960s became increasingly characterised by high-rise tower blocks that were deemed to provide better housing density. The rise of homeownership, and especially the introduction of Right to Buy in the 1980 Housing Act (see below) by the Conservative Government, together with design faults and reduced investment led to sharp reductions in popularity and tenure. Council housing became associated with poor quality standards inhabited by poor households. The housing stock transfer programme provides an opportunity for councils to attract inward investment into council housing through establishing different types of management arrangement. Both Labour and Conservative governments have encouraged this.

Housing associations

Housing associations (sometimes referred to as registered social landlords) are the main providers of new and affordable homes to rent and buy in England. They operate on a not-for-profit basis and any surplus generated is invested into housing management and maintenance and helping to finance new housing developments. There are over 1500 housing associations in England managing over two million dwellings and housing over four million people. Some housing associations were first established over 100 years ago but many were founded in the 1960s and 1970s. The Housing Corporation is the regulatory agency that supports, provides investment and measures performance of housing associations.

Macpherson Report

The Macpherson Report is sometimes known as the Lawrence Report and was published in 1999. Chaired by Judge William Macpherson it was the culmination of an inquiry into the unlawful and racist killing of Stephen Lawrence in South London. The Report was important because it highlighted the institutional racism in the failure of the

Metropolitan Police in successfully complete their investigation leading
to the non-conviction of the alleged perpetrators. The Macpherson
Report was hugely influential in establishing a framework for race
equality in the UK.

NASS

The National Asylum Support Service is the government agency that
has responsibility for people who are seeking asylum in the UK.
Limited support is provided with accommodation and other areas
of support. Importantly, once a decision has been made on status,
people that have been seeking asylum have only 28 days to leave NASS
supported accommodation which may increase the risk of
homelessness.

NHF

The National Housing Federation is the trade body for 1400 independent
and not-for-profit housing associations in England. It promotes the needs
of members to government and other key agencies, influences the public
policy agenda on housing and supports its members through briefings,
conferences and workshops.

Right to Buy

The 1980 Housing Act first introduced the Right to Buy Scheme. It
enables local authority tenants with at least two years tenancy to buy
their homes at below market rates. More than 1.6 million tenants have
exercised their Right to Buy since 1980. For some the policy has helped
to create mixed income and mixed tenure neighbourhoods but others
suggest that it has also increased polarisation and led to further erosion
of council housing stock.

The Housing Corporation

The Housing Corporation is the government agency that funds new
affordable housing and regulates housing associations across England.
This is achieved by investment through the approved development
programme to housing associations, being the statutory regulator for
housing associations and helping to influence housing policy nationally,
regionally and locally.

Homes and Communities Agency
The HCA is the national housing and regeneration agency for England that is charged by government to increase economic growth, supporting communities and delivering affordable housing.

7/7
This refers to the series of planned attacks on London's transport system on the 7 July 2005. Fifty six people were killed including the four bombers and more than 700 people injured.

ODPM
This is the Office of the Deputy Prime Minister which was established in 2001. It was replaced by its successor The Department for Communities and Local Government in 2006. As a government department ODPM was responsible for communities and local government.

CIC
The Commission for Integration and Cohesion was launched by the Labour government in 2006 in the aftermath of 7/7. Its remit was to look at how local areas can manage the challenges of increased diversity in the UK. The CIC final report 'Our Shared Future' was published in 2007.

Equality and Human Rights Commission (EHRC)
The EHRC was established came into being in 2007. It promotes and enforces equality and anti-discrimination laws in the UK.

FBHO
The Federation of Black Housing Organisations was the national race and housing charity which supported the work of black and minority ethnic housing associations through lobbying, research and training.

CRE
The Commission for Racial Equality was the national non-governmental agency charged with promoting race equality and addressing racial discrimination. It emerged in 1976 and was merged into the EHRC in 2007.

Connecting Communities

The Connecting Communities initiative was a £12million programme launched by the Labour government in 2009. It was designed to promote cohesion, address deprivation and increase empowerment in deprived communities.

A8 Migrants

The A8 are the eight countries in Eastern Europe who joined the European Union in May 2004. Migrants from these countries had the right to work and travel to the UK.

SUS

The sus law (suspicious person) was name given to the stop, search and arrest powers given to the police by the 1824 Vagrancy Act. Some have viewed this as a way of racial profiling and harassment of minority communities.

ASBO

The Anti-Social Behaviour Order was introduced by the Labour government in 1998. It is a civil order designed to address anti-social behaviour and has been associated in the main with young people.

Acknowledgements

I would like to thank my colleagues and friends at former and current places for their help and support in writing this book. My perspectives have been sharpened by debates in the worlds of policy, practice and academia.

In particular, I would like to thank and acknowledge the Joseph Rowntree Foundation and Birmingham City Council for supporting research on difficult and sensitive topics that have helped shape some of the chapters in this book.

This book would not have been possible without the help of my friend Arlene Conn in the United States. Her encouragement, generosity and spirit of challenge cannot be repaid by any act on my part. I would simply like to place as permanent record my deep appreciation for Arlene's many skills and moral fortitude.

My family are my constant in life in so many ways. Your support, love and challenge constantly inspires me to become a better husband, father and academic.

Sarah: any words on my part are really academic but I could not wish for a better person to share ideas and life.

Jemima, Alys, Jess and Thom: your very being makes me proud to be your father.

1

Race, Housing and Community

Introduction

This book seeks to critically analyse the story of race, housing and community cohesion. They have different meanings for different audiences. This is not surprising since race, housing and community cohesion do not especially lend themselves to a sterile analysis. The problem with these debates is that there is very little end product resulting from the critique of race and community cohesion.

Some have argued that community cohesion should be regarded as the antithesis of multiculturalism. As we will see in more detail later in this chapter, community cohesion is sometimes viewed as bleaching race from public policy debates and replacing it with a much more insipid fluid. There is a level of concurrence with this perspective. However, community cohesion should not be regarded as neutral. Rather the opposite. It is a highly ideological response to race during a remarkable and politicised period in our history. The concept has been influential in public policy debates in shaping the direction, content and trajectory of travel.

Race, Housing & Community: Perspectives on Policy & Practice, First Edition. Harris Beider.
© 2012 Harris Beider. Published 2012 by Blackwell Publishing Ltd.

Housing has been a key metaphor for race and community cohesion. Indeed, housing publications have illuminated the discourse on race and more latterly, community cohesion. Policy analysts have generated research, guidance and impact measures on race and community cohesion. Practitioners need to utilise academic research and policy guidance in making sense of conflict for public resources between and within communities.

So much for the reduced significance of race and community cohesion in recent years. There has never been a prescient time to discuss these concepts in relation to housing. The book provides an interpretation of housing, race and community cohesion in a highly politicised and fluid policy context. It is designed to initiate discussion and debate. This should not be esoteric and limited to a group of academics. Rather, the objective is to bridge academic and policy audiences in the hope that this fusion provides a basis for a new agenda to discuss these topics.

This first chapter will place the book in context. We will assess how academic contributions to race and housing reflected national policy imperatives and provided a context to discussion about the impact minorities have on housing and neighbourhoods. This is not so much about passive responses but the contention is that academic research was shaped by public policy. To make sense of this and also provide a context, housing and race will be explored from 1945. Necessarily we will be selective but the timeframe we review is important given that the first phase of minority migration to the UK took place during the 1950s and 1960s. The contributions will be grouped into four distinct categories: passive culturalism, choice and constraint, social conflict, politics and power, and cultural resistance. They are not clinically sequential but do reflect broad periods in the post-war period. Race and housing research has been shaped by the choice/constraint paradigm. Here it is argued that this has been more of a hindrance rather than a help.

An early note about race

Before continuing on to discuss race and housing, it is important to clarify our understanding of the term race. This is a deeply contested concept. Though extensively used in literature, the roots of race suggest that it is flawed as an analytical concept (see Back and Solomos, 2000, for an overview of theories of race).

It could be argued that earlier studies of minority communities accepted the notions of both race and race relations (Banton, 1955; Glass, 1960; Patterson, 1963; Rex and Moore, 1967). Though there was disagreement about the precise locus and development of 'race,' these publications shared the view that race could be analysed, largely within a framework of interaction between the dominant white communities and new immigrants from the Caribbean and Indian sub-continent.

Research and subsequent publications influenced a discussion about phenotype differences between groups. It has been suggested that the concept of race is based on a biologically determinist concept (Miles, 1982). Indeed, Britain's imperialist adventures in the nineteenth century had been partly predicated on the application of race in this way. The concept of race and 'racial' ideology supported the subjugation of people and communities across the British Empire, the assumption being that British people (being white) were superior to these groups (being non-white). Indeed, Patterson's title *Dark Strangers* is loaded with political and racist imagery (Patterson, 1963). Banton (1967, 1997) has been an influential proponent of race relations theory. The focus of his work is the study of diverse groups in society based on cultural difference, the development of relations between different racial categories and a narrative about the usage of race. Developing this framework further he argues that six stages of race relations can be deduced: institutionalised contact, acculturation, domination, paternalism, integration and pluralism (Banton, 1967). This theoretical paradigm (sometimes known as the race relations problematic) appears to closely parallel public policy priorities on race relations.

Rex's theory of race relations is grounded in the seminal publication *Race Relations in Sociological Theory* (Rex, 1983). His model is based on social conflict. It views race relations as being structured by conditions existing within society including competition over scarce resources (such as access to housing), class exploitation, cultural segregation, varying group access to power, and minorities filling the role of an underclass within an urban context. This type of analysis borrows significantly from the work of Weber (1976). As we will see later when reviewing race and housing literature, Rex and his associates were especially interested in differential access to housing, education and employment markets and how racial discrimination led to the formation of political action that was disconnected from class conflict (see Rex and Tomlinson, 1979).

Though employing different approaches to race relations theory, both Banton and Rex acknowledge the concept of race and the existence of race relations. This has been strongly disputed by a number of academics and activists. For Miles (1982; 1995) race is an ideologically constructed term that forms the basis for racism and the domination of groups of people. Those that use the term have given it a dangerous legitimacy. The problem with race as an analytical category is best summarised by Guillaumin:

> Whatever the theoretical foundations underlying the various interpretations of 'racial' relations, the very use of such a distinction tends to imply the acceptance of some essential difference between types of social relation, some, somewhere, being specifically racial. Merely to adopt the expression implies a belief that 'races' are real or correctly apprehensible, or at the best that the idea of race is uncritically accepted ...' (cited in Miles, 1995: 72)

Miles further suggests that the concept of race is a distraction from the importance of class. Whilst recognising that capitalist societies need a mobile and reserve army of labour (which may be racialised) to meet requirements of capital accumulation, there is no room in the analysis of race as driver for progressive change (Miles, 1982). Miles concedes that race is a term that is used in everyday language. He also agrees that the term has been reclaimed by black activists since the 1960s as a form of resistance against racism. However, it remains an ideological construct and only serves to confuse the primacy of class and economics.

The importance of the economy is further stressed in explanations for post-war migration to the UK. Castles and Kosack in a classic study of the subject viewed immigration from poor to rich countries as an essential tool to support capitalist expansion (Castles and Kosack, 1973). The same point is made by Sivanandan who suggests that Britain's imperialist past effectively underdeveloped the Caribbean and Indian sub-continent (Sivanandan, 1982). The economies were in such poor condition by the time of decolonisation that they created 'push' factors for people to migrate to seek new jobs. Peach suggests that Caribbean migration was closely linked to the needs of the British economy in the post-war period. People settled in areas where there was a labour shortage. Once labour shortages had eased Caribbean migration slowed down (Peach, 1968).

Reviewing patterns of minority settlement in the UK demonstrates the validity of economic explanations of migration. Minorities continue to be concentrated in metropolitan areas. In effect, they were a replacement labour force for the British economy (Miles, 1982; Smith, 1989).

The analysis by Miles is the most concerted attempt to theorise an explicitly Marxist analysis of race but there are weaknesses in his approach (see Solomos, 1986 for a detailed discussion). The reluctance to discuss the progressive role of culture and ideology is a serious problem. Black politics both in the United States and the UK have used these components to reference radical initiatives against the State. For example, the Notting Hill Carnival started as a celebration of Caribbean culture but became a point of resistance against heavy handed police tactics in the 1970s and 1980s. More recently Islamaphobia in the UK has led to Islam being employed by some British Muslims as a form of cultural resistance against growing acculturation. Whilst accepting that race is a pejorative concept in common sense usage, culture and ideology (that may be bounded by references to a generic black identity or faith) are key agents for change and resistance used by minority groups. Miles' reluctance is based on a Marxist reductionism which superimposes class as the most important reference point for discussing race. This, too, is limiting in the same way as the earlier discussion of race is redundant.

The ready acceptance of race as a concept has also been criticised as reifying group behaviour for 'racial' groups. To this end it fuels debates that research has led to 'common sense' understanding of minority groups based on racist and stereotypical assumptions (Sivanandan, 1982; CCCS, 1982, especially chapters by Lawrence). There are a number of specific charges levelled at Rex and Banton. The most important is the pathologies used to account for the behaviour of minority groups. For example, 'Afro-Caribbean' youth are variously described as having a 'criminalised dreadlock sub-culture' (cited in Lawrence, 1982). Asian groups are at once viewed as being passive and yet possessing cultural bootstraps that will support them in British society. The contrast with 'Afro-Caribbean' groups is striking.

> If the West Indian is plagued by self-doubt ... and seeks a culture which will give him a sense of identity, the Asians have religions and cultures and languages of which they are proud and which may prove surprisingly and suited to the demands of a modern industrial society. (Rex and Tomlinson, 1979: 117)

Normative assumptions and ascribed group behaviours may considerably weaken race as a concept. Rex and Tomlinson's reification of African-Caribbean and Asian communities is a case in point. Research does not analyse the differences within a group shaped by gender, age and class. Neither does the research focus on the modes of collective resistance within minority communities against racism, harassment and fascist attacks in the post-war period (Sivanandan, 1982; Lawrence, 1982; Gilroy, 1987).

The reification of minority groups has been a strong influence in public policy debates. This, combined with the importance attached to culture and resistance within black politics from at least the 1960s, helps to explain why concepts of 'white', 'black' and to a lesser extent 'brown' are still widely used (for example the Housing Corporation's *Black* and Minority Ethnic Housing Policy; *black* led housing associations).

It is advisable to take a practical and informed view of race. First, research has shown the importance of culture in informing the identity of minority communities across the country. Sivanandan provides a vivid account of culture and black resistance in the post-war period. It seems that that culture dissociated from the racist and biological use of race needs to be included for meaningful discussion (see Sivanandan, 1982; Fryer, 1984; Gilroy, 1987). Second, culture should also be celebrated in its own right as adding diversity within communities and providing choice. A cultural approach in social housing helps to meet specific and nuanced needs within groups. Third, culture should also be viewed as a form of social resistance when collective interests are challenged (Bourne and Sivanandan, 1980; Sivanandan, 1982; Lawrence, 1982). For example, this was utilised by minority groups to champion black led housing associations as a response to the failure of housing providers to meet needs; it informed analysis of riots and rebellions, most noticeably in 1981 and 1985, as well as culture, which can currently be seen in the way Islam is being used as a rallying point for Muslims in the fevered political climate in which we now live. Finally, race and racism are used in everyday language within policy and practice communities. These terms are unavoidable and should be at least acknowledged and justified by researchers working in the field.

An understanding of race is critically important. Race has been, and remains, a highly contested concept. However, it is, along with culture, vital in moving debates forward. This is especially crucial within the current policy and political climate given the discussion about identity, citizenship and territory as ushered in by the 2001 riots (Home Office, 2001), the September 11 attacks on New York and Washington, and the 2005 bombings on the transport network in London. Race and culture should not be regarded as esoteric concepts but fundamental to the future direction of society.

This book is about race and housing. At the outset we need to understand the framework for key debates and to this end we will now review a selection. In doing so we suggest that there are four different typologies on race and housing literature. This closely mirrors public policy interventions that help to understand sequencing and content.

Passive culturalism

It could be argued that the first and earliest strand of research on race and housing has been termed passive culturalism and is often associated (though not exclusively) with studies undertaken in the 1950s and 1960s. The approach is characterised by an anthropological method to studying newly emerging minority communities and an absence of the discussion of power, conflict and racism.

The context is large scale immigration from the Caribbean and Indian sub-continent in the post-1945 period which was concentrated in major urban centres of England. At this point it should be noted that a black presence in Britain had been recorded for many centuries and publications have celebrated the role, presence and resistance of these established groups before 1945 (for example, Fryer, 1984). However, the point we are making here is that post-war immigration helped to fuel the perception about adverse neighbourhood change in urban centres. This became so unsettling to politicians and policy makers in the 1950s that Churchill considered using the slogan 'Keeping Britain White' to mobilise popular support at a General Election (Layton-Henry, 1984). A common misconception was that the 1950s was a benign political environment. This was far from the case. Indeed, MPs repeatedly intervened during Parliamentary debates in the 1950s to call for restrictions on immigration from the Caribbean and Indian sub-continent (see Carter et al., 1987).

Despite immigration helping to sustain a post-war economic boom by providing an accessible army of labour for shortages in key industries, these newly emerging minority communities presented a policy dilemma for the State, namely to politically restrict immigration from the Caribbean and Indian sub-continent at a time when cheap labour was required to maintain growth. National debates on race were being justified on the basis of the 'problem' that immigration was generating in towns and cities. The image of neighbourhoods being transformed became popularised during this period and continues to resonate in the discourse on race and immigration. Indeed, immigration played a significant role during the 2010 General Election and was highlighted at several times in the televised leadership debates. During the 1950s, concern was expressed partly because it was believed that immigrants were in competition with white communities for housing, health and employment. It should be noted that public housing was generally perceived as tenure of aspiration for a broad range of people living in the UK. It compared favourably with private sector housing to rent which was unregulated, of poor quality and located in neighbourhoods of economic decline (Malpass and Murie, 1994; Pawson and Mullins, 2010).

We contend that a passive culturist approach framed studies of race and housing during this period. Leading publications on race (Little, 1947; Richmond, 1954; Banton, 1955; and Patterson, 1963) emphasised that the conflict was due to cultural differences between immigrant and host communities. Over time, conflict would ease because of increased interaction between groups and the goal of integration reached. As we have discussed, Banton (1967) developed a theory of race relations predicated on increased cultural understanding leading to stability. These earlier studies focused on minority communities living in urban centres. For example, Little and Richmond concentrated on describing the conditions of Somali groups living in Cardiff and Caribbean migrants in South Liverpool respectively. There was very little discussion about discrimination by public and private sectors or harassment of new migrants by established communities. Instead researchers appeared to approach race as a psychological problem. The main aim of Little's study was to: '...examine the social interactions and reactions resulting from the specific presence of coloured people in Britain...and the patterns of coloured-white relations could add to the political awareness and understanding of a social problem.' (Little, 1947: 1).

A notable example of the passive culturist approach can be viewed in Patterson's *Dark Strangers* (Patterson, 1963) which is a study of relationships between Caribbean migrants and white communities in Brixton. This publication exemplifies, as suggested by its title and content, the impact of immigration on traditionally white neighbourhoods. The terminology is grounded in the immigrant-host praxis and identifies the problem of race to be with Caribbean migrants rather than racism in housing and wider society. 'Common sense' narratives help to construct race and immigration as critical issues that need to be addressed by local and national policy. Here, it could be construed that minority communities are viewed as a threat to stability, housing resources and established white residents.

> Open doors, its friendly room to room visiting, the noise of music and conviviality, the quarrelsome voices from rooms in which gambling, ganja-smoking and drinking goes on may be enough to drive out all but the elderly, lone white tenant. (Patterson, 1963: 167)

The onus appeared to be on minority communities to either 'trade off' minority identity for a British cultural view or, alternatively, wait until relations between different groups were stabilised over a period of time. Competition for housing between established communities and new migrants is considered by Patterson and other publications during this period. Discrimination is discussed but is largely contextualised within a host-immigrant framework (Patterson, 1963).

These passive culturist studies only serve to demonstrate the problems of reification and stereotyping of groups that impact on race and housing. Of course, largely anthropological accounts are based on location and observation. They provided little in the way of critical appraisal of government policies or interventions by housing providers that led to the concentration of migrants in the most disadvantaged neighbourhoods of cities and living in the most overcrowded and poorest parts of the private rental market. In addition there are three further problems with the passive culturist literature. First, race is viewed within a socially constructed lens. This helps to support political debates on racial hierarchy and dominant modes of culture and living. The onus is on minorities to adapt to British culture rather than addressing problems of structural and institutional racism. Second, there is an almost total absence of discussion on power, conflict and resources in critical areas such as housing. One reason could be that that the Welfare State was viewed as a key mechanism to resolve conflict between groups in different public policy areas. Finally, the passive culturist perspective portrays minority groups as submissive recipients of services rather than activists. Indeed this comes up again in the choice-constraint debates where some (Ballard and Ballard, 1977) suggest that minorities are much more active in housing decisions than others suggest.

Taking this into account we are left with the conclusion that earlier studies of race and housing had a fixed view of minorities that did not consider needs and aspirations of communities, and how these change over a period of time.

Social conflict, politics and power

Growing evidence of racism in the UK during the 1960s and 1970s led to a different type of approach to race and housing. During this period, research showed that structural constraints prevented minorities from exercising housing choice. Rather than take a passive view of 'immigrant-host' relations, this framework was based on social conflict between groups competing for scarce and valued resources such as public housing. John Rex's two seminal publications on race and housing in Birmingham helped to transform academic and policy debates (Rex and Moore, 1967; Rex and Tomlinson, 1979). Apart from these specific accounts of race and housing we will also make reference to an important strand of literature on race, communities and politics generated by key interventions by American academics. This includes Katznelson (1973) as well as the debates on community power (Bachrach and Baratz, 1970) and social capital (Bourdieu, 1986; Putnam, 2000). This chapter, and indeed the thinking of this book, suggests this literature may provide a productive way to make sense of race and housing in a modern setting.

The context for Rex and Moore's study of race and housing in Sparkbrook was increased conflict between different groups in a city. Birmingham in the 1960s was as it is today—a city that attracts immigrants to different forms of employment. In their study, Rex and Moore employed a Weberian approach. Here, class theory is based on groups of people sharing the same life chances because of their economic power in labour *and* additional markets. Rex and Moore wanted to show that people within the same class could be allocated different types of housing because of competition over this scarce resource. Sparkbrook demonstrated that minority groups were denied access to good quality public sector housing because of racism by local authority housing officers. Moreover this was replicated by landlords and agents operating in the private sector. The consequence was minorities occupying poor quality housing in areas of economic and social decline (the so called zones of transition). In this way the differential position of groups is based on resources available to them (financial, political and social) and leads to Rex's and Moore's central theory of housing classes. This institutional approach subsequently influenced a number of housing studies (for example, Saunders, 1990).

The later work of Rex with Tomlinson developed the themes of *Race, Community and Conflict*. On this occasion the focus was the Handsworth area located in the north west of Birmingham. Here too, the concern was to demonstrate that competition for housing, education and employment had left minority groups occupying the poorest housing as well as suffering disadvantage within schools and the local labour market. Rex and Tomlinson suggested that whilst white workers had improved their economic and social position through representation by trade unions and the Labour Party, the position of minority workers had deteriorated. Moreover, they were not represented by the Labour movement and would find it difficult to improve their economic position through these channels. In effect, minority communities were detached from working class institutions even though they occupied housing in the same neighbourhoods. They had become an 'underclass'.

> The concept of underclass was intended to suggest ... that the minorities were systematically at a disadvantage compared with their white peers and that, instead of identifying with working class culture and politics, they formed their own organisations and became effectively a separate under-privileged class.' (Rex and Tomlinson, 1979: 275)

Having located minorities as being the most exploited class, Rex and Tomlinson then suggested that this group could become a 'class in themselves' and be imbued with revolutionary potential. Political inspiration would come from struggles against imperialism and colonisation in the developing world. Rex and Tomlinson further suggested that political strategies would vary for different groups. The process for Asian communities was securing economic and social capital leading to improved opportunities in housing, education and employment. In contrast 'West Indians' are likely to withdraw from the State and seek to develop a black identity (Rex and Tomlinson, 1979: 245).

The conflict model used in Sparkbrook and Handsworth developed from a Weberian perspective. It was not associated simply with class and the State but also competition over a number of policy and political areas such as housing. Rex and his associates accepted the notion of race because it was used in common discourse and viewed minorities as being rooted in poor housing located in declining neighbourhoods. Crucially the analysis emphasised the role of housing organisations and individuals to shape the outcomes for minority groups.

Despite being seminal studies, there are weaknesses in Rex's work which need to be explored. First, it could be argued that this is a culturally deterministic approach. Though the concepts of class, power and politics are discussed, Rex and Moore (and later, Rex and Tomlinson) make grouped assumptions about minorities that rest on culture and behaviour. This could be viewed as associated with deterministic theories and not so far removed from the simplistic anthropological studies previously discussed.

Lawrence (1982) criticised Rex and Tomlinson for arriving at 'common sense' assumptions on minority culture that borrow heavily from racist stereotyping. For example, the comparison between successful entrepreneurial Asians to 'West Indians' who withdraw altogether from society is a crude form of grouped assumption. Minorities are not passive recipients within society. Neither should they be reified into groups nor ascribed collective behaviour based on assumed cultural preferences. A second concern with Rex is the fixed assumptions made about housing classes. The studies of Sparkbrook and Handsworth suggested that minorities are parked in the same rigid housing market over a period of time. However, research shows that minority groups have moved out from housing markets. This is because of increased prosperity for some groups (Harrison and Phillips, 2003) and by housing organisations seeking to meet needs and aspirations (see Ratcliffe et al., 2001). Differential aspiration for housing is dependent on a number of factors including income, education and employment performance (Harrison et al., 2005). Finally, there is little or no consideration of the way in which the State can respond to meet needs. Social housing organisations, whether local authorities or housing associations, have been forced to consider the housing needs of minority groups and address the problems of racism. Initially this was embedded within the 1976 Race Relations Act. Later the Housing Corporation supported the growth of black led housing associations as well as developed anti-discriminatory measures in social housing (see Harrison, 1995). This important and interesting period shows that the State can act in a benevolent as well as malevolent way on race and housing. We will critically analyse this idea as well as the black led housing sector later on in this book.

Rex did consider the role of race and local politics but this was largely framed on minorities and party political competition (see in particular Rex and Tomlinson, 1979). Katznelson's comparative study of race and politics goes much further by reviewing the role of the State, minorities and community based organisations. He suggests that local authorities create buffer institutions such as community relations councils to mediate the politics of race. Radical activists join these organisations and get absorbed by the State and its bureaucracy. Protest is neutralised and race equality progress slowed down by working within a bureaucratic framework (Katznelson, 1973). Moreover, minority politics may be compromised as some groups are given access whilst others remain excluded. This builds on the community power literature most notably Bachrach and Baratz (1970). Studies into local politics in the United States showed that conflict could be managed by a differential application of power. Disputes were limited because local political decisions were limited to neutral issues. More problematic areas such as race did not make it onto the agenda for discussion. Power was used to minimise conflict by reducing discussion to non-decision making arenas. Power, access, restricted agendas are all important areas for discussion on race and housing. This is even more the case given that growing diversity has led to increased numbers of minority groups attempting to access power and resources for local initiatives and projects. These will be explored later in the book with reference to the concept of recycled racism and the relationship between different minorities.

We mentioned social capital earlier in this chapter. The term is associated with Putnam who defined it as 'connections among individuals – social networks and the norms of reciprocity and trustworthiness that arise from them' (Putnam, 2000). The more recent strain of social capital has been influential to public policy debates especially during the Labour Government of 1997–2010. It provided a form of analysis that powered debates on social exclusion and addressing neighbourhood disadvantage. There are considerable problems with the work of Putnam when viewed through race. Assumptions are made that prosperous neighbourhoods (mainly white) have greater levels of social capital than poor neighbourhoods (mainly minority as well as poor whites). In an echo to previous debates, there is a tendency for Putnam to reify communities by both class and race in that his analysis suggests that poor neighbourhoods need a fix of social capital to support renewal. However, minority groups have strong social networks and indeed this is one of the reasons that influence housing decisions. Moreover, research has found that minorities may not want to join local organisations because they do not meet their current needs or future aspirations (Mullins et al., 2004). Bourdieu's radical perspective on social capital helps to understand the role of minorities better (Bourdieu, 1986). Here we see social capital as a contested concept between different groups within society. There are four forms of capital; economic, cultural, social and symbolic. The importance of ideology, resources and power leads to a much more inclusive discussion. For example, cultural capital is explained as building up knowledge, skills and credentials through upbringing and education.

This helps to maximise economic capital and enables people for example to decide upon different forms of housing choice. New minorities may be adversely affected in a two ways. First, knowledge and skills are limited because they are new arrivals. Barriers exist in the form of language, lack of awareness by government and housing agencies of their needs. Second, they may also be excluded from decision-making machinery that decides on housing investment in local areas. They cannot choose because they do not have a choice.

We will return to the debates of race, housing and social capital in the concluding chapter of this book. We will attempt to make a case for these to be included as part of the new research agenda for race and housing.

Choice and constraint

It has been stated that the 'choice-constraint' debate is the most important theme in the academic literature on race and housing (Ratcliffe, 2000). One of the most enduring issues has been to explain housing based segregation in towns and cities across the country (Robinson, 1986; Smith, 1989; Ratcliffe, 1996; Phillips, 1998). The narrative was based on the importance of power (held by the State), residence (shaped by discrimination and/or class) and choice (limited). It could be argued that these publications followed in the tradition of Rex et al. and stated that minorities were denied a housing choice because of racism operating within public and private sector housing markets.

Housing affordability is one the most significant structural constraints that confronts minorities. These groups are disproportionately represented within the poorest sections of society (Social Exclusion Unit, 2000; National Equality Panel, 2010), face the greatest levels of housing need (Harrison and Phillips, 2003) and are more likely to have low wages or be out of work (DWP, 2007). In the main, minorities remain concentrated within the poorest neighbourhoods in towns and cities because they cannot afford better housing located elsewhere. In these circumstances housing reach is limited. The housing booms of the 1990s onwards have widened the affordability gap between poor minority groups and the rest of the population which the periodic slumps in housing price have not rectified.

Those who are committed to the theory of constraint argue that the relatively poor position of minority communities reflects the discriminatory barriers placed by housing organisations and individuals. There is little or nò room to manoeuvre for individuals when presented with these structural barriers. The opposite view is taken by those who put forward a choice model who believe that minorities are not passive actors within the housing market. Individuals act with a degree of freedom in making decisions about housing and this may reflect the importance of accessing community infrastructure, family and friends (see for example, Dayha, 1974).

Proponents of the constraint school suggest that institutional racism, poverty and harassment in some neighbourhoods limit the housing choice available to minorities. This was the main cause of racial segregation within towns and cities across the country. We have seen that Rex and his associates (Rex and Moore, 1967; Rex and Tomlinson, 1979) viewed structural constraints in employment, education as well as housing that resulted in minorities concentrated in the poorest neighbourhoods. Their analysis showed little optimism for the State to act in a positive way to empower minority groups in the housing market. Lee's account of housing segregation in London during the 1970s demonstrated that discrimination in public sector housing combined with perceived harassment from people living in some neighbourhood's reinforced concentration of 'coloured' communities in Brixton and Streatham. Dispersal was happening but there was a general reluctance by minorities to become 'pioneers' in new housing markets (Lee, 1977). The structural barriers in housing are again stressed by Smith (1989). Constraints are considerable and enduring spanning inequality within employment, discrimination in society and of course, housing.

> ... segregation is not a neutral expression of cultural preference. It is ... the fulcrum of racial inequality – in the labour market, in the housing system and ... in access to wide range of opportunities ... such inequality is sustained by the operation of the housing system and by the restructuring of welfare rights that has accompanied the economic and ideological change of the late twentieth century. (Smith, 1989: 18)

For Smith these structural inequalities lead to increased racial polarisation with the tacit support of the State. Referencing housing policies to the 'common sense' images of minorities as being problematic means that there is little incentive for politicians to develop a progressive policy on race and immigration. The theme of systematic inequalities reproduced by the State is some distance from the discriminatory role of housing officers identified by Rex and Moore as being so crucial to the development of housing classes in Sparkbrook (Rex and Moore, 1967).

The race and housing debate was developed by Henderson and Karn in their influential study of public housing in Birmingham (Henderson and Karn, 1987). Despite the passing of the 1976 Race Relations Act and related anti-discriminatory housing policies their research identified that minority communities were still being offered the poorest housing. Like Rex and Moore before them, Henderson and Karn point to the role of housing officers in rationing this scarce product. Minorities lose out in the allocation process because of the 'common sense' view that they either do not want to be housed in some areas or direct discrimination. A housing system which seeks to act on the basis of need does not function for minorities because of the pervasive nature of racism operating within society. Problems with running a dispersal policy in Birmingham for minorities are also identified by Flett (1979). This floundered because of fears of a tenants' revolt against the movement of minorities into predominantly white neighbourhoods. Rather than address the issue directly, housing policy was circumvented despite the realisation that integration was the solution for the city as a whole (Flett, 1979: 189). Similar problems of racial inequality in housing were uncovered by Simpson (1981) and reports conducted by the Commission for Racial Equality (CRE) reviewed a number of local authorities, most notably Hackney and Liverpool (CRE 1984a; CRE, 1984b).

Structural constraints are embedded within the housing system and overlain by racism. These factors lead to the pattern of minority segregation across the country that is still in place today. A very different view is provided by supporters of the choice (or agency) approach. As mentioned, one of the best known and earliest examples of this approach is the study by Dayha of Pakistanis living in Bradford (Dayha, 1974). Whilst acknowledging the importance of discrimination in restricting choice, Dayha nevertheless suggests that Pakistani communities voluntarily choose to live in close proximity to each other. This provides social, economic and political support. Housing decisions are made on a rational basis (Dayha, 1974: 112). The choice interpretation has been supported by Burney (1967) and Ballard and Ballard (1977) in their studies of Pakistani and Sikhs respectively. Minority communities are active in their housing decisions and value the importance of community infrastructure. As Ratcliffe succinctly points out in reviewing different theories of race and housing: 'The fundamental argument here was that social actors are not simply pawns of the market: they are knowing actors with aims, objectives and aspirations.' (Ratcliffe, 2009).

Interestingly the theme of 'choice' has been inverted somewhat by the much more recent debates on community cohesion which will be picked up in this and subsequent chapters. Some commentators criticise minorities (mainly Muslim Pakistanis) for not doing enough to integrate themselves within towns and cities even though many of the structural constraints have been reduced (Home Office, 2001; Phillips, 2005). Community infrastructure in this scenario is not seen as providing support but perpetuating segregation (see Robinson, 2007 for a community cohesion critique; also Flint and Robinson, 2008).

The dualism between choice and constraint and the relative importance of structure and agency is interesting but ultimately very limiting. There is a danger of race and housing debates leading to an intellectual cul-de-sac. Recently there have been signs of a much less rigid stance. For example, Harrison has suggested that policy debates on race and housing have inevitably been highly normative in suggesting that minority residential concentration is a problem. 'The idea that concentration is a damaging process-produced by external forces, accident, or social pathologies – also may undervalue the importance of action and choice within minority communities.' (Harrison, 1995: 58).

The choice and constraint models have a great virtue in their simplicity. However, as Ratcliffe notes, the problem with these theories (and indeed much of the debate on race and housing in general) is that they provide very little room for taking on a dynamic approach to structure and agency (Ratcliffe, 2000; Ratcliffe, 2009).

Giddens helped to move away from the dualism of structure and agency by suggesting that rather than being fixed and durable concepts they are both subject to change over a period of time. Individuals (agents) can influence the State (structure) and both are interdependent (Giddens, 1976). As he states: 'Structures must not be conceptualised as simply placing constraints upon human agency, but as enabling.' (Giddens, 1976: 60).

One of the more interesting attempts to take this debate forward with reference to race and housing was undertaken by Sarre and his colleagues (1989). The study of minorities in Bedford focused particularly on the Italian community. Advancing Giddens' structuration theory, they sought a model that would reconcile choice and constraint. The structures within society that limit choice of housing available to minorities are not independent. They may be influenced and changed through the actions of individuals within society. It could be argued that Giddens freed up the 'log jam' in race and housing by constructing a framework to consider dynamic and interdependent relationships between structure and agency

(Giddens, 1976). The Bedford study showed how agency can influence structure. For example, private lenders that prevented Italians from securing competitive loans to buy homes lost out on this business as this group moved to organisations that had a more progressive outlook. This helped to change patterns of lending and residence in Bedford (Sarre et al., 1989: 320). More recent examples of changing behaviour of housing institutions has been mainstream lenders such as HSBC offering Islamic mortgages in a specific appeal to get the custom of the growing number of Muslims in the country (CIH, 2005). Similarly a provider perspective is the role of housing associations in trying to work with refugees to renew neighbourhoods and communities in areas of economic decline (Mullins et al., 2007). As we can see, the value of structuration theory is that it brings dynamism to the debates. Of course, it too can be criticised for providing a 'fudged' solution to choice and constraint but nevertheless the interdependence between structure and agency may provide a positive way forward for discussion of the subject.

The constraint approach that has dominated much of the discussion has a number of weaknesses. First, it could be argued that the focus on structure is a one sided analysis of race and housing. There is an assumption that minorities want to move from inner urban areas to access better housing, education and environmental outcomes in contiguous neighbourhoods. This makes an erroneous assumption that housing markets remained fixed. That is, it takes the view that housing pathways will always be uni-directional from inner urban to outer urban areas. In fact, minorities may want to continue living in housing markets because of the presence of community infrastructure but also fear of harassment in some outer neighbourhoods (Henderson and Karn, 1987). Second, the structure and agency approach is a static model that does not take into account how the State can respond to political mobilisation (Ratcliffe, 2009). Whilst some have argued that housing organisations have been institutionally racist (CRE, 1984a) and helped to reproduce racial inequality (for example, Flett, 1979), there have also been interventions to promote race equality. For example, the Housing Corporation has had a specific policy to develop minority housing associations and more recently ensuring the social housing sector as a whole meets the needs of minority consumers (see Harrison, 1995; Housing Corporation, 1998). Regulators now have sanctions in place to ensure outcomes in these areas are met (Housing Corporation, 2002). It is also important to note the impact of the Macpherson Report (Home Office, 1999) on helping to prioritise race equality in the social housing sector. Measures against racism should help to increase housing choice. It should be noted, however, that sometimes race equality initiatives (such as 'colour blind' or treating people the same) reproduce and entrench inequality. Third, the race and housing debate is still characterised by reification of minorities and ascribing of collective modes of behaviour that was problematic within the passive culturist approach. Rex and his associates have been criticised for arriving at stereotypical and racist assumptions of minority groups but this is a charge that can be levelled at much of the race and housing debates (see Lawrence, 1982; Sivanandan, 1982; Burnett, 2004). The reification is much more problematic given the impact of migration combined with post-Fordism and breaking down groups into diverse and atomised communities (Gilroy, 1987). Finally, the structuralism approach to race and housing was partly based on the assumption that minority communities had a desire for public sector housing. This does not take into account the growing deterioration of this type of housing in the post-war period. As Forrest and Murie rightly point out, a combination of increased access to mortgage finance, reduced investment in public housing and central interventions such as the right to buy legislation contributed to public sector housing being seen as tenure of last resort (Forrest and Murie, 1983; see also Pawson and Mullins, 2010). Council estates were soon regarded as places that households with aspirations did not want to live and, therefore, largely became occupied by the very poor, very old and low skilled (ODPM, 2004). Public housing was also largely rejected by minority communities and became stigmatised as being places where racial harassment was a frequent occurrence (Chahal and Julienne, 1999). Reduced reliance on public housing coincided with private sector owner occupation being regarded as leading to increased choice, power and economic capital in the housing market for minorities.

It could be argued that housing classes still operate within the housing market. Minorities are denied housing in certain neighbourhoods by factors unrelated to class including harassment and the actions of organisations, agencies and individuals. In reality the dynamic nature of housing markets, differential prosperity and progressive housing organisations weaken the classic interpretation of housing class theory.

Cultural resistance

The fourth strand of race and housing literature is closely associated with Stuart Hall and the Centre for Contemporary Cultural Studies (CCCS) formerly based at the University of Birmingham (CCCS, 1982). Though not explicitly considering the role of housing, the theories configured on cultural resistance have been noted within a number of studies on race and housing including Smith (1989), and Sarre et al. (1989). This tradition (sometimes known as the Birmingham School) was developed by Hall and others who considered culture as an important point of resistance for minorities (Hall, 1980).

In one respect, those who took on this perspective viewed race as a valid analytical category that is dynamic and contested (CCCS, 1982; Gilroy, 1987; Solomos, 1993). The problem with race was that it had been previously defined by the State, local authorities and housing organisations as being problematic. The process of race formation occurs when minority groups become organised on a political, ideological and institutional basis. Race does not replace class but should be regarded as an additional category and point of resistance for minorities. In short, race was being reclaimed from the passive culturists and used as a basis for minorities to mobilise and challenge the State to change policies and practice. Gilroy further explains the process of race formation as;

> ... the manner in which 'races' become organised into politics, particularly where racial differentiation has become a feature of ... institutional structures as well as individual interaction ...race formation can also relate the release of political forces which define themselves and organise around the notion of race to the meaning and extent of class relationships.' (Gilroy, 1987: 35–36)

Cultural resistance and the reconceptualising of race as an analytical term marked a significant departure from the work of Rex and his associates and also the earlier studies of Banton. In some instances both were parodied as being part of a dated 'sociology of race relations' that reinforced racist stereotypes, ascribing causal behaviour within generic groups of minorities and assuming that groups in part or whole would assume a passive position vis a vis discrimination in general and racism in particular. The problems were compounded by the lack of reference to class (although Rex and Tomlinson would dispute this), power and conflict (see Bourne and Sivanandan, 1980; CCCS, 1982). Indeed Lawrence summarises the critique of the sociology of race relations succinctly:

> The ideas about 'identity crisis', 'culture conflict' and 'intergenerational conflict' which power the accounts of race/'ethnic relations' sociologists

have been constructed in large part without reference to the struggles that the parents have been involved in before and since coming to Britain. They have been characterised as passive, acquiescent victims of racism wanting only to 'integrate'; as recalcitrant 'traditionalists'; suspicious and bewildered by white society, who 'withdraw' wilfully into their own 'ethnic' or 'religious' enclaves ...' (Lawrence, 1982: 132)

In contrast to earlier political orthodoxies which viewed the Welfare State as resolving conflict, this perspective suggested that the needs and aspirations of minorities could not be met by government or agencies. Hence, the onus was on minority groups themselves to self-organise and critically use culture as a form of resistance. It could be put forward that Sivanandan was at the forefront of this model (Bourne and Sivanandan, 1980; Sivanandan, 1982) which viewed minorities as the most radical section of society using their experiences both in this country (racially) and abroad (culturally) as the engine for social change. To Sivanandan restrictive policies on minority immigration were an attempt by the State to regulate labour to meet the demands of the economy. Race relations policies were then used to manage this potentially revolutionary sector of society.

Theories of cultural resistance may seem detached from the review of race and housing but they can be used to explain a number of developments in the housing sector since the 1980s. Recognising the importance of culture and race as an analytical concept and basis for resistance helps to understand the growth of the black led housing association movement. The stimulus for growth was the failing of social housing providers to understand the needs and aspirations of minority communities. In addition, community activists lobbied the Housing Corporation for practical support for minority led housing providers and eventually initiated the cycle of Black and Minority Ethnic Housing Policies (see Harrison, 1995: 82–110; also see Chapter 4 on black led housing associations later on).

The important role of culture (as opposed to class) in shaping housing needs and aspirations has been evidenced by a number of recent housing studies (Somerville and Steele, 2002; Mullins et al., 2004; Niner, 2006). First, minority groups may express their housing preference as being in close proximity to social and community infrastructure, demanding that housing providers increase choice within a neighbourhood, and perhaps help to access culturally specific loan finance. Second, minorities may use community based organisations as a conduit to represent their needs and aspirations to housing providers (Mullins et al., 2004). Third, culture and race may be mobilised and used as source of resistance when minorities feel that they are under attack. The 2001 riots in Burnley, Oldham and Bradford could be seen as a response to fascist groups trying to create conflict in these predominantly Muslim areas (see Burnett, 2004). A politically charged climate may limit the options available for minority communities preventing them from accessing housing in some neighbourhoods.

Culture is becoming more relevant to housing. However, there are a number of critiques that can be placed against this strand of race and housing literature. Culture, and especially minority based culture, is now viewed by the State as being highly problematic. The report into the 2001 disturbances partly blamed housing providers for increasing segregation between groups living in the same places (Home Office, 2001). The black and minority ethnic housing sector was undermined by the criticism of providing grants to support minority organisations. As a consequence, it could be said that Housing Corporation backing for the black led housing sector has now gone into reverse. Indeed, since 2003 there has been no specific policy for black led housing associations by the new Homes and Communities Agency. The number of minority registered housing associations has declined with many being forced to merge with larger mainstream providers. Further, the establishment of the Commission for Equalities and Human Rights could be said to have effectively sounded the death knell on race being regarded as the critically important area for discussion and debate in the housing sector.

Growing atomisation within minority groups is also problematic for cultural theorists. Rather than becoming a collective entity grounded on common experiences of class and racist disadvantage, the opposite seems to be the case. In an increasingly diverse and heterogeneous society it is becoming difficult to expect different minorities to be politically bound under a single identity. Competition for housing, education, funding and neighbourhood 'turf' lead to an ever more complex situation where conflict could be between different minority groups. The 2006 Lozells disturbances have been described as a 'race riot' between Caribbean and Pakistani groups living in that disadvantaged part of Birmingham (Black Radley, 2006). Of course the truth is always more difficult to comprehend but the impact of diversity on race and housing seems to be one of the key areas which requires more research. We start this process later on in this book.

About this book

We have attempted to provide a context by reviewing key trends in housing and race. As we have seen, research parallels societal, demographic and political changes moving from passive culturalism, social conflict, and cultural resistance overlain by the spectre of choice and constraint. These are not neatly sequential but are shaped by different concerns from the 1950s onwards. By selectively reviewing publications we need to acknowledge how the debate on race, housing and community has developed and grown. Importantly, it could be argued that notions of power, conflict and resistance have become part of the analysis of race and housing. However, there is a continuing need to challenge and take forward the debates on these critical issues. Community cohesion and housing will be discussed in the next chapter but it could be argued that its emergence since 2001 in public policy debates has made it much more difficult for black led housing associations. Moreover the spectre of rising support for the Far Right Parties such as the BNP at the ballot box has happened at the same time as the growth of community cohesion and the establishment of the Equality and Human Rights Commission. A cause and effect is not suggested but at least needs to be investigated. All of this shows that debates on cohesion, race and housing still form a combustible part of academic and policy debates. In this book we seek to put a different perspective on themes that have been discussed in this first chapter and add to our knowledge in areas that have not been developed through subsequent chapters.

The following chapter is titled *Housing Policy and Practice*. The task is to go into more detail about housing policy interventions on race. Specifically we will critically assess the role of the Housing Corporation as the regulator and investment agency for housing associations during a period of change in meeting the needs of black and minority communities. This included the active support to create black and minority ethnic housing associations across England to support housing needs but also encourage black and minority ethnic leadership. The Housing Corporation has given way to the Homes and Communities Agency which has been less enthusiastic on continuing to develop programmes for the black and minority ethnic housing sector. Similarly, the impact of the Commission for Racial Equality on housing debates will be reviewed and the role of the Equality and Human Rights Commission on policy and practice analysed. The focus on policy and practice is framed by the emergence of the

Housing Corporation BME Policy in 1986. The debate on race and housing has been punctuated by two important policy interventions: Macpherson in 1999 and Cohesion in 2001 (see Home Office, 2001). Both in isolation were influential but they could be seen as part of a continuum which is part of a retreat from race and housing and a move from specific to generic policy and practice.

In Chapter 3 we look at localised responses to housing and race. There has been a strange consistency in the terms and narratives on housing. By this, it could be argued; frameworks and practical responses have intertwined race and housing with discussions on the adverse transformation and impact on neighbourhoods. Thus, understanding and appraising localised responses should be an important part of any book on this subject. However the chapter will not focus on black and minority ethnic communities. Instead the emphasis will be to explore community cohesion, housing and the experiences of white working class communities. It will be stated that these communities have been conspicuous by their absence in the race and housing literature and this has enabled stereotypical and unflattering images to be developed in both popular culture and policy. Building on recently completed research the chapter will discuss the perspectives of these groups on community cohesion and housing.

We have already mentioned the emergence of the black led housing sector and which is the focus of Chapter 4. This has been one of the most interesting developments in the social housing sector since the 1980s. Most were registered by the Housing Corporation and reached a peak of over 60 organisations by 1999. They have variously been regarded as beacons of black and minority leadership, providing culturally sensitive services and creating space for black employees, board members and tenants to engage with housing issues. Yet, there have also been a number of issues and challenges for the sector. First, it could be argued that performance has been patchy. Indeed on occasions this has led to the Housing Corporation using statutory powers to intervene in the running of the association. Most recently, Ujima (the first and largest black and minority led housing association) has been taken over by a mainstream housing provider after concerns about performance. In addition macro policy shifts from a model of multiculturalism to community cohesion has further called into question the role of black and minority ethnic housing associations. The focus is not so much on narrow concerns of race but a wider agenda of equalities. Related to this are questions on the appropriateness of using labels such as 'black' to describe an increasingly fragmented society. Are we seeing the declining significance of race and housing or a move to a differ-ent type of discussion where race is still important?

As we have seen earlier on in this chapter, race and housing is populated with important and influential publications. One of the objectives of the book is to increase knowledge and understanding in areas that have not hitherto been discussed in detail. To this end, in Chapter 5 we focus on *Housing, Communities and 'Recycled Racism'*. Part of the premise of the discussion here is that Britain has witnessed an unprecedented phase of migration during the last 20 years. Much of this has been the result of enlargement of the EU in May 2004. More than 800 000 people have arrived in the UK to live and work. In addition people have come and settled in the UK from other parts of the world including places of conflict such as Iraq, Somalia and the Balkans. Taken together these new communities have questioned assumptions of 'black' as a generic term, challenged housing providers to deliver services sometimes in areas that had seen very little immigration and led to competition between established and emerging communities for housing and related services. This has been termed 'recycled racism'. This chapter will explore the impact of migrants on the housing market, competition and conflict between different communities and the extent to which this can be termed 'recycled racism'.

In the concluding section of the book, Chapter 6, an attempt will be made to review and identify possible new directions for race, housing and community. We will also lay out the challenges and opportunities for researchers in this field. In so doing, we will suggest that existing theory and practice continues to use outmoded models of analysis that are no longer appropriate or relevant in organising housing services. Fixed notions of race and representation need to be modernised and set within an increasingly dynamic and fragmented society. In short we need to: get beyond representation and race which has limited debates and has led to positions that may be perceived as protecting self interest; help reconfigure BME housing organisations into community agencies of change; critically find alternatives to 'community leaders', who have disfigured some of the more recent debates on race and housing; and, finally, move towards a more inclusive and shared vision of race, housing and community.

It is important to acknowledge the rich contribution of housing and race research as we have done in setting a framework for the discussion in this chapter. More importantly, there is a need to review and assess the last 25 years of housing and race so that it will help to chart a new vision in an increasingly turbulent political climate.

2

Housing Policy and Practice

Introduction

Housing operates within the shifting sands of public policy. Housing organisations are vested with funding to meet housing demand and yet at the same time address wider societal challenges. This chapter will review public policy approaches to race, cohesion and integration through the prism of time. During the 1980s the housing sector supported multiculturalism and valued difference. It should be noted the Housing Corporation devised and delivered a positive action programme from 1986 to 2003. In retrospect the black and minority ethnic housing policy spawned new organisations, developed leaderships and profoundly influenced wider debates on equality. During this expansive phase of policy the 1999 Macpherson Report (Home Office, 1999) kept the focus on race equality and spurred greater action from housing organisations and representative bodies. The 2001 disturbances in Burnley, Oldham and Bradford ushered in community cohesion. It will be put forward that the concept was in direct contrast to multiculturalism. Admittedly, community cohesion did suggest that diversity should be valued but in reality the focus was much more on common and shared norms between different groups. Difference was not promoted. The agenda on race equality and housing

Race, Housing & Community: Perspectives on Policy & Practice, First Edition.
Harris Beider.
© 2012 Harris Beider. Published 2012 by Blackwell Publishing Ltd.

faced a number of challenges on viewing black and minority ethnic associations as a solution rather than a problem, making the case for specific investment for groups and creating space for positive action to be debated. The organisational memory on race equality from 1986 was in danger of being erased. Community cohesion moved the policy agenda in a different direction to Macpherson. Race was simply part of wider range of equality strands. Indices were developed across government to measure belonging, interaction and how different communities perceived to get on with each other. It now seems that cohesion will be replaced by a much harder variant of integration. A new government was elected in 2010. Rejecting multiculturalism as sowing division and diminishing cohesion as being too passive, a much more active approach to integration is in the offing. The Housing Corporation has been replaced by the Homes and Communities Agency and the Black and Minority Ethnic Housing Policy has been rejected in favour of Valuing Difference. The transition has been stark: Macpherson to Cohesion; CRE to EHRC, Race Relations Act 2000 to Equality Act 2010 and BME Housing Policies to Valuing Difference. It will be suggested in this chapter that these could also be viewed as a shift away from race specific to more generic solutions, a move away from single group funding based on ethnicity and a transition to an overarching regulatory regime. The contention is that new institutions and approaches have been strongly influenced by policy and this is likely to increase rather than decrease. Predictions are always risk laden but there seems very little likelihood of returning to multiculturalism even at a time of unprecedented super-diversity.

Policy context

It could be argued that policy related discussion on race specifically and community generally reached a pinnacle following the publication of the Macpherson Report into the murder of Stephen Lawrence in 1999 (Home Office, 1999). Moreover the intervention had an important impact on housing leading to the National Housing Federation sponsored Race and Housing Inquiry (2001) and incorporation of the Race Relations Amendment Act into the regulation of social landlords across the country. The focus of the Macpherson Report into new definitions of a racist incident and for the first public endorsement of the concept of institutional racism led to the social housing sector looking at the way in which the needs of black and minority ethnic stakeholders were being met.

As the regulator of housing associations in England, The Housing Corporation had an impressive record in promoting race equality. Since 1986 until 2003 the quango had initiated three five-year strategies on black and minority ethnic housing issues (see Beider, 2007a). This resulted in investment leading to the registration of more than 70 black led housing associations, designing new regulatory measures to ensure proportionate representation on non-executive and executive positions, and ensuring that satisfaction levels of black tenants matched those of their peers. Hence the social housing sector was well regulated on racial discrimination (Harrison et al., 2005). It is clear that the Macpherson Report was a profoundly important document for public policy in the UK. However, the social housing sector had already pioneered initiatives and ideas that predated 1999. Further, it should be remembered that the Housing Corporation initiated these policies largely under a Conservative government that was regarded as being regressive on social policy issues. There were three key reasons behind this approach. First, the critical role of black housing activists who formed the Federation of Black Housing Organisations (FBHO) in 1984 to represent the needs of black and minority ethnic communities. The organisation became a critical support and ensured that race and housing issues were publicised and debated in the sector. Second, a new type of municipal socialism emerged in major cities during the 1980s. Three successive and heavy defeats for the Labour Party at the General Elections in 1979, 1983 and 1987 led to a retrenchment of radical politics in local government. Anti-racism became an important part of the local agenda and this made it easier for the Housing Corporation to develop national frameworks on race and housing knowing that policies would be supported at the local level (Solomos, 1993). Third, as suggested earlier, senior executives at the Housing Corporation were committed to equality of opportunities for ethical and business reasons.

Housing had an impressive record on race equality before the Macpherson Report. This is not to underestimate its impact following publication in 1999. Institutional racism was now set within the context of systemic and collective failures of organisations. This needed fundamental cultural change within institutions, understanding the needs of diverse communities and effective engagement to counter direct and indirect discrimination. The focus was on social justice, specific interventions and resultant outcomes. For these reasons it could be argued that Macpherson was the high-water mark for British race relations. As Sivanandan states:

Macpherson, in that sense, was not just a result but a learning process for the country at large and, in the course of it, the gravitational centre of 'race' relations discourse was shifted from individual prejudice and ethnic need to systemic, institutional racial inequality and injustice. (Sivanandan, 2000)

Housing regulation became tighter and specific. Developing a race equality policy should ensure that any organisation is 'fit for purpose'. This meant meeting the guidance set by the Housing Corporation Good Practice Note and made explicit in Section 2.7:

Housing associations must demonstrate, when carrying out all their functions, their commitment to equal opportunity. They must work towards the elimination of discrimination and demonstrate an equitable approach to the rights and responsibilities of all individuals. They should promote good relations between people of different racial groups. (Housing Corporation, 2002)

Regulators shifted from a concern on processes to outcomes on equality issues. Housing associations needed to demonstrably show how they met this policy and practice agenda. Simply having policies in place was not good enough. Discussion, consultation, project development and evaluation were required. Moreover, race equality (as opposed to other forms of equality such as gender and disability) was seen to be driving the agenda.

Racism and discrimination were viewed as critical policy areas that had to be prioritised by housing associations and the Housing Corporation. Less than five years later the tone and scope of the housing sector has changed from the heights reached by the Macpherson Report and its aftermath.

It is suggested here that the transitioning from race equality commenced with the response to the 2001 summer disturbances in Burnley, Oldham and Bradford. The Cantle Report (sometimes known after the inquiry chair) set out to explore the causes of the disturbances in the three places but also conducted visits, interviews and meetings across the country. The final report made 67 recommendations, many largely concerned with practical interventions. A recurring theme was the depths of polarisation and separation in terms of education, housing, social and cultural networks (Home Office, 2001). In effect, the separation of communities in the same towns and cities was akin to people living 'a series of parallel lives' with real differences in education, employment and housing. The focus had moved away from processes and institutions that had held sway on debates on race and housing up to and including the Macpherson Report. Indeed, the sense of a bootstraps-led approach oozes from the Cantle Report.

> It is easy to focus on systems, processes and institutions and to forget that community cohesion fundamentally depends on people and their values ... many of our present problems seem to owe a great deal to our failure to communicate and agree to a set of common values that can govern behaviour. (Home Office, 2001)

If the problem was fragmented and ethnically polarised groups, then the task for organisations was to build 'cohesive communities'. These have been defined:

> As where there is a common vision and a sense of belonging for all communities; the diversity of people's different backgrounds and circumstances is appreciated and positively valued; those from different backgrounds have similar life opportunities; and strong and positive relationships are being developed between people from different backgrounds and circumstances in the workplace, in schools and within neighbourhoods. (LGA, 2004)

Community cohesion promotes contact between different groups because it serves as a driver to increase tolerance and reduce parallel lives. Deprivation and social justice are not ignored but the emphasis is on building shared values, civic ownership and responsibility. In this way the concept could be viewed as having classic New Labour ingredients: the aforementioned bootstrap approach, civic responsibility and centrally developed policies and indicators.

Housing and community cohesion: a critique

More specifically, community cohesion allowed housing and the role of housing organisations to be viewed as critically important in constructing shared norms. The Cantle Report stated that housing agencies should review their policies and strategies to provide more mixed housing areas, together with supportive mechanisms for residents who faced intimidation and harassment.

New developments, whether in the public or private sector, provide the basis of social interaction and thereby the development of common norms that is the cornerstone of much of the community cohesion rhetoric.

Indeed housing access and leasing policies were partly blamed for the creating of 'parallel lives'. Cantle returns to the theme in the context of concentration of communities in housing markets. Whilst acknowledging that a level of clustering may be needed to support services (though this is not quantified) he goes on to warn that: 'Once this tips over into an exclusive, or mono-cultural, environment based upon 'parallel lives', the opportunities for cross-cultural contact are diminished and the potential for the demonization of those communities appears to be greatly increased.' (Cantle, 2008: 217).

Community cohesion has been a cross-cutting policy initiative throughout government. The key principles of inter cultural contact, shared norms and reciprocity have driven performance in schools, colleges, universities, policing, and housing. Given the influence of community cohesion there is a need to challenge the concept generally and more specifically the application to housing.

First, there is an explicit assumption that neighbourhoods and/or communities become pathologised once they get to a yet to be defined tipping point. Here communities cease to connect and communicate with each other leading to 'parallel lives'. Yet this appears to be a simplistic and blunt analysis. Communities and neighbourhoods are diverse beyond race or faith. They can be differentiated by class, gender, employment and tenure. Research demonstrates that housing markets function in so called 'mono cultural environments' but this is just one aspect of a much more complex situation (Goodson and Beider, 2005). Communities will come into contact through different forms of consumption including retail, culture and virtual communities. Second, community cohesion approaches to housing are culturally loaded. Repeatedly the literature is fixated with inter cultural dialogue that will increase intolerance. Accepting that access to different communities may be important there is also evidence from contact theory that increased inter cultural contact may lead to reduced tolerance (Phillips and Harrison, 2010). Disadvantage and alienation together with power and conflict are absent from community cohesion discussion. Housing associations need to increase the choice of products for different communities both within perceived 'mono-cultural' and 'non-mono-cultural' markets. This has very little to do with culture and places much more emphasis on access to public services and goods. Third, it could be argued that the emergence of community cohesion has coincided with the demise of the Black and Minority Ethnic Housing Policy that drove ideas and investment since 1986. The new Housing and Communities Agency (HCA) amalgamating the Housing Corporation and English Partnerships has instead moved onto a Single Equalities Scheme. Reviewing the document it becomes evident that race equality has all but been erased from policy debates. The focus is on a generic approach emphasising equality and cohesion.

Given the emergence of black led housing associations from 1986–2003 we need to consider their role in a policy environment shaped by community cohesion. It should be noted that many were birthed in a multicultural policy environment bookended by the riots of 1985 and the Macpherson Report of 1999. The Cantle Report was published in 2001 but the impact for black led housing associations has been significant. Legislation and regulation has weakened the position of this group. Transitioning from the CRE to EHRC together with the 2010 Equality Act has shifted the policy focus away from black led housing associations. In short it could be argued that the imperative for the social housing sector to act on racist discrimination became less important within a more crowded legislative environment of gender, disability, age, sexual orientation and faith. Housing associations had to demonstrate commitment to wider equality issues. Additionally it could be suggested that the legislative and regulatory pressure from 1986–2003 led to increased representation of black and minority senior managers and board members. Progress had been made on key indicators and housing professionals questioned the need for a continued focus on race and housing.

Housing and 'race' equality has given way to housing and concern about community cohesion. The shift has its origin in the critique of Macpherson as an example of 'political correctness'. Institutions, organisations and individuals cannot operate freely without the fear of being branded a racist. The progressive 'race' equality group CARF summarises this thinking: '... The whole Right position on Macpherson: the Lawrences were exploited and Macpherson was misled by pressure groups which sought to establish black people as victims of a white society that cared little about the death of a black man.' (CARF, 2001).

So Macpherson and its recommendations appear to be in descent. Indeed, some have described the reaction against the Report as tantamount to a burial (CARF, 2001). The focus now is not so much about 'race' equality but differences between groups living in neighbourhoods. Once housing organisations stop discussing specific actions to prevent racism and commence a discussion about differences we are walking the precipice of a racialised context. Instantly the problem is not about racism, inequality and power but about identity, roles and responsibilities. Even more problematic is that the onus to change and integrate within 'common norms' falls on people rather than the institutions and organisations who are supposed to serve them. This seems to indicate a status hierarchy of deserving and non-deserving migrants in society with established minority groups at the top followed by new economic migrants, and refugees and asylum seekers at the bottom. The ordering of different groups in such a way and linked to welfare rights has even been suggested by some New Labour groups (for example, see Goodhart, 2004).

Many housing organisations regard creating sustainable and diverse neighbourhoods as a key policy driver. However there are a number of problems with community cohesion as a concept and also how it works in practice. First, the responses to the disturbances in Oldham, Bradford and Burnley in 2001, together with the negative debates on asylum and immigration, could be seen as counter-productive to the goals of shared identity and citizenship. New and old migrants are less likely to feel any obligation to contribute to community cohesion (and thus engagement) when they are being identified as being part of the problem. Second, the search for common identity can also be viewed as problematic. Minority residents who have moved from traditional neighbourhoods to contiguous neighbourhoods in urban areas have to decide on a trade off: moving away from accessing community infrastructure but securing better quality housing. In reality they may not be prepared to fully trade minority identity for unclear notions of citizenship within an increasingly secular society. Access to shops, places of worship and family networks may remain important to these economically mobile residents.

The changing nature of debates on 'race' and housing has helped to shift the policy discussion as well. The imperative is integration. As we have seen the agenda is driven by building shared norms, common identity and stable communities, by expecting diverse groups to 'buy into' British institutions, organisations and processes. Relationships with government and institutions based on loyalty and reciprocity were seen as the cornerstones of community cohesion (Robinson, 2007). This could lead to improved understanding, better services and greater mutual tolerance.

Since the emergence of community cohesion, we have not only seen a reduced importance on race equality but also a decline in the number of registered black led housing associations and symbolically the closure of the Federation of Black Housing Organisations (FBHO), which since 1985 has been the representative voice of these associations and has taken on a wider campaigning role on race and housing. It would be too simplistic to state a direct link between community cohesion and the collapse of FBHO. However, the focus on shared norms, common spaces together with a critique of multiculturalism eroded the rationale for black led housing associations and FBHO. This accelerated following the publication of the report from the Commission for Integration and Cohesion (CIC, 2007) which questioned amongst other areas the need for single group funding.

> All agencies, including Local Authorities and affordable housing providers, should operate inclusive allocations and lettings policies. Unless there is a clear business and equalities case, single group funding should not be promoted (see Annex D). In exceptional cases, where such funding is awarded, the provider should demonstrate clearly how its policies will promote community cohesion and integration. (CIC, 2007: 124)

The language on black led housing associations had slipped (Worley, 2005). More questions were being asked about these organisations (Beider, 2007a). These included the added value to black and minority ethnic housing consumers and their role in broader representation and leadership on race and housing issues in the sector as whole.

> They were relevant when they were set up, and then maybe for 10 years afterwards ... what has happened is that as other housing organisations have grown bigger they have taken up quite a lot of BME housing need as well. (Inside Housing, 2009)

The sense of being irrelevant to an evolving sector is couched both in the mainstream housing sector improving performance on race equality and the changing policy to community cohesion and equality. Indeed it could be argued that some representatives of the black led housing sector assumed an entrenched and defensive perspective in the midst of regulatory, policy and wider societal changes as a result of free movement of people Eastern Europe after the 2004 enlargement of the EU. Community cohesion focused on increased contact between communities and black led housing organisations were viewed as being problematic in terms of delivering shared norms and understanding. Given this perfect storm of retreating policy commitment, reduced investment and changing housing priorities it is no surprise that FBHO closed.

Looking ahead: a new agenda?

Recognising the weakness of community cohesion generally and specifically when applied to housing should not result in simply turning the clock back to 2000. Multiculturalism did advance representation, addressed specific needs and generated new ideas on race and housing. It could also be argued that the concept and organisations supporting key tenets did not sufficiently acknowledge the impact of new and different migration flows on housing needs and advocacy. The dominant domain was a binary analysis of race together with a resistance to working with the State yet at the same time being the recipient of investment and support based on race. Resourcing models did pit communities against each other in a deficit sum theorem that inevitably led to disconnection and alienation from groups who were unsuccessful.

Discussion of race and indeed class in housing seems strangely sterile and fixed in the past. The assumptions on equalities and legislation need to be reviewed in the search for new models and ideas that can drive forward analysis. Community cohesion could be viewed as a response to multiculturalism but also public management which focused on processes which seemingly embed disadvantage. Policies based solely on representative outputs will inevitably lead to a 'tick box' mentality. Minority organisations and individuals had long fought implicit and explicit accusations of favouritism after successfully securing employment or resources. In these circumstances, leadership should have connected interventions to address disadvantage. There remains a need to emphasise the diversity dividend on personal and organisational development. Instead, excluded individuals and organisations feel disconnected from the politics of race.

We should also resist calls for a simple class reductionism allied to a malevolent view of the State. Discussions on race have long argued the relative merits of class, race and the State (CCCS, 1982; Miles, 1982; Sivanandan, 1982). It could be argued that all were entrenched in fixed notions of class and the State and an alignment to a dualistic approach to housing that prevented discussion from moving forward. The dualism between choice and constraint and the relative importance of structure and agency is interesting but limiting. There is a danger of the race and housing debates leading to an intellectual cul-de-sac.

The seminal work of Giddens provided the basis for race and housing debates to move away from the dualism of structure and agency by suggesting that rather than being fixed and durable concepts they are both subject to change over a period of time. Individuals agency can influence the State (structure) and both are interdependent (Giddens, 1976). As he states: 'Structures must not be conceptualised as simply placing constraints upon human agency, but as enabling ...' (Giddens, 1976: 60).

Recent research on the subject appeared to take a less rigid stance on choice and constraint. Harrison has suggested that policy debates on race and housing have inevitably been highly normative in suggesting that minority residential concentration is a problem (Harrison, 1995). However as Ratcliffe notes the problem with these theories (and indeed much of the debate on race and housing in general) is that they provide very little room for taking on a dynamic approach to structure and agency (Ratcliffe, 2009). One of the more interesting attempts to take this debate forward with reference to 'race' and housing was undertaken by Sarre and his colleagues (1989). The study of minorities in the small town of Bedford particularly focused on the Italian community. Advancing Giddens' structuration theory they sought a model that would reconcile choice and constraints. To Giddens the structures within society that limit the choice of housing available to minorities are not independent. They may be influenced and changed through the actions of individuals within society. For example, private lenders that prevented Italians from securing competitive loans to buy homes lost this business as it moved to more progressive organisations. This helped to change patterns of lending in Bedford (Sarre et al., 1989: 320). A more recent example of this can be seen through mainstream lenders such as HSBC offering Islamic mortgages in a specific appeal to capture the business of the growing number of Muslims in the country (CIH, 2005). Similarly, a provider perspective can be seen through housing associations working with refugees to renew neighbourhoods and communities in areas of economic decline (Mullins et al., 2007).

The value of structuration theory is that it brings dynamism to the debates. The interdependence between structure and agency may provide a positive way forward for future research. Community cohesion, similar to many government generated concepts, remained frozen in the policy context of 2001 rather than progressing.

A major limitation of the 'race' and housing research has been the view that communities have fixed identities and are bounded within neighbourhoods. These are not simply associated with cultural theorists but include those who would claim to be Marxists. The focus is on collective action and behaviour within a rigid and stratified society. There are a number of weaknesses with this approach. First, fixed identity ascribes collective actions predicated on biological determinist models of behaviour. Grouping individuals together suggests that people are related by ethnicity (arguably this is on the continuum of biological determinism) and cannot move out from this perspective. Second, the idea of minorities living in bounded neighbourhoods has been an enduring characteristic of housing studies. Many have suggested that minorities have had very little choice to move away from traditional areas of settlement because of housing based discrimination. We are not for a moment suggesting that discrimination has not impacted on choice and shaped residential settlement across the country. However, minorities are active in deciding on their housing options and housing careers.

Housing and spatial context has moved on since the work of Rex and his associates. Our criticism of the models of 'race' and housing was partly based on the fixed models of housing markets leading to minorities being concentrated in poor housing. Spatial development and housing has since progressed. Housing markets are much more dynamic because of interventions such as Housing Market Renewal and the City-Region. In some cases, minorities are being viewed as a key driver for stability and growth in new types of neighbourhoods contiguous to traditional housing markets. In others, minority communities themselves have revived once derelict neighbourhoods through investing in shops, organisations and other types of infrastructure (Goodson and Beider, 2005). In both cases of institutional intervention and community action the emphasis is on neighbourhoods of opportunity rather than those where housing choice is limited.

We should have dynamic notions of identity and space. Minorities have different forms of identity that varies in different contextual situations such as the home, work or school and a social setting. The emphasis placed on 'race' and identity should consider these different circumstances. Minorities are multi-layered and there should be further research that explores the impact of gender, class and age within these groups. From undertaking such an exercise the non-reification of minorities will follow and mark a complete break from the normative labelling that has characterised 'race' and housing.

Research has focused on how the State has acted in a way that excludes minority communities from participating in housing organisations, including access as board members and in employment opportunities. These and other actions have led to minorities living in the worst housing conditions in the poorest neighbourhoods. However we also need to understand that the State can respond and indeed lead reform on 'race' and housing. For example, direct discrimination has been outlawed (1976 Race Relations Act), the pervasive nature of institutional racism acknowledged (Macpherson, 1999) and minority based housing organisations viewed as an example of black leadership (Housing Corporation, 1998).

The State has responded to external drivers for change. Access to decent housing services, gaining employment opportunities particularly at the most senior levels of management within housing organisations and gaining support for housing activities remains a problem but it is important to recognise that the State has evolved on minority issues in housing. Representation has been criticised in this narrative as a measure for success in housing but there has been clear progress on the number of minority senior manages in the sector as a whole together with the measures on 'race' as part of regulation.

Macro policy on 'race' has been contradictory for much of the post-war period. Restrictive policies to curb immigration, problematic labelling of minorities and State acculturation have been in an uneasy embrace with measures against discrimination, supporting minority based housing providers and promoting positive action in housing. More recently there has been a contested debate about community cohesion and its applicability to the UK.

In the same way as identity is dynamic we need to consider the capacity of the State to be both restrictive and expansive on 'race' and housing. It should not be seen as a fixed repressive force but one which can adapt and change to meet different circumstances.

Declining interest in race and housing: from Macpherson to cohesion

Policy and political discussion on race, housing and community in the UK gained a high political profile following the Macpherson Report into the murder of Stephen Lawrence in 1999 (Home Office, 1999) and the Cantle Report that investigated the disturbances in Burnley, Bradford and Oldham in 2001 (Home Office, 2001; Harrison et al., 2005). These policy interventions have shaped discussion on race equality in the UK and presaged legislative changes. Interestingly race equality debates have shifted considerably from advocacy and positive action to one that is couched in terms of roles, responsibilities and shared norms. As we will discuss next, this policy trajectory from Macpherson to Cantle helps to provide a context for the discussion on race and representation in the housing sector.

It could be argued that the Macpherson Report was simply another stage in identifying the embedded nature of racism and discrimination in British civic society. Britain had witnessed many celebrated policy interventions that scoped black and minority disadvantage. These include the Policy Studies Institute Reports (Madood et al., 1997) and also the Scarman Report into the 1981 'race' riots (Scarman, 1981; Benyon and Solomos, 1987). In the first Blair government the Social Exclusion Unit demonstrated that black and minority ethnic communities were amongst the most disadvantaged groups in society.

> ... People from minority ethnic communities are more likely than others to live in deprived areas and in unpopular and overcrowded housing. They are more likely to be poor and to be unemployed, regardless of their age, sex, qualifications and place of residence. (Social Exclusion Unit, 2000: 7)

The Macpherson Report was not focused on disadvantage per se. Its remit was to uncover the failure of the Metropolitan Police to convict the people who killed the black teenager Stephen Lawrence in South London. However, this was never going to be a routine murder investigation. The 70 recommendations, along with the acknowledgement about the scale of racial violence and the existence of institutional racism, distinguished this report from previous interventions. For example, Scarman had barely acknowledged racism after the 1981 riots by suggesting that police officers had, on occasions, shown personal prejudice (Scarman, 1981). Macpherson swept away these notions to discuss institutional racism within the context of systemic and collective failures within organisations. Countering direct and indirect discrimination required effective engagement, fundamental cultural change within institutions, and an understanding of diverse community needs. The focus was on social justice, specific interventions and resultant outcomes. In this context, Macpherson was the high-water mark for British race relations. As Sivanandan states:

> Macpherson, in that sense, was not just a result but a learning process for the country at large and, in the course of it, the gravitational centre of race relations discourse was shifted from individual prejudice and ethnic need to systemic, institutional racial inequality and injustice. (Sivanandan, 2000)

Publication of the Macpherson Report ushered in a series of changes on race equality. The most fundamental of these was the Race Relations (Amendment Act) 2000 which compelled all public funded bodies (not just the Police) to meet a specific duty to promote race equality. An example of this was the recruitment of a representative workforce ensuring that policies did not indirectly discriminate against certain specified groups (Blackaby and Chahal, 2000).

Apart from providing a new legal framework, Macpherson had a significant impact on housing. As discussed previously, the social housing sector had a track record of promoting race equality. Indeed there have been three distinct housing and race equality policies since 1986 that have helped to create over 60 BME housing associations, managing over 2000 housing units and spending over £500 million in capital funds (see Beider, 2007b for more detailed discussion of policy and BME housing associations). The Macpherson Report led to housing initiated Race and Housing Inquiry, which was managed by NHF and concluded that much still had to be done in meeting the housing needs of black and minority ethnic groups (National Housing Federation, 2001).

Housing Corporation regulatory practice on race equality is set within this context. Specifically, the Corporation comes under the jurisdiction of the Race Relations (Amendment) Act 2000 and has a statutory duty to 'eliminate racial discrimination, promote equality of opportunity and promote good relations between people of different racial groups' (Housing Corporation, 2002). In practice this meant that the Housing Corporation regulated housing associations in order to demonstrate to government that it was promoting race equality. The Race Equality Good Practice Note established three standards on meeting needs and requirements, which covered both internal governance and external engagement of different minority groups. The Housing Corporation clearly regarded race equality as an important policy priority in the aftermath of the Macpherson Report and the Race Relations Amendment Act. Developing a race equality policy should ensure that any organisation was 'fit for purpose'. This meant meeting the specific guidance set by the Corporation and made explicit in Section 2.7:

> Housing associations must demonstrate, when carrying out all their functions, their commitment to equal opportunity. They must work towards the elimination of discrimination and demonstrate an equitable approach to the rights and responsibilities of all individuals. They should promote good relations between people of different racial groups. (Housing Corporation, 2002)

Regulators shifted from a concern on processes to outcomes on equality issues. Housing associations had to demonstrate how they met this agenda; simply having policies in place was not good enough. Discussion, consultation, project development and evaluation were required. Race equality (as opposed to other forms of equality such as gender and disability) was seen as driving the agenda.

Macpherson was a symbolically important policy intervention that led to the Race Relations (Amendment Act) 2000. Racism and discrimination were viewed as important policy areas that had to be prioritised by housing associations and the Housing Corporation. The focus was on recognising the contribution of BME housing associations, compelling mainstream housing associations to improve performance on race equality, and recognising that ethnic diversity was good for the sector as a whole. An example of the Housing Corporation taking positive action measures is the financial help provided to BME housing associations to assist with reducing their rents in line with government policy. This amounted to £15 million distributed amongst ten housing associations (Housing Corporation, 2004a).

In less than five years, the tone and scope of the housing sector has changed from the heights reached by the Macpherson Report and its aftermath of the 2000 Race Relations Amendment Act. Earlier in this chapter we discussed the transition from Macpherson to the community cohesion agenda. In practice, the Macpherson Report, together with its recommendations, has been viewed as swinging the pendulum too much in favour of minorities. To detractors it has been viewed as an example of 'political correctness'. In short, preventing politicians and policy makers speaking out against some interventions on race equality because of the fear of being branded a racist. Of course, to supporters the Macpherson report was a radical and far reaching publication that led to positive changes in the police and wider society.

Community cohesion established a very different position. Difference based on ethnicity, which was seen as a positive and enriching symbol of multicultural Britain, was now regarded as potentially problematic. The focus on shared values could be viewed as moving to policies that promoted cultural integration alongside rights and responsibilities. In this context the focus of the 'problem' inevitably moves to British citizens who were regarded as being different. In short, British Muslims who followed a different faith and set of beliefs. After 9/11 and 7/7 community cohesion ceased to be about passive concerns about shared values and norms. Policy became highly politicised with the transition from race equality (Macpherson) to culture (community cohesion).

The new framework to discussing race equality in housing and elsewhere is based on the concept of community cohesion. This concept began to inform discourse following the disturbances in northern towns and cities in 2001. The subsequent inquiry led to a wide-ranging debate on the role of housing improvement in relation to ethnically segregated neighbourhoods in urban areas.

A key recommendation of the report was to urge housing agencies to review their policies and strategies to provide more mixed housing areas, together with supportive mechanisms for residents who faced intimidation and harassment. It was also noted that funding for housing improvement could distort regeneration programmes as it is capital intensive, and suggested that some change of emphasis may be needed to develop a people focused, rather than what was termed a property needs approach to areas. Community cohesion is important in public policy discussion because it drives initiatives across a number of cross cutting areas such as housing and neighbourhood renewal and also triggers wider debates on citizenship.

By contrasting the Macpherson and Community Cohesion Reports, it may help to clarify some of the problems with housing, race and representation. Table 2.1 shows how policy interventions have led to legislative changes that eventually impact on the way in which housing organisations manage diverse communities.

Macpherson was laced with discussions on racism, social justice and power that gave rise to the 2000 Race Relations Amendment Act with the specific duty to promote race equality. The housing sector responded with initiatives such as the Race and Housing Inquiry, which helped to keep the focus (and pressure) on race equality and change. Black and minority ethnic housing associations had a key role as advocates and were seen as dispensing good practice. Moving on five years and we see a dramatic change. Community Cohesion generated debates with the emphasis on difference, identity and cultural norms. It could be argued that race was simply a sub-text in these wider narratives. Indeed, cohesion suggested that all groups had a responsibility to promote community cohesion. Sometimes the apparent reluctance of minority groups to change 'their ways' led to problems with neighbourhood-based integration. The legislative outcome was the movement from the Commission for Racial Equality to the Equality and Human Rights Commission and the 1976 Race Relations Act to the 2010 Equality Act. The focus is not on race but subsumed within wider concerns such as gender, disability and religion. These have 'crowded out' race equality measures from public policy discussion and may have left some housing organisations to

Table 2.1 From Macpherson to cohesion: policy, legislation and housing impact.

Policy	Legislation	Housing impact
Macpherson Report	2000 Race Relations (Amendment) Act	• Race specific • Duty to promote race equality • Race and Housing Inquiry • Good Practice Note 4 specifically to address race equality
Community Cohesion Report	2010 Equality Act	• Shared identity and norms • Race as a problem • Conclusion of BME Housing Policy • Good Practice Note 8 to address wide range of equalities

become sanguine about achieving the type of change that Macpherson demanded. Indeed, the Housing Corporation did not develop another five-year race equality strategy after 2003 but instead opted for a wider equality and diversity approach that reflects the importance of community cohesion. Black and minority ethnic organisations are no longer seen as advocates and beacons for best practice but rather as problematic in terms of performance and role (Lupton and Perry, 2004). Indeed, the number of independent black housing organisations has declined sharply reflecting concerns about role, viability and identity (Beider, 2007b). The policy transformation sets the parameters of action on race equality and housing.

The changing nature of debates on housing and race discussed above has helped to shift the policy discussion as well. Black and minority communities have become a problem. The imperative is integration. As we have seen the agenda is driven by building shared norms, common identity and stable communities, by expecting diverse groups to 'buy into' British institutions, organisations and processes. Relationships with government and institutions based on loyalty and reciprocity were seen as the cornerstones of community cohesion (Robinson and Reeve, 2006; Beider, 2007b). This could lead to improved understanding, better services and greater mutual tolerance. However, the diagnostic and outcomes are problematic.

Housing had an impressive record on race equality before the Macpherson Report. This is not to underestimate its impact following publication in 1999. Institutional racism was now set within the context of systemic and collective failures of organisations. This required fundamental cultural change within institutions, understanding the needs of diverse communities and effective engagement to counter direct and indirect discrimination. The focus was on social justice, specific interventions and resultant outcomes. For these reasons it could be argued that Macpherson was the high-water mark for British race relations.

The turning of the wheel: 'muscular liberalism' and integration

The view being put forward in this chapter is a movement from progressive policies to regressive on race and housing. The Labour Government of 1997–2010 promoted a range of progressive interventions including sponsoring the Macpherson Report (1999) and Social Exclusion Unit (2001) as well as the 1998 black and minority ethnic housing policy (Housing Corporation, 1998) and investment for black led housing associations to support rent regulation (Housing Corporation, 2004a). Alongside this has been a move away from race equality and towards community cohesion. As discussed in this chapter, and also in relation to black led housing associations in Chapter 4, the impact on race and housing has been to focus on common norms and shared values during a period of super-diversity (Vertovec, 2007). Moreover, the diminution of race generally and in social housing comes in the midst of research that demonstrates the scale of minority disadvantage (EHRC, 2010). In many of key indicators such as housing affordability, overcrowding and access to decent housing, minority groups are more vulnerable than other sections of the population. Yet the policy of community cohesion has been implemented to gloss over differences and narrow the norms and shared values across the country. As we have noted this has been influential in moving the direction away from race equality in housing. Governance on race and housing is now very much embedded in the model of integration and common values. Of course community cohesion was birthed under the Labour government and this has given way since the 2010 General Election to a Conservative-Liberal Democrat coalition. Pronouncements on race and housing have been limited but this has not stopped wider discussion about the nature of multiculturalism. The portents seem to suggest a much more robust version of community cohesion emphasising integration and acceptance of common values. The speech by David Cameron at a Munich security conference in

February 2011 linked common values as almost akin to a value based society of rights and responsibilities:

> Under the doctrine of state multiculturalism, we have encouraged different cultures to live separate lives, apart from each other and the mainstream. We have failed to provide a vision of society to which they feel they want to belong ... We need a lot less of the passive tolerance of recent years and much more active, muscular liberalism. (Cameron, 2011)

This seems to suggest that Macpherson and Community Cohesion were driven too much by the State. Further, a top down approach does not work in promoting shared values but there is no sense of who or what will be promoting 'muscular liberalism' that is being advocated. Belonging, a mainstay of community cohesion since 2001, remains an important component but there has been a failure of a common vision. There is a contradiction. 'The doctrine of state multiculturalism' implies that Government had been zealous in promoting this particular brand of policy but there is no indication that the State will be taking a minor role in the promotion of 'muscular liberalism'. Here we see neither multiculturalism nor community cohesion but a hard edged integration policy with the problems associated with the letter and none of the benefits of the former.

A very real danger would be to regress to some of the debates of the 1950s and 1960s discussed in Chapter 1 with references to 'Dark Strangers' (Patterson, 1963). The critique of multiculturalism in the speech and promotion of integration seems at odds with the now model definition of the same term provided by Roy Jenkins, the Home Secretary in the Labour government of 1964–70: '... not a flattening process of assimilation but equal opportunity accompanied by cultural diversity in an atmosphere of mutual tolerance.' (Jenkins, 1967: 216).

Contrasted with 'muscular liberalism' and more recent varieties of community cohesion, Jenkins' integration promotes two aspects that seem to have been lost in the debates about shared values and belonging. First, equality of opportunity or simply social justice. Communities and groups start of from different points in society. As evidenced by substantive recent research (EHRC, 2010; National Equality Panel, 2010) the UK has different levels of inequality measured by income, tenure and ethnicity to identify just three indices. Becoming part of societal values is much more problematic when equality of opportunity in law is not part of the reality of life. Addressing economic equality should be the prerequisite to build the foundation of belonging. Second, Jenkins recognised the importance of cultural diversity. In fairness, diversity and difference forms part of the definition of community cohesion (Home Office, 2001) and the two further national iterations (CIC, 2007; CLG, 2008). However, the focus on difference is eclipsed by the move towards shared values and integration. Diversity is seen as problematic in community cohesion (Kudnani, 2002). This is exemplified by the decline of black and minority led housing associations which is discussed in more detail in Chapter 4. Indeed, some have suggested that cultural diversity may weaken social capital in society (Putnam, 2007).

It seems perplexing that the increasing super-diversity (Vertovec, 2007) has been accompanied by a response to promote common indices of belonging whether this is based on cohesion or integration. The wheel has turned to previous debates. A prescriptive form of integration seems to have been heralded but devoid of content and reality of the modern and diverse society which is such a strong feature of the country. In the next section the role of the transformation of policy will be framed by the role of the HCA.

The Housing Corporation had a progressive policy towards black and minority ethnic issues. This is the explored in greater depth in Chapter 4 but goes back to the first Black and Minority Ethnic Housing Policy launched in 1986. This sped up the development of black and minority ethnic housing associations and also black and minority ethnic leadership in the sector (Harrison, 1995). Progress was accompanied by a macro policy context of increased investment in inner urban areas through schemes such as City Challenge, Single Regeneration Budget and New Deal for Communities. The Housing Corporation intervention may have been instigated by the rioting in poor, disadvantaged minority neighbourhoods in London, Manchester, Birmingham, Liverpool and Bristol during 1981 and 1985. There is little doubt that the growth of the black and minority housing movement was helped by the publication of the Macpherson Report (Home Office, 1999) and the 2000 Race Relations Amendment Act. These interventions prioritised race equality and ensured that policy focus remained in this sector. The Housing Corporation Black and Minority Ethnic Housing Policies went through three iterations, completed in 2003, and led to significant progress on race equality in housing.

In 2008 the Housing Corporation was replaced by Homes and Communities Agency which became responsible for housing and regeneration across the country. Also the heady optimism of the Macpherson Report has been replaced by the sober reality that multiculturalism could be problematic in skewing housing investment and embedding difference between different groups in the same town or city. As discussed community cohesion was a challenge to race equality in housing and especially on the role of black and minority led housing associations. Supporting single group funding (as black and minority ethnic housing associations were categorised) was identified as a cause of tension between different groups in later reports on community cohesion and integration (CIC, 2007).

These changing policy environments meant that the HCA developed a less race specific response to housing. In formulating policy on diversity, equality and cohesion the HCA published *Diverse Interventions* (HCA, 2009). Compared to the bold commitment to race equality showcased by the Housing Corporation in 1986 the new approach straddled statutory duty towards race but also gender and disability. In addition the HCA also focused on age, faith and sexual orientation. The new equality strands squeezed race and heeded the policy transformation of race and housing discussed above. Indeed less than six years after the conclusion the last Black and Minority Ethnic Housing Policy there is not a single mention of BME housing associations in *Diverse Interventions*. Instead the HCA seeks to promote a broad approach to equality through influence of the *Single Conversation* which has been described as:

> ... a place-based approach that .will take the vision and ambitions of local authorities and help them achieve their plans through a shared investment agreement. Delivery will be achieved through a more streamlined use of investment and resources, including using expertise from the HCA to address specific challenges. Through this process, the HCA as the national housing and regeneration agency, will act as the bridge between local ambition and national targets. (HCA, 2009)

Many of the processes focus on supply side measures on equality. Increasing awareness of diversity amongst key partners externally and promoting diversity champions internally to inculcate the message. It could be argued that the HCA approach marks a clear break from the Housing Corporation. In short, race equality became less of priority. Black and minority ethnic housing associations found it difficult to meet new economic challenges on rents and efficiency. Some of the leading housing organisations became the subject of regulatory intervention and the representative organisation, FBHO, closed down because of a steep decline in membership (see Chapter 4).

In tone and delivery the HCA has moved towards a much more integrated approach to managing equality. After the 2010 election the agency, similar to many other government sponsored organisations, had to make substantial budget cuts as part of a wider public expenditure cuts. The £230 million reductions included scrapping £30 million of the gypsy and traveller programme that were highlighted as a key group in *Diverse Conversations* (Inside Housing, 2010). Given these circumstances of policy direction and economic constraints there seems no immediate prospect of the supporting the next generation of black and minority ethnic housing associations.

Conclusion: a housing journey through multiculturalism, cohesion and integration

In this chapter we have seen the direction of housing policy from multiculturalism to cohesion and now integration. This spans the period from 1986 when the first Black and Minority Ethnic Housing Policy was introduced by the Housing Corporation to 2009 to the publication of *Diverse Interventions* by the HCA. Bookended between these two different policy statements are a number of policy initiatives that had a profound impact on race and housing. An expansive period of support for black and minority ethnic housing associations reached a policy peak with the Macpherson Report which spoke about racism, power and the need for change. Difference was actively encouraged by the Housing Corporation. Not only was funding provided to housing associations to meet the specific needs of black and minority ethnic communities but the agency also sponsored research, conferences and seminars exploring the extent of black and minority ethnic disadvantage. Housing associations not only had to be seen to delivering change but were regulated against race equality objectives. In part, community cohesion could be viewed as a rejection of the multiculturalism approach. The desire to meeting specific needs resulted in investment decisions that prevented communities from interacting with each other. In some instances this led to different groups leading 'parallel lives' and increases in local tensions. Rather than predicating housing policy on different communities the priority should be on creating cohesion based on common and shared values. Community cohesion shaped public policy after its introduction in 2001. It heralded an approached that diminished the role of race in housing. Since its inception, the number of black led housing associations fell to a historic low, the representative umbrella organisation, FBHO, closed and the Housing Corporation did not instigate a new black and minority ethnic housing policy after 2003. It has been suggested in the chapter that community cohesion, whilst instigating a different process on race, had not led to increased levels of tolerance or a sense of shared values. This seems to have been endorsed by the current government who have been critical of multiculturalism but also previous integration policies. These have been labelled as passive rather than interventionist. A new and harder edged approach to integration is being developed. This could focus on shared values and norms but will insist that groups and organisations actively support common perspectives. Housing organisations will remain the conduit to support integrated groups and communities. However, it remains uncertain on how this goal will be achieved at a time of ever increasing super-diversity. In these circumstances housing policies that focus on belonging will require an elastic approach to integration in order to make this a reality.

3

Developing Cohesive Neighbourhoods in UK Cities: White Perspectives

Introduction

Community cohesion has become the key driver to discussing segregation and integration in UK. This followed disturbances between immigrant and white communities in Northern towns and cities across England in 2001. The focus since then has been on building common norms and shared spaces and increasing inter-cultural dialogue. However, the contention is that the number of studies on the white working class, cohesion and housing has paled into insignificance compared to those of minority groups. This has created a policy vacuum as well as a tendency for a social construction to be developed based on normative assumptions and collective behaviours that underpin approaches in white working class communities.

In this chapter a number of issues will be addressed. First, a study of white working class communities will be placed in context by reviewing academic and policy contributions. Second, consideration will be given to the importance that is placed on housing in white communities and, specifically, the role of social housing. This is based on a synopsis of a research study in three neighbourhoods of England. Third, and given the first two themes, recommendations will be suggested on the importance

Race, Housing & Community: Perspectives on Policy & Practice, First Edition.
Harris Beider.
© 2012 Harris Beider. Published 2012 by Blackwell Publishing Ltd.

of including white communities in discussions about cohesion and housing. This chapter should be seen as exploring new ideas and themes in housing and cohesion and in this vein chimes with the overall ambitions of the book as a whole.

Race, culture and change

The premise of this chapter is focused on white working class communities in the context of community cohesion and housing. In this sense it is unusual. Generally, it should be noted that discussion on race has been shaped by studies focusing on the experiences of minority groups (Fryer, 1984). A body of literature has been generated that goes back to at least the post-1945 immigration from the Indian sub-continent and Caribbean. Before we review policy and academic approaches on white working class communities, it is important to summarise key themes on race literature. There are similarities in content, approaches and policy applications for both minority and white groups.

The minority based literature goes back to the 1940s and can be broadly summarised in three distinct phases. The first of these may be described as *cultural difference* and is associated with a largely anthropological approach to new immigrant communities. This commenced with studies of emergent minority communities in different urban spaces during the 1950s and 1960s. The leading publications on race during this phase (Little, 1947; Richmond 1954; Banton, 1955; and Patterson, 1963) emphasised that conflict was due to cultural differences between immigrant and host white communities. Over time, interaction between groups would reduce tensions and achieve the goal of integration. Of course, the role of cultural interaction easing tensions between different groups is one of the key themes of community cohesion, which will be explored later in this chapter. Patterson's *Dark Strangers* (Patterson, 1963) exemplifies the impact of immigration on traditionally white neighbourhoods in South London. The terminology is grounded in the immigrant-host praxis and identifies the problem of integration to be related to Caribbean migrants rather than racism within the broader society. Common sense narratives are quickly developed where minorities are positioned as a threat to stability, norms and behaviours of a white neighbourhood (for example, see Table 3.1 later in this chapter)

During the 1960s and 1970s, the focus shifted to understanding discrimination operating within the State and wider society. Debates were anchored in addressing *racial discrimination* together with policies that prevented minority communities from gaining access to services, employment and goods. It could be argued that the most celebrated publication was Rex and Moore's *Race, Community and Conflict* (1967). This study of racial discrimination operating within housing markets in Birmingham allowed discussion of power, conflict and exclusion to be included in the debates on race relations. This was a new departure and contrasted with the largely passive approach of cultural difference previously discussed in literature. Rex and Moore also provided a framework that suggested that conflict could exist between different groups outside class relations. Further studies on the theme of racial discrimination in public policy include Rex and Tomlinson (1979), Smith (1989) and Henderson and Karn (1987). The narrative in each of these important studies is that the State and related institutions were responsible for growing segregation within towns and cities because of racism, especially in public sector housing.

Importantly there is a reification of white communities. The dominant theme is one where this group is pitted against minority communities in competition for jobs, housing, education and political rights. Racial discrimination is viewed as benefiting white working class communities. Further the advantageous position is supported by representative bodies such as trade unions and the Labour Party (Rex and Tomlinson, 1979). Here the white working class are viewed as being resistant to change, hostile to new migrants and stubbornly maintaining power and control. Grouped assumptions are made about white communities. The legacy remains and it is suggested here that the perception of white communities protecting interests in social housing and related policy domains and mobilising against minority communities has not been helpful. Reality is much more complex. In contrast, minorities are generally considered passive recipients of discrimination and form a type of underclass that is detached from mainstream society. Of course, both could be considered as false representations based on reification and collectivised behaviours. A more nuanced approach is required.

In response to Rex et al., an academic literature based on *cultural resistance* developed from the 1980s. Here minority groups were not viewed as passive instruments of institutions but could organise themselves to resist racism. The agency of minority culture and a radical approach to political activism marked this approach as different to the paradigm developed by Rex. Moreover a critique was also made of Marxist writers such as Miles (1982) who promoted class as the key model of analysis. This was too restrictive and reductionist.

Seminal publications during this period were Sivanandan (1982) and the Centre for Contemporary Cultural Studies (CCCS, 1982). The key concepts are about power, discrimination and urban crisis. Cultural difference should be celebrated and encouraged as a form of political organisation. This literature has been influential in opening discussion on race by developing new debates on racism, culture and social construction. However, there is once again a lack of understanding and context about whiteness or white identity. Solomos and Back (1995) recognise the shortcomings of literature on whiteness and suggest that it is important to understand how the term is constructed and applied in everyday discourse. Despite this, they still warn against focusing too much on white working class communities in case it leads to the diminution of anti-racism policies and practice. Indeed cultural resistance literature could be criticised for using normative assumptions in the same way Rex et al. were critiqued for reification of minority communities.

So far we have attempted to demonstrate that discussion on race and racism has been a largely minority experience. Academic literature has vicariously viewed immigrants as being problematic, victims and latterly the most radical points of organisation in society. In contrast, analysis of white communities has been largely absent. They are variously depicted as perpetrators of harassment or viewed as hostile to immigration because of a combination of racism and labour protection (Miles and Phizacklea, 1984).

Connecting communities: a focus on white working class communities?

Our review demonstrates that there is a gap in knowledge and understanding about the white working class and community cohesion. Compared to research on minority communities there have been relatively few studies on how this group have engaged with race and cohesion. However, publications on the two groups do follow a similar trajectory: a strongly cultural focus and subsequent downplaying of inequality and disadvantage; prescriptive and collectivised behaviour ignoring differences by gender, age, sexuality and tenure; and blaming communities for keeping themselves apart or not participating in building common norms. Previously we have discussed the interplay between the social construction of problematic or dangerous labels to minority and white communities. In the former this led to criminal behaviour such as mugging being perpetrated and addressed by SUS (police are able to act on suspicion to stop and search a person); in the latter a predilection toward disruptive behaviour has led to ASBOs (anti-social behaviour orders). Both groups have been described as residing within confined and separate boundaries. For the most part this means poor quality private sector housing in urban conurbations for minority communities and peripheral council estates for white working class communities. Communities are easily identifiable because of collectivised behaviour, cultural underpinning and residence.

Between 2010 and 2011, the terms of reference on white working class communities changed with the government announcement of *Connecting Communities* (CLG, 2009). This was a £12 million national programme which targeted more than 160 neighbourhoods across the country badly hit by the 2007 recession. These areas vary in size and location but it is noted that they share three themes in common. First, a decline in manufacturing that adversely impacts white communities; second, increased immigration, perceptions of neighbourhood change and competition for jobs; third, problems with crime and general anti-social behaviour. At the core of *Connecting Communities* is focusing on the needs of white working class communities and preventing the rise of support for far right parties such as the British National Party (BNP). In this way cohesion and resilience will be increased.

Local authorities were being tasked with developing programmes in advance but each initiative needed to demonstrate how *leadership* could be improved, 'giving people a voice' and increased connectivity with local councillors and community activists with *opportunities* to access jobs, training and learning. Language on *Connecting Communities* symbolically talks about rebuilding neighbourhoods and leadership to prevent the rise of extremism.

> … none of this will work unless on the doorstep, in pubs and community centres local people know and see that someone is speaking up for them and fighting their corner. They need to know that the jobs being created are the jobs they can get, the houses being built are the homes they can live in, and the library, the school and the hospitals are being built for them, their families and their community. (Denham, 2009)

This seems an acknowledgement that government policies on race, cohesion and related areas had ignored a white working class constituency. Some have suggested that threat of the far right in these areas has been exaggerated (Goodwin, 2009). Though the British National Party has increased the number of elected councillors in places such as Barking and Stoke, support in white working class neighbourhoods is levelling off with real growth in contiguous semi-skilled areas (Eatwell and Goodwin, 2009). The association of the white working class follows an established (and false) narrative going back the rise of Oswald Moseley in the East End of London (Harris, 2010). Since this time, the white working class has been labelled as hostile to race and immigration (Teddy Boys in the 1950s; Dockers in the 1960s; Skinheads in the 1970s; Rise of BNP after 2000). As Goodwin points out, support for the Far Right covers a gamut of issues including social disadvantage, ineffective leadership and representation result which lead to scepticism on the role of the State (Goodwin, 2009).

Connecting Communities arrived rather belatedly after 13 years of Labour Government. During this period we have noted how white working class communities have been socially constructed by policy and popular culture as a problematic ethnic group. There has been little analysis of differences, inequality and ideology of neighbourhoods and communities. It could be argued that the absence of empirical studies of white working class communities equates to the emergence of pathologies on collective behaviours which merely demonstrate how these groups deviate from societal norms.

The focus of policy and practice on norms and inter community contact has emphasised culture in the discussion of race, minorities and the white working class. The absence of terms such as power, conflict and disadvantage has led to a cultural reductionism. More than this, the problems may have been the result of economic restructuring and poor political leadership but white working class communities need to resolve these challenges by a boot strapped communitarian approach. The recession means that more and not less will be expected of local communities and organisations as the State is scaled back by political will and economic necessity.

Whiteness: culture and pathology

It is suggested here that the lack of focus in the literature helps the construction of white communities as an ethnic rather than class group. In a sense, the group becomes an empty vessel that has filled with normative and cultural ingredients. Typically white working class communities are viewed as being problematic, dysfunctional and living in annexed council estates. Collectively they are viewed as hostile to change and being the vanguard of support for extremist parties. This type of fixed construction is viewed as erroneous. Garner has argued that the reality is one of fluid and dynamic communities (see Garner, 2009).

An emerging literature on whiteness has started to deconstruct the term. Some start from the position of whiteness as being the normalised position within society. It could be argued that difference, identity and power are measured against this norm and indeed has shaped discussion and policy interventions on integration. To put it more bluntly, everything that is not white necessarily has to be deviant (Dyer, 1988). This is consolidated by research on white working class communities in the south west of England (Garner, 2006; Garner, 2009). Apart from viewing whiteness as the 'dominant normalised racialised location in British society' the key themes for this group are invisibility, norms, loss and empire.

Neighbourhood change and loss are key markers as a recurrent theme in the study of whiteness. Inevitably this becomes coupled with immigration and access to social housing. In this way whiteness literature shows parallels with studies on minority communities who could be viewed as agents of change (see Patterson, 1963 earlier). For example, Hoggett discussed how white communities in London's East End lamented the impact of a growing Bangladeshi population on previous neighbourhood norms (Hoggett, 1992). This has also been taken up by other studies of white communities such as the National Community Forum's overarching research on perceptions of minority communities (National Community Forum, 2009). In the following quote there is a real and urgent sense of cohesive white working class communities coming under pressure to change and, as a result, reacting in a visceral way.

> ... We're trying to stick up for ourselves. We are white, we are ... this is our country, and as they are coming in they should be taught, there should be said "alright, what can you offer, how do you feel ... living among white people? Will it be, you know, a hindrance? Will you be able to get on with your neighbours if they are white?" And if not, they shouldn't be allowed to come. (National Community Forum, 2009: 28)

Much of the discussion about white working class communities has been focused on cultural characteristics. In the past, interpretations could be viewed as simplistic. For example, Roberts focused on working class values as being the reward for hard work, aspiration for family improvement, solidarity, security and support for the needy. He contended that these were common values which could be found in working class neighbourhoods in different contexts and locations (Roberts, 2001). This is also developed by Joyce (1995). The emphasis is on mutual reciprocity and solidarity in disadvantaged communities. Skeggs (2009) has a rather different interpretation where class is inevitably antagonistic because it is shaped by exploitation.

One of the key themes of literature is the heavy cultural and normative inculcation of white working class communities. Much of this has shaped a negative social construction. Being white and working class is viewed as being problematic. Charles Murray popularised the term underclass in his polemical but influential article in the *Sunday Times* (see Murray, 1996). He suggested that Britain was experiencing a white working class problem in the UK that was getting worse. This was the result of an over generous welfare state, reduction in common norms and increasing crime.

> 'There are many ways to identify an underclass. I will concentrate on 3 phenomena that have turned out to be early warning signals in the U.S.: illegitimacy, violent crime, and drop out from the labour force.' (Murray, 1996).

Though Murray's research has been challenged (see Levitas,1998) his intervention shaped a discourse on white working class communities that constructed imagery of council estates marked by indicators of rising illegitimacy, crime and unemployment. We once again see the ascribing of collective and dysfunctional norms which are out of step with society. These perspectives quickly became incorporated into policy and practice. New Labour's establishment of the Social Exclusion Unit was a spatial and combined response to the challenges in some white working class neighbourhoods (Social Exclusion Unit, 2000). Peter Mandelson, a senior government Minister and one of the architects of New Labour, was explicit in his analysis of the challenges in Britain:

> We are people who are used to being represented as problematic. We are the long term, benefit-claiming, working class poor, living through another period of cultural contempt. We are losers, no hopers, low life scroungers. Our culture is yob culture. The importance of welfare provisions to our lives has been denigrated and turned against us; we are welfare dependent and our problems won't be solved by giving us higher benefits. We are perverse in our failure to succeed, dragging our feet over social change, wanting the old jobs back, still having babies instead of careers tuck in outdated class and gender moulds. We are the challenge that stands out above all others, the greatest social crisis of our times. (cited in Haylett, 2001)

There is direct correlation between social exclusion, problems associated with white working class and deviant places loaded within a problematic cultural construction. Recent interventions such as the term 'chav' has helped to shape the conventional view of white working class communities through cultural concerns (normative) rather than social inequality (subjective). These communities are thus located as being outside accepted norms within society. Moreover, it could be argued that embedded and fixed values are prescribed to communities. Interestingly Nayak contrasts the culturally and spatially restrictive white working class community with the dynamic middle class: 'cosmopolitan citizens no longer rooted to archaic images of whiteness.' (Nayak, 2009).

Pathology, whiteness and class

It is suggested here that the absence of a coherent policy or academic literature on community cohesion and whiteness has created a vacuum that has been filled by depictions on whiteness in popular culture. In the main these have been negative with the representation of whiteness focused as a lumpen proletariat, dysfunctional or dangerous or a combination of all three. Programmes on British TV such as *Shameless* and *Little Britain* provided a comedic framework; the *Jeremy Kyle Show* has been described as 'proletarian porn' and again emphasises the cultural gulf between norms of behaviour amongst white working class as compared with the rest of society (Nayak, 2009).

Taking this further, theorists have suggested that white working class has become a distinct 'other' within Britain. Similar to minority communities and especially Muslim Britons, the white working class can be viewed as different to mainstream, with common and shared norms, living in problematic council estates rather than 'segregated' inner city neighbourhoods. Mockery in popular culture is viewed as part of this 'othering' (Raisborough and Adams, 2008) and a process where class distinctions become less associated with economic accounts and engrained in cultural reproduction. We have previously noted that the absence of social inequality in the debates on community cohesion has led to prominence of normative cultural factors shaping policy and practice frameworks. Inter community contact, shared norms and spaces have become the main points of configuration. Importantly Bourdieu (1986) has stressed how culture can be used to exclude communities and encourage the formation of hierarchies of dominance. The point is emphasised by Skeggs who suggests that culture and taste can be used to differentiate and distance groups in society especially from working class communities:

> ... to move beyond (but still with) the economic ... into understanding value more generally to understand how class is made through cultural values premised on morality, embodied in personhood and realized (or not) as a property value in symbolic systems of exchange ... (Skeggs, 2005: 969)

The cultural configuration of white working class culture as being problematic has been prominent in the media and not simply confined to the Right. The popular press coined the construction of deviant group but this was also taken up by commentators in broadsheets and political class. For example, the editorial in *The Independent* states:

> Generations are being brought up on sink estates mired in welfare dependency, drug abuse and a culture of joblessness. And the majority of children born in such wretched circumstances are simply not making it out in later life. This is not a class problem: it is an underclass problem. And it is the failure of these sections of society to get on that is responsible for the fact that social mobility is in decline. (cited in Sveinsson, 2009)

Interestingly we have the fusion of class, whiteness and pathology. More than this there is an echo to the way that minority communities were depicted in a variety of publications discussed earlier. Apart from cultural classification of white communities as being problematic we should also emphasise that the onus is on groups themselves to resolve the societal problems. This is a communitarian approach which underpins much government policy since 1997.

In the midst of a largely negative and cultural depiction, recent documentaries have tried to develop an informed approach to white working class; the BBC *White* Series and also films such as *This is England* and *Somers Town* attempted to discuss themes such as class, identity loss and racism in the context of political, cultural and economic change. *This is England* in particular symbolises tensions within working class culture on race and immigration. These communities are not projected as being collectively racist and exclusionary but instead celebrating aspects of multiculturalism. The group of young people at the centre of the film are composed of both black and white members and celebrate black culture and ska music. This is some distance from the stereotypical image of the racist groups who attack minority communities. It could be argued that the portrayal of white working class communities in recent film making is far more balanced than policy and media literature and should be optimised in discussions on these issues.

Similarities exist in the narratives of minority and white working class communities. Both have been viewed as being problematic and posing challenges to social order. This is from a culturally normative perspective that considers communities as being difficult to integrate into societal norms (see Patterson 1963; Murray 1996).

In the previous sections we have seen similarities in the literature. Discussions on race and cohesion have emphasised cultural solutions as more important than debates on economic inequality. Promoting interaction between different groups should lead to increased tolerance and diminution of 'parallel lives'. However, acceptable 'norms' in a societal context are problematic because they are subjective and shaped by a perception of acceptable and unacceptable behaviours and attitudes.

Policy prescriptions have focused on the ethnic dimension of minority and white communities rather than class or indeed inequality. It could be argued that white working class communities are viewed as resistant to change and developing behaviours that are far from norms. Table 3.1 shows how the discussion and policy prognosis of both communities has developed.

Table 3.1 Reviewing literature and policy approaches to minority and white communities.

Key themes in literature	Policy responses
• Cultural difference • 'Deviant' from societal norms • Spatial boundaries Normative assumptions/collectivised behaviours	• Integration • Social exclusion • Community Cohesion • Connecting Communities
Critique of literature	**Pathologies of policy and social construction**
• Muted on white working class communities • Reification of groups • Limited discussion of diversity within communities • Limited discussion of institutions, power and representation	• SUS (black youth) • ASBO (white youth) • Prevent (Muslims) • Connecting Communities (white working class communities)

Both minority and white working class communities may be perceived to deviate from acceptable norms. As we have seen, it is regrettable that both have been pathologised by some research and policy interventions as being problematic. Minority communities are increasingly occupying inner city neighbourhoods and white working class groups housed in annexed council estates. A sense of closed neighbourhoods imbued with criminality, loose morals and resistance to integration is constructed. Policy interventions could be viewed as attempts aimed at both groups to acculturate to mainstream norms and integrate into wider society. Debates on cohesion and integration have evolved since the Macpherson Report (Home Office, 1999) and the Home Office Inquiry into the disturbances in Burnley, Oldham and Bradford (2001). However, the direction of travel has been towards minority groups doing much more to integrate themselves into British society. Implicit is the view that multiculturalism has failed to deliver a cohesive society. Indeed, David Cameron's Munich speech suggested that 'State multiculturalism' has led to increased division. A much more robust policy of integration should be advanced by the government (Cameron, 2011). As far back as 1997 we saw the launch of policies to address social exclusion across England. This was premised on the growing gap between the poorest neighbourhoods and mainstream society and showcased by spatial programmes trying to close the gap in education, jobs and health as well as housing (Social Exclusion Unit, 2000). As we have seen, *Connecting Communities* was the first coherent attempt by the Blair and Brown led governments to focus on white working class neighbourhoods. Challenges on employment, crime and community engagement were fuelled by increasing support for Far Right political parties in local and European elections.

Similarities exist in policy and social intervention. Some have stated that the 'SUS' laws were used by the police to target and control black youth in the 1970s (Sivanandan, 1982), criminalising black communities as robbers and muggers. In the same way, anti-social behaviour orders were designed to crack down on the sense of youth lawlessness in inner city neighbourhood and council estates during the 1997–2010 Labour Government. The media portrayal commonly showed young people from council estates indulging in behaviour that was unacceptable to societal norms and helped to deepen the pathology of these groups and neighbourhoods.

The discussion about white working class communities and community cohesion has been unsatisfactory. There is an absence of evidence and coherent research which has allowed a vacuum to be filled by studies that focus on cultural pathologies. Hence the group is regarded as being one dimensional and generally negative. Complexity in white working class communities in terms of tenure, class, age, ethnicity and sexuality is muted. Alongside the reification there is limited discussion on concepts of power and the role of the community organisations and institutions in supporting community cohesion. Representation is often limited to the connection of white working class communities to support for Far Right parties. In short, debates on white working class communities, cohesion and housing need to be encouraged to redress the balance of studies limited in scope and depth.

Community cohesion, institutions and white communities

In common with the general lack of academic focus on white working class communities, there is also an absence in explaining the role and function of community organisations and community cohesion. Of course there have been numerous studies about working class culture, seminally Young and Willmot's study of families in the East End of London during the 1950s (Young and Willmott,1957).

More recently two studies have emphasised how white working class communities are lagging behind most other groups in British society. First, the National Equality Panel reported that income inequality had significantly grown during the last 30 years. This accelerated under the Conservatives during the 1980s and has significantly narrowed in the New Labour years of 1997–2010. Now the richest 10% of the population are more than a thousand times better off than the poorest 10% (National Equality Panel, 2010).

Second, a Barrow Cadbury Trust study on how Birmingham was coping with recession found that white working class neighbourhoods had fewer community and civic organisations to cushion the blow of increased poverty compared to predominantly minority neighbourhoods (Fenton et al., 2010).

These recent publications, together with the *Connecting Communities* programme introduced by the last government in 2009 and the focus on class in the 2010 Equality Act, show renewed interest in poor white neighbourhoods. Yet the focus is on a communitarian approach that at best downplays the significant economic collapse in white working class neighbourhoods. Earlier we suggested that community cohesion is

embedded in an approach that blames communities for segregated housing markets, mutual intolerance and the potential for further riots and
disturbances. There is little analysis of how government policies have
contributed to a declining manufacturing sector and fewer jobs. More so,
community cohesion does not focus on social justice and equality of
opportunity. Rather the emphasis is on bringing different communities
and cultures together to increase understanding. 'Myth busting', community mapping and toolkits will make places cohesive. Of course the
absence of social justice, economic analysis, power and politics are fatal
to the community cohesion concept. It simply becomes a convenient
bandage to cover up the key challenges in income inequality, class and
race in society.

The recent *Connecting Communities* initiative does at least
acknowledge effective local leadership in white working class neighbourhoods. As we have seen, the decline of public sector housing, trade
unions and manufacturing as well as the national political shift to the
mainstream meant that there was scant attention paid to these groups.
The economic vacuum still needs to be filled but political representation
was replaced in some of these neighbourhoods by the rise of voting for
Far Right parties such as the BNP. Depicting themselves as an old style
Labour Party, the BNP gained votes and political representation at
municipal and European level (see Goodwin, 2009). The recent May 2010
General Election did not lead to a breakthrough of Parliamentary representation. Indeed, the BNP lost local political representation. Despite
this, more than 500 000 people voted for the BNP which is more support
for a Far Right party than any previous General Election (BBC, 2010). The
point is that community cohesion interventions since the 2001 disturbances has coincided with increased intolerance and vote share for the
BNP rather than a communitarian renewal of civic and shared
leadership.

There is much work to be completed on white working class groups and
leadership. Disengagement from mainstream politics seems to be the
trend but what of the role of community based organisations? Emerging
findings show that these organisations do exist and show two different
trends. First, leadership could be described as formal and informal.
Formally they are community centres with dedicated staff that work with
different groups and are funded by the local authority. Community
activists tend to be engaged in a number of overlapping organisations and
have extensive links to the local State. More interestingly, the informal

frameworks and leaders who come together on specific issues and not aligned to any group. It could be argued that these individuals provide potential for expanding different forms of organisations and leaderships that could support wider attempts at community cohesion. Second, in majority minority neighbourhoods, white working class communities see themselves as excluded from political representation by the operation of machine politics. They are simply not large enough to make their votes count. In these circumstances, white communities may form proxy community organisations to ensure that issues and concerns are placed on policy and political agendas. The proxy organisations are focused on specific sub-neighbourhood issues but utilise the media and networks to ensure that the local State takes heed of the issues that are generated. The application of places and groups that bring together white communities needs more consideration. The decline of traditional organisations such as the church, trade unions and the Labour Party signifies that the concerns of this group must be accommodated elsewhere. To this end we need to explore the role of social institutions such as the public house and working men's clubs (both in steep decline) as well as the role of sports such as football as a conduit to express the views of the white working class.

It is ironic that the new government continues to espouse communitarian approaches to policy making in areas such as education, health and crime. Yet the impact of economic restructuring and social reforms has resulted in many working class organisations disappearing from neighbourhoods. Rebuilding these groups and activists within will take time and there is no guarantee that they will have the capacity and knowledge to deliver macro policy on behalf of a much smaller state.

Housing, fairness and equity: case studies of three neighbourhoods in England

Research context

In this section, the focus will be on white working class perspectives, cohesion and access to housing. The analysis is based on the views of white working class residents and local stakeholders to community cohesion and neighbourhood change in three different neighbourhoods across England. As noted in the chapter, much research on community cohesion is undertaken in minority communities. There are very few studies on white working class perspectives on community cohesion. The research project strives to generate evidence on white working class communities and community cohesion and look at how these groups may positively contribute to debates. These groups sorely need a voice. The research was not meant to be representative or lead to generalisations given that no more than 150 people were interviewed. Nevertheless, the research provided depth and opportunities for white working class communities to participate in discussions about cohesion.

The study deployed a qualitative approach. There were three stages to the process. The first was *scoping*, which began by establishing links with community organisations and agencies. Principally this was achieved by meeting with lead officers from three local authorities. Second was the *active* stage; underpinned by different types of qualitative intervention. Researchers worked with community organisations to recruit residents for community study days and focus groups. Three community study days were organised to allow for reflective discussion. This was followed with three focus groups. In total, 100 residents and nearly 50 stakeholders participated in interviews, study days and focus groups. Fieldwork commenced in October 2009 and was completed in October 2010, covering the period of the General Election in May 2010. The third and final stage was *reflection*. A policy workshop was organised to enable residents to hear report findings and debate the results.

In spite of the analysis and commentary from the section above, the fundamental theme was that members of the white working class do not feel they have been treated fairly by government. In employment, social services, community development and most notably housing there was a strong and consistent view that residents lost out to minorities and new migrants. The narrative suggests that white working class communities have been politically marginalised and ignored.

Challenges for community cohesion

Despite the ending of *Connecting Communities* (discussed above) and uncertainty about government spending and policy interventions, the challenges in terms of applying community cohesion to these three neighbourhoods remained significant. There was a clear division in the levels of awareness between stakeholders and residents. The former were able to understand core meaning and discuss how cohesion was developed. These were individuals who were in part responsible for developing and implementing policy. The majority of residents had not heard of the term but a minority knew its meaning.

Discussion with both stakeholders and residents demonstrated a number of challenges with community cohesion as a concept, its perception and usefulness as a model of intervention. Many stakeholders found community cohesion a problematic concept. Some associated the term with a top down approach to community development. It was nebulous in the sense that both community and cohesion can have different meanings dependent on locality, ideology and composition of communities.

> People just glaze over. It's an expression of forced mixing of communities on people from a height. Not mixing from the bottom up. It's only sociologists and council staff that use the term. It's not an experience, community cohesion; you don't hear people asking about cohesion. You hear them asking if so and so went to the village fete. (Neighbourhood A stakeholder, male)

In this context, community cohesion was regarded as a generic instrument imposed on local authorities, neighbourhoods and residents by national government. Policy makers appeared to have an understanding of the key tenets but recognise limitations in application. Its association with national government, and its cross cutting reach, leaves the concept exposed at a time of dramatic reductions in government spending.

> Community Cohesions equals authority, it's a negative. It's not necessarily about race ... working class are quite a tolerant group of people, in X we have Polish, Ukraine, Asian, Irish, West Indian, Somalian. (Neighbourhood A stakeholder, male)

Stakeholders welcomed new and practical interventions to support community renewal. Many suggested that community cohesion happened in these neighbourhoods prior to the concept being inculcated into government policy.

After a decade of policy guidance and local interventions there is a still reluctance on the part of national government to recognise how difference is manifested. Difference couched in terms of immigration and competition for resources such as housing may lead to a racist discourse. Community cohesion was viewed as shutting down discussion about the composition of communities.

> We close down debates about race … conflict is not always bad and difference can be good and leads to change. (Neighbourhood C stakeholder, male)

Community cohesion presented a conundrum to stakeholders during the project. It was perceived as being a government instrument that is about forcing different communities together. However there was recognition of its influence in shaping policy albeit it was not seen as easy to implement. Local stakeholders gave examples of what they thought were community cohesion initiatives in the study areas. These ranged from working with schools on hate crime (Neighbourhood B), supporting new arrivals (Neighbourhood B), and organising street festivals (Neighbourhood C).

The research demonstrated that the real issues and challenges within neighbourhoods are not so much about bringing people together on common and shared norms, but about accepting the value of difference and how this is manifested within the arena of power and conflict such as competition for social housing or support for community projects. This resonates with resident findings Here residents felt that their views were muted compared to other groups. Concerns were not being listened to by government. More than this conflict over resources, such as social housing in Neighbourhood C and Neighbourhood B, pointed to cohesion challenges. Principally that the concept has become preoccupied with cultural explanations and less about difference and conflict. This view is summarised by a stakeholder who has responsibility for delivering cohesion policy:

> Groups of people have issues and they want to make themselves distinct from other groups. We are going against this by smothering over differences. Conflict is not really bad and difference is good although it is a challenge. (Neighbourhood C stakeholder, male)

In contrast to local stakeholders most residents had not heard of community cohesion. This is not altogether surprising because it is not an outward facing concept. It could be contended that definitional challenges on community cohesion should only concern those who work directly in policy. The minority of residents across the three areas who stated that they understood the concept suggested that it was about bringing people together:

Using community centres to bring people together, varieties of cultures, positive ways of bring people together. (Neighbourhood A resident, male)

Yes I have heard of it as I go to a lot of meetings, it's about networks of activities, local people working together to improve things. (Neighbourhood B resident, female)

It's everyone getting together, working together, bringing down barriers to include everyone, race, culture it all being welcome. (Neighbourhood C resident, female)

Although most had not heard of the term they were prompted to think further about its meaning. There was a consensus that community cohesion was about bringing people together. Beyond this basic assumption there was very little about norms and shared spaces. Rather, the opposite was the case. Much of the discussion with residents was focused on how government policies on race and equality at local and national level had not connected with white working class residents. These policies were proxy for political correctness. In short this meant that some residents viewed equality of opportunity as simply supporting minority groups at the expense of the majority. Political correctness was raised on a number of occasions during the course of the project and was seen as diminishing the rights of white working class communities.

It means that we do what they want. (Neighbourhood A resident, male)

Segregating groups – like X – the Asian women's centre. Everyone should have access – they segregate themselves and whatever funding they get they kept. It's PC to throw money at them. (Neighbourhood C resident, female)

We could be sanguine about the fact that many residents did not know about community cohesion. This was after all birthed by government and largely discussed by the policy and academic communities. A more substantive point is about policy disconnection with white working class communities. Despite attempts to build community cohesion in Neighbourhood A, Neighbourhood B and Neighbourhood C, people felt disenfranchised. The perspective of white working class communities had been excluded from debates on immigration, race and community. Moreover, government (and community cohesion was framed in this way) seemed uninterested and favoured minorities instead.

More community interaction needed

Residents wanted to increase interaction with different people in their neighbourhood. This was more evident in Neighbourhood A and Neighbourhood C than in Neighbourhood B. The latter is overwhelmingly a white working class neighbourhood and there are far fewer minority communities. This being the case the focus was on creating spaces for community interaction to take place. People lamented that the Neighbourhood B Carnival had not happened for many years and community development work had declined.

> The Carnival in Neighbourhood B stopped twenty years ago, the community centre in St. Margaret's closed. People are not prepared to do something for nothing. Most people now take rather than give back. It really has gone downhill. (Neighbourhood B resident, female)

Community interaction is recognised as being beneficial. It seems that the basis for valuing diversity is predicated on the role of neutral spaces and institutions such as community organisations, schools and street festivals. These are embedded in the community, trusted and credible and non-political. Thus community organisations encountered during the research are valued for providing services such as advice on welfare issues, access to childcare and signposting services. Similarly schools are focused on improved educational outcomes for young people and families living in disadvantaged communities whilst festivals provide a space to participate freely in a range of arts and cultural activities. These are examples of community advocacy which is provided freely and fairly to all groups within a neighbourhood.

> My son is the only white kid in his class – he is seven this year – he loves it – his sister and one other are the only white kids in the school. Mainly Black, Somalian, Asian and mixed race – they like it – we have only had one incident where someone shoved dirt in his face. I think it's good for him. (Neighbourhood A resident, female)

> Brilliant. Its community based no one cares; it's about being good people. We have had lots of Kosovans and Chinese move into the area. (Neighbourhood B resident, female)

> In the school I was working in, a lot of Bengali and Somalia community, you might have five British working class whites in the whole school. We did a lot of work, weekly events – got a whole group going for everyone – it

didn't feel agenda based. If you keep the fairness going, everyone was equal to come and get on. (Neighbourhood C resident, female)

Community interaction happened in each of our research neighbourhoods but at an informal rather than formal level. In shops, junior schools and in parks, people came across each other in routine situations. In this way community cohesion takes place as a series of routine interactions set against the everyday life of a neighbourhood. It is organic. Residents expressed the desire for these conversations with people who are different by race and class or both.

> The places people meet each other are the doctor's surgery, the market, the pub. That's where you'd bump into someone in the street and hear that so-and-so's just died, or got married, and you'd get all your information that way – you wouldn't have to read it in a Journal. (Neighbourhood C resident, female)

Access to social housing and equality

The case study areas demonstrated a disconnect between policies such as community cohesion on white working class communities. Residents in all three areas suggested that they were the invisible minority, not heard or taken seriously by policy makers. Research showed that residents felt they were being treated unfairly and lacked a voice. They regarded themselves as the forgotten group. Government had not listened to them in the past, nor does it show any signs of doing so currently. Language appeared to be racialised yet residents interviewed would take umbrage at this suggestion. Racialised commentary should be seen through the prism of neighbourhood loss, political disconnection and competition for scarce resources such as social housing. Residents did not express support for far right parties. Indeed these groups were seen as outside the norms of working class culture.

Being treated unfairly was most vividly seen in the specific debates on social housing. Many were proud to be social housing tenants and resented the portrayal of these neighbourhoods as council estates beset by social problems. Indeed, social housing tenants were largely content with their housing. It was affordable, regulated and maintained. In short, social housing was seen as an important resource and identified with by the working class. Many saw social housing as a right that was being denied to them by the local authority or housing association.

Social housing has largely been associated with white working class communities and has been viewed by some as the 'wobbly' pillar of the welfare state (Malpass, 2008). As we have seen Rex and Moore (1967) suggested that minority communities were excluded from accessing social housing by racial discrimination. Such policies led to segregated housing markets by income and ethnicity. Social housing has been replaced by owner occupation as the tenure of choice. Recent surveys showed that 70% of white households were owner occupiers compared to 17% in social housing and 13% in private rented accommodation. However, minorities had improved access to social housing with 26%, compared to 50% in owner occupation and 24% in private rented accommodation (Shelter, 2000). The figure for social housing masks differences between minority groups with the tenure housing only 7% of Indian communities compared to over 40% for Caribbean and African communities (Shelter, 2009). Characteristics on social housing are most marked in terms of economic profile with only 34% of people working and households having the lowest mean and median gross income compared to other tenures.

The supply of social housing has become tightly restricted and allocated to those individuals in greatest need. Given the above, it is not surprising that access to social housing became a touchstone of wider concerns about neighbourhood change. The commonly held view in the three case study neighbourhoods was that minorities and immigrants were preferentially allocated social housing. This was changing 'neighbourhood character' or, putting it more simply, certain areas were becoming ethnically diverse. Loss was personal and recounted through testimonials. A pattern emerged. Residents were told that they did not have high priority on social housing waiting lists and were forced to live in poor conditions only to see a minority family being allocated a unit. In reality, council housing departments and housing associations were simply following agreed lettings policy and meeting housing need. On the ground it appeared that these communities were being housed faster than white working class residents.

> If you've got five kids then you get a big house and the only people that have five kids nowadays are the Bengalis and the Somalis and so they get all the big places. (Neighbourhood C resident, female)

> I was told I didn't have enough points – they haven't been here two minutes and they get a house, we have to wait years. Why should we have to? (Neighbourhood B resident, female)

My cousin is black. She was here for two years and now has a beautiful house. I have been here for eight years ... I don't. I'm still here. It's about skin colour. (Neighbourhood A resident, female)

The inference is clear. The housing system disadvantages white working class communities and its values and, by allocation, favours all other groups. In each of the research sites there was ignorance and media fuelled speculation with the process of housing allocation and the points system. This was not determined locally but as part of a wider housing and social policy which demonstrated that minority communities and immigrants are in greatest housing need. Added to this was the impact of housing policies such as the right of tenants to buy council housing at a discounted rate and the subsequent problems of replacing social housing stock.

The 'buy to let' boom created by loosening of credit facilities may act to reduce cohesion and stability. Private sector landlords, unlike their counterparts in the social housing sector, are not driven by the need to promote community cohesion and mixed neighbourhoods. Rather, the overriding objective is to maximise profit. More than this, at least two of the research sites could be described as reception housing markets. They provide an opportunity for those with limited income to rent or buy a property. These factors did not seem to resonate with residents who viewed housing as crystallising the sense of loss and disconnection discussed earlier. It was unfair, they were not being listened to, and others were being given an advantage that was not deserved.

Interestingly local stakeholders who were part of the case study were sympathetic to the problems associated with accessing decent housing. There were two problems. First, housing regulation was predicated on priority need. It was evident that other groups had more need than white working class communities for this limited resource. Second, there was very little that the local housing department could do in the private sector. Landlords could charge and let properties to a range of tenants from single men to students to mobile workers. The transitory nature of these groups means it is unlikely that they will contribute to community cohesion.

Problems with accessing affordable housing combined with the depletion of housing stock emphasised the powerless position of white working class communities. Residents in all three areas expressed a view that social capital was being eroded. Specifically, young people could no longer afford private sector housing nor could they access social housing. Thus housing was the vessel that directly demonstrated the concerns of residents: breaking up of families, loss of networks and a dilution of core values that held many residents together.

> If you can't get on the housing list and you aren't a priority case, then you have to move away and that breaks up families. None of my children and grandchildren live around here. (Neighbourhood C resident, female)

Policies on housing were seen as unfair. The perception was that housing organisations rewarded groups who did not appear to add anything positive to neighbourhoods. The contrast between cohesive and values driven working class communities and those of resistant minority communities as well as other groups such as students was telling. A message was being relayed that dependency and failure would be rewarded.

> I was told that unless I was an alcoholic or a druggie, then I wouldn't get a place. (Neighbourhood C resident, male)

Housing was symptomatic of the wider concern about the future of white working class communities. These residents viewed themselves as hardworking, values led communities who had missed out on housing opportunities because of an unfair system. They could not compete for housing when it came to family size or social problems and these were viewed as the gateway to securing an affordable form of tenancy.

Previously, we discussed how residents took exception to the view that white working class communities were a disconnected, parochial and dependent group in society. This could also extend to being depicted as racist or supportive of the Far Right. Despite the vehemence of the discussion, many accepted that neighbourhoods were multicultural and understood the benefits of this diversity.

In this way unfairness could be separated from racism. Equality of opportunity was welcomed but in practice the legal framework led to adverse outcomes for white working class communities. Key issues were not addressed, and, unlike new arrivals, they did not seem to have anyone advocating on their behalf.

> Equal opportunities are anything but. We are bottom of the pile now. (Neighbourhood C resident, male)

Aston Pride's ran by Asians for Asians. (Neighbourhood A resident, male)

And the England flags, the council are worried about the political correctness of it. It's England- if we can't be proud in England ... (Neighbourhood B resident, female)

People rejected the view that they were racist or had a dislike of foreigners. Rather the blame was placed on activists who promoted equality of opportunity which led to 'political correctness'. The latter term was seen as preventing free discussion of the issues of identity, race and neighbourhood. Many thought political correctness had a stifling effect on people as they did not want to be thought of as racist or espousing views that were deemed inappropriate.

It's not a problem them being here, just the rights they have over us. (Neighbourhood B resident, female)

Minorities now hide behind the race card. When Camden Town was full of Greek and Irish people, it wasn't like that. Everyone mixed and fitted in. The new lot don't do that. (Neighbourhood C resident, male)

A policewoman called me racist – I said you must be mad! I've been to a Paki wedding, to an Indian wedding, a Russian wedding ... who made that word? [racism] We didn't learn that word when we were at school!; (Neighbourhood A resident, female)

It is important to stress that political correctness has become a pejorative term that becomes dismissed too easily by commentators drawn from the media and research communities. However, there is a need to emphasise the reasons behind the emergence of race equality policies. These policies came about as a result of evidence that minority communities faced discrimination due to the ethnicity of its members (Daniel, 1968). During the 1970s racist language was mainstreamed into society by its use in peak time UK TV programmes such as *Love Thy Neighbour* and *Mind Your Language*. Hence equality policies have played an important role in moving us away from discrimination and racism and should not be viewed as political correctness. There is a need for free debate but this should not be to the detriment of the progress made since 1975 and 1976 (passing of Sex Discrimination and Race Relations Acts respectively). Communities needed to voice their concerns and fears, but within a framework of equality of opportunity and permissible behaviours.

In this way residents viewed equality of opportunity as part of government interference in private domains. Predictably they were resistant to interventions because the benefit that these policies would bring to neighbourhoods was not clear. They were tolerant of diversity and understood this as the reality of living in a modern Britain. This may be seen at odds with the views expressed previously but can be explained in terms of fairness. This concept applied to all groups. Many had no problem living alongside people of different backgrounds.

> My street is a microcosm … Next door is Polish, then Indian, then African and then an obese white family and an Irish woman a little further. There is no hostility. Everyone largely muddles along. (Neighbourhood A resident, male)

> I've found them some of the nicest people, but if I listen to what other people say I wouldn't have even spoken to one. (Neighbourhood B resident, female)

> People and the media call X racist but it isn't. We never even used to notice the differences. When I was at school, about 60 years ago, a Greek boy who spoke no English at all started and we were told by the teacher to be kind to him … and we were. He still lives round here now. The indigenous population has always been accepting and we never felt threatened. Some people are threatened now but everyone is scared to say anything for fear of being called racist. I stuck up for black people … recently a black guy had to stick up for the white groups … in a housing meeting because it would have been seen as racist if a white person had said what he said. It has gone full circle. (Neighbourhood C resident, male)

Housing and neighbourhood were key touchstones in the case study research on white working class communities. The findings suggest that residents in these areas felt disconnected from policy and politics. Voices were not being heard and housing policy was leading to the breakup of families and neighbourhoods. Access to social housing was rightly mediated on needs and this led to increased numbers of minority households in previously white working class neighbourhoods. Complaints were as much about local government as minority communities. Indeed residents were concerned that they may be perceived as being racist. It was pointed out in all three neighbourhoods that there was little or no support for the Far Right and difference was welcomed. People simply wanted to be treated fairly and be heard.

Complexity of whiteness

The research into case study neighbourhoods countered the stereotype presented by some of the literature on white working class communities. They are seen as a feckless group: resistant to change, problematic in terms of social norms and behaviours, and living in annexed council estates that are mired in unemployment, high teenage pregnancy rates and poor educational performance. The research demonstrated that there was another type of social construction being developed. Residents identified white working class as being associated with a strong work ethic, respect, collective values and reciprocal support. People resented the negative stereotype:

> They think that we are all on the giro. They think we are all the same. (Neighbourhood A resident, male)

> I may be from the nineteenth floor of a tower block, thirty and have a child but I am not stupid! I see the news. My father's got O and A levels and all that. I get fed up with being seen as thick. (Neighbourhood C resident, female)

White working class groups were not from a narrow ethnic group. In contrast, residents acknowledged cultural diversity. Some recounted that they were of Irish, Scottish or Welsh backgrounds and this continued to be part of their identity. A small proportion had family members who were drawn from minority backgrounds. This was not a blunt one dimensional group. Rather it was multi-faceted and many expressed that difference could be beneficial. Some raised and celebrated the concept of 'a melting pot' as something that should be embraced.

> I grew up around Birmingham; I have coloured black friends and I've got a bit of Indian in me but I don't know much about that culture. (Neighbourhood A resident, male)

> I can't be racist as I have seven half-Bengali step children ... there is no division because this is their home. (Neighbourhood C resident, male)

These views suggest that equality in the allocation of public resources such as housing was central in supporting cohesion in these neighbourhoods. To substantiate the point the challenges linked to white minorities such as migrant workers from Eastern Europe and students were raised in all three study areas. Both groups presented challenges in terms of integration, housing and employment. In addition, students are also viewed in a negative way in terms of cohesion and restricting access to housing. Creating cohesive neighbourhoods was complex and needed to take into account the range of views from white working class communities. It is not simply about imposing government models on collectivised groups.

Conclusion

In this chapter we have tried to review the literature on white working class communities and cohesion. By using three case studies from recently completed research we contextualise the role of housing, neighbourhood change and cohesion. Here, residents wanted to be heard. They were the forgotten group in society and believed that social housing was being preferentially allocated to other groups. Families and the neighbourhood were becoming fragmented and their sense of place was being lost. A number of key points emerge. First, in comparison to studies on minority communities and race there is relatively little discussion on the topic. Second, white working class communities are framed as an ethnic rather than class group which supports a cultural analysis. Third, and because of this, pathologies of white culture are developed which emphasise exclusion from mainstream society in terms of norms and space. Fourth, there is scant discussion of the complexity of white working class communities in terms of tenure, gender, ethnicity and age or focus on key concepts such as power, conflict and leadership. Fifth, recent media and film representations has helped to support a new and arguably more nuanced conversation about white working class communities. An empirical approach is required to test our research questions in connection to white working class communities, community cohesion, institutions and housing. Sixth, white working class neighbourhoods have been hardest hit by the economic policies and social reforms undertaken by successive governments. The communitarian approach being advocated by the Conservative -Liberal Democrat government needs to appreciate that the local economy needs to be rebuilt and community organisations need investment and time to achieve community cohesion in partnership, rather than instead of the State. Above all there is a need to challenge the evidence gap, myths and collectivised pathology that these communities have had to endure for far too long.

4

The Emergence of the Black Led Housing Sector

Introduction

One of the most interesting developments in the social housing sector has been the growth and development of so called black and minority ethnic housing associations. Most were registered by the Housing Corporation after the first Black and Minority Ethnic Housing (BME) Policy in 1986 and reached a peak of over 60 organisations by 1999. They have variously been regarded as beacons of black and minority leadership, providing culturally sensitive services and creating space for black employees, board members and tenants to engage with housing issues. Yet there have also been a number of issues and challenges for the sector. First, it could be argued that performance has been patchy. Indeed on occasions this has led to the Housing Corporation using statutory powers to intervene in the running of the association. Most recently, Ujima (the first and largest black and minority led housing association) has been taken over by a mainstream housing provider after concerns about performance. Second, macro policy shifts from a model of multiculturalism to community cohesion has further called into question the role of black and minority ethnic housing associations. The focus is not so much on narrow concerns of 'race' but a wider agenda of equalities. Third, there are

Race, Housing & Community: Perspectives on Policy & Practice, First Edition.
Harris Beider.
© 2012 Harris Beider. Published 2012 by Blackwell Publishing Ltd.

questions on the appropriateness of using labels such as 'black' to describe an increasingly fragmented society. An assessment and review of the black and minority ethnic housing sector helps to make sense of wider debates on 'race', housing and communities. Thus, this chapter will review the role of the social housing sector in England in engaging with minority communities. Specifically it will scrutinise the impact of the Black and Minority Ethnic Housing Policies implemented by the Housing Corporation from 1986 to 2003. These policies led to the development of over 60 registered black and minority led housing associations which were viewed as a key mechanism for community engagement, capacity building and meeting the housing needs of minority communities. Our review will discuss the impact and outcomes of the policy through the lens of black and minority housing associations and also in the context of macro policy from the Macpherson Report (positive action) to the Cantle Report (community cohesion). We will argue that whilst the Housing Corporation Policy was an innovative programme the impact and success have been mixed with few demonstrable outcomes. Instead there has been a decline in the significance of race in housing generally and the role of black and minority led housing associations specifically. A number of reasons will be put forward including changing macro policy priorities, organisational performance and regulatory focus. Finally we will suggest a need to develop a new type of housing organisation that represents, advocates and cuts across different policy boundaries.

The rise of race and housing

The rise in discussion, debate and policy salience needs to be set in the context of the anti-racist movement of the 1970s (Sivanandan, 1982). Racism provided the basis for community mobilisation in black communities. One of the key elements was to secure a better housing deal for these groups. Grassroots activism was important but there are two additional factors that should be considered. First, the Section 71 Amendment to the 1976 Race Relations Act placed a duty on local authorities to eliminate unlawful discrimination and promote equality of opportunity. It could be argued that this helped to support local anti-racist campaigns for improved access to housing and placed external pressures on local authority housing departments and housing associations alike to put these issues onto policy agendas (Solomos, 1993: 104). Second, the 1981 riots in Liverpool, Birmingham and Brixton between mainly minority youth and the Police (see Benyon and Solomos, 1987) had a catalytic impact in linking race and disadvantage. These events shaped responses at the national level on race and public policy, leading to investment in programmes on inner city renewal. Hence the increased importance of race and housing should be set within the frame of legislative changes, urban disturbances and grassroots political campaigns.

In 1986, ten years after the 1976 Race Relations Act and five years after serious urban riots, the Housing Corporation launched a Black and Minority Ethnic Housing Policy designed to 'encourage, run and create separate black run organisations as a channel for providing rented housing' (Harrison, 1995: 88). The language is stark and contrasts with the current policy approach to equalities in its radicalism. Public investment in supporting minority black led housing associations was an early and radical example of positive action in practice. The 1986 BME Housing Policy was about capacity building black leadership and providing alternative sources of housing for minority communities. Implicit in this was the recognition that the so called mainstream (or white led) housing associations had not addressed the issue of race equality. The outcomes were dramatic. Between 1986–1991 direct and targeted investment by the Housing Corporation resulted in the registration of 44 BME housing associations. This was important for two reasons. Symbolically, these community based organisations were given an opportunity to address housing and related disadvantage in minority communities by creating new dwellings and leveraging investment into neighbourhoods, leading to renewal. Practically, BME housing organisations created opportunities in employment and management openings for minority activists as either employees or committee members. In short, the first phase could be regarded as being based on empowerment, meeting the housing needs of minority communities and increasing representation of minority groups within the wider voluntary housing sector (Harrison, 1995: 91).

A second five-year plan – *An Independent Future* – began in 1992 (Housing Corporation, 1992). The theme was less about empowerment and much more about making BME housing associations financially viable. One of the consequences of the 1988 Housing Act was freeing up housing associations to get investment from the private sector to build and manage housing. The terms of reference for social housing changed, especially for BME housing associations, leading to the possibility of high rents for tenants and making inner city renewal a much riskier proposition than even a few years before. This was problematic for BME housing associations because their lack of longevity meant that they did not have sufficient time to accumulate the level of funds required to subsidise rents and their housing stock was located in poor inner urban neighbourhoods (Royce, 1996). Asset value, management capacity and governance were the key indicators taken into account by financiers. Black and minority ethnic housing associations were viewed as a high risk.

The final Housing Corporation Policy – *An Enabling Framework* – from 1998 to 2003 was shaped by the desire to meet the needs of minority consumers irrespective of whether they were tenants of a BME housing association. To this end the focus was on meeting the needs of minority tenants of all housing associations:

> ... towards ensuring that the expectations of black and minority ethnic communities are achieved, whether through the provision of adequate social housing by the full-range of landlords (only some of which will be black-led) or through enabling members of the community to effectively participate in the delivery of services, through equality in the workplace, in management and in board membership. (Whitehead et al., 1998: 5)

Improving governance and business performance rather than either consolidation or empowerment were the key watchwords from 1998 to 2003. In short the policy moved from producers to consumers. In retrospect there are several reasons for the declining significance of race in the three five-year BME Housing Policies developed by the Housing Corporation. First, BME associations were small organisations and at risk to changes in policy and economic climate. For example, rent capping had an adverse impact because BME housing associations did not have the financial reserves in place to subsidise rents. The perception of high rents ensured the Housing Corporation regulatory spotlight was firmly placed on this sub-sector. (Whitehead et al., 1998). Second, development costs became complex and expensive, requiring investment in human capital, partnership agreements and legal scrutiny. Housing development is an important component of sustainability and became much more problematic for BME housing associations after the 1988 Housing Act. Third, equality legislation combined with inspection by the Housing Corporation (latterly the Homes and Community Agency) and the Audit Commission led to improved performance on these issues by the social housing sector as a whole. A debate developed on the added value BME housing associations. (Lupton and Perry, 2004).

Organisational or system failure?

The growth of the black led housing sector was much more than the result of policy interventions. It could be argued that the extensive role of black community activists and community organisations has not been given enough prominence in comparison to policy debates or indeed the numerous analyses of housing needs of minority groups. An attempt will be made here to begin to redress this balance moving the discussion forward after Harrison's important contributions to this subject (Harrison, 1995; 2001). First, we will consider the role of community activists in shaping the agenda on race and housing prior to the 1986 Housing Corporation Black and Minority Ethnic Housing Strategy. Second, we will reflect on the role of the Federation of Black Housing Organisations (FBHO), the representative organisation for black and minority ethnic housing organisations. How was it able to influence the debates on race and housing? What were the reasons for its decline and demise? Third, and related to the last point, we will critically analyse the downfall of Ujima Housing Association, amongst the first and largest black led housing organisation, and the symbolic impact this had on the sector generally.

We noted in the opening chapter the tendency of some research and researchers to describe black communities as passive recipients of racism by the State. Taking this further, research has been focused on top-bottom rather than bottom up approaches. The long line of government interventions related to race and housing show a similarity in terms of development, regulation and evaluation being driven from Central Government. Regeneration and renewal interventions that came after serious rioting in 1981 and 1985, including City Challenge, Single Regeneration Budget and New Deal for Communities, were administered by central and regional government. Race and housing interventions such as the Housing Corporation Black and Minority Ethnic Housing Strategies from 1986 to 2003 and the Audit Commission Key Lines of Enquiry and Community Cohesion, could all be described as blunt, centralised top-down measures to address localised and nuanced challenges. It is especially important to consider community cohesion given its significant influence on race policy since 2001. This has been explored in more depth in Chapter 2 but suffice to say that it is a good example of centralised command and control that has helped to regress rather than progress the agenda on race. The importance of understanding and importing grass-roots perspectives on race has never been more important given the rise of intolerance towards immigrants and asylum seekers as well as the organised Far Right during the last ten years. Goulbourne has succinctly summarised the epistemological challenges:

> The failure of much of British 'race relations' research and writing to move into this gear runs the danger of developing and cementing a tradition of scholarship in which … we see victimization but not the victim, we see the forces of anti-racism, but not the anti-racist, we see the processes of institutional change, but not the groups and individuals who fight for such changes. (Goulbourne, 1990: 3)

In recent years the gap in bottomup perspectives on race has started to be closed. For example, Harrison has completed interesting and informative studies of the black led housing sector (Harrison, 1995; Harrison et al., 1996; Harrison and Davis, 2001) but there is still a need to focus on the role of black community activists in political mobilisation in general and in housing specifically.

The Federation of Black Housing Organisations (FBHO) was established in 1983 under the banner of a *Better Housing Deal for Black People*. However, it was not the first national voluntary organisation with the broad message on race equality in housing. The Federation of Black Hostels (FBH) began in 1982 to meet the chronic situation of black youth homelessness that rose to prominence during the 1970s (Black Housing, 1998). Whilst single black homelessness remained, community activists wanted an organisation with a broader remit that could address a range of challenges on race and housing. Moreover, it could be argued that the FBH focused its appeal not only on a single issue but to Black Caribbean communities. The founder members of FBHO wanted a broad alliance of members drawn from a diverse range of communities. In this context, 'black' meant taking up issues relevant to Caribbean, African and importantly Asian communities. From the outset FBHO was a coalition of organisations and community activists which had two immediate priorities following its formation: the registration of 100 black led housing associations and increasing the number of black people working in white or mainstream housing associations (Black Housing, 1998).

In retrospect, the formation of a national black housing agency could not have happened at a more opportune time. The country had experienced the most serious spate of urban rioting since 1945 only two years previously, in 1981. Primarily these took place in disadvantaged black neighbourhoods blighted by high levels of unemployment, decline in manufacturing industries and high levels of overcrowding in housing. The riots had led to these issues being forced onto the political agenda of the Conservative Government led by Margaret Thatcher. A second round of rioting in the same types of areas during 1985 led the Prime Minster to comment in the immediate afterglow of her 1987 election victory that 'we must do something about those inner cities' (cited in Jacobs, 1988). Race and public policy was also being championed by some Labour led local authorities, most notably the Greater London Council (see Solomos, 1993). Thus the impact of urban rioting led to renewed interest and investment in neighbourhoods by a radical and Right Wing Conservative national government that was supported by equally radical and Left Wing Labour local authorities who were politically committed to race equality and increased representation. These two factors combined with the black political mobilisation discussed earlier ushered in the birth of FBHO.

It should be noted that the 1966 Local Government Act contained powers under Section 11 to sponsor black led initiatives and programmes (Harrison et al., 2005). However it was 20 years later that the Housing Corporation launched the first five year Black and Minority Ethnic Housing Strategy in 1986. The role of the Housing Corporation in supporting race and housing issues has been discussed elsewhere in this chapter. As Black Housing rightly stated, 'The Strategy aimed to increase the provision of housing for black people and also the participation of black people in the voluntary housing movement.' (Black Housing, 1998: 12). The results were startling; 19 black led housing associations registered, with capital allocations increasing from £12 million in 1986 to £97 million in 1991 (Black Housing, 1998). Harrison has described the growth of black led housing associations as 'internationally an almost unique example of successful separate organisational development' (Harrison et al., 2005: 80). For FBHO, the Housing Corporation was a vindication of the community mobilisation and the key aims enshrined in its launch. Public support, personal commitment and grassroots mobilisation had generated a new chapter in organisational development in the social housing in the UK.

Some have argued that the Housing Corporation two further five-year plans on black and minority ethnic housing issues supported the growth of FBHO (see Beider, 2007a). By 1997 there were more than 60 black led housing associations with the 23 largest managing over 20 000 housing units and a collective turnover of £82 million (Harrison et al., 2005). The growth helped FBHO to generate an income stream (fee income was collected from member housing associations on the basis of size and units in management),which led to a programme on research and seminars to engage and disseminate learning and good practice. More than this FBHO became the independent voice of the black led housing sector. Thus by 2001, the organisation's turnover had moved beyond £300 000 and membership was in excess of 200 organisations including white led housing associations. Conferences were attended by more than 400 delegates and FBHO had informed public policy and practice through publications on racial harassment in the UK (see Chahal and Julienne, 2000). FBHO was also invited to advise the Social Exclusion Unit led by Tony Blair's New Labour Government (see FBHO Annual Report 2000).

These were important achievements and marked the transition of FBHO from being an outsider to an insider organisation. On reflection this was not surprising. The representative national organisation was undergoing the same transformation as its membership. Both were once radical and grassroots organisations steeped in black nationalist politics. Many people involved and active within black led housing organisations were community development workers who had engaged with young people involved in rioting in 1981 and 1985. However the investment which flowed from the Housing Corporation Black and Minority Ethnic Policy in 1986 together with the encouragement to start new housing associations changed the terms of reference. New skills, structures and organisational cultures were needed to manage complex associations. It could be argued that radicalism and community politics were jettisoned by black housing associations to meet business plans and targets. At a national level, FBHO was no longer perceived as critical of mainstream housing providers and outside central debates but was viewed as more constructive and open to partnership with mainstream housing associations and indeed the Housing Corporation. To a large extent this was driven by pragmatism to secure an income stream and support activities as much as it was the politics of moving away from community politics.

By 2000 FBHO had reached a peak in terms of membership and income. In 2008, FBHO could not pay its bills and had cancelled its once mighty annual conference because of a lack of support and sponsorship. Twenty five years after FBHO was started by a group of community activists it had ceased to exist as an organisation. Moreover, membership had dwindled and the organisation was struggling to assert its relevance (Inside Housing, 2009). There are many reasons for the fall of FBHO. This has more than a passing symmetry to its rise. First, as has been discussed elsewhere in this book, the macro policy environment became less supportive to black led housing associations and thus

FBHO. For example, the Home Office Inquiry Team, established to look into the 2001 disturbances, blamed housing policy as contributing to 'parallel lives' and increased tensions between different groups (Home Office, 2001). Indeed, the Chair of the Inquiry team had reportedly questioned the future role of black led housing associations at a national housing conference. This resulted in a letter being sent to the Housing Minister by FBHO, in which the Inquiry Chair was criticised for 'having little or no understanding of the cohesive nature of BME associations.' (Inside Housing, 2001). Community cohesion and the movement of government policy from race to equality certainly played an important part in the demise of FBHO and black led housing associations. The move from Macpherson to community cohesion has been discussed in some detail in Chapter 2 of this book. The former regarded black community organisations as critical to developing new ways to address racist victimisation and institutional racism in society. The latter viewed black community organisations in an all too different light. Second, and related to the first point, macro policies combined with robust inspection by the Housing Corporation and later the Audit Commission, led to increased levels of representation and good practice on race equality in the mainstream sector. Black staff were recruited as senior staff in housing associations and also within the Housing Corporation itself. It could be argued that there was less need for grass-roots mobilisation when some of the activists had secured employment in the housing sector. The Federation of Black Housing Organisations had succeeded in meeting one of its key aims. Third, modernisation had swept through social housing and politics from at least the election of New Labour in 1997. There was less emphasis on radical grassroots political strategies and more of an onus on partnership building and new public management. Some suggested that FBHO had not grasped the need to change as an organisation or indeed its message. It was seen as parochial, defensive and reliant on patronage of government. This sense of refusal to change is summed up in the following quote: 'I don't think they were up to speed as an organisation or a group of staff … They were relevant when they were set up, and then for maybe ten years afterwards.' (Inside Housing, 2009).

In explaining the fall of FBHO, we should also consider the decline of black led housing associations. This goes beyond vertical integration of these bodies joining larger mainstream providers discussed elsewhere in this chapter. Here we want to focus on the collapse of Ujima Housing Association, the largest black led housing association, in 2008. It is a story beset by claims of poor leadership, governance, regulation and rancour with claims of racism.

In 1977 a group of black community activists formed a housing organisation in North London called Ujima which means working together in Swahili. This was pre-FBHO and also pre-urban rioting of 1981 but the concern of the founding members was about providing decent housing accommodation primarily for disadvantage black communities. This was an excellent example of black community mobilisation in raising concerns about racism in housing and the importance of self-help to resolve these challenges. By 1980 Ujima was registered by the Housing Corporation and from 1986 benefitted from the Black and Minority Ethnic strategies developed by the Housing Corporation. It grew to become the largest black led housing association in the country with more than 4,500 homes in London and the South East. After being registered, Ujima had received £300 million of public investment and had more than £200 million in borrowings (Housing Corporation, 2008). Indeed it was so highly regarded by the Housing Corporation that in 2005, under the new commissioning arrangements, Ujima was granted £47 million to build social housing (The Guardian, 2008). Yet less than three years after this, and some 30 years after its foundation, Ujima had created a different type of history by becoming the first housing association to go bust.

The Housing Corporation invited an independent inquiry into the fall of Ujima. The reasons for failure became clear. First, there was an idealistic and risk laden expansion plan launched in 2006 to take over smaller black led housing associations and increase homes in ownership and geographical coverage. Ironically named 'Project Jerusalem', the plan led the organisation far from the Promised Land into the rocks of receivership. The stark evidence shows that rental income could not cover loans taken by Ujima to support expansion. Moreover, the independent review showed that Ujima had been coming under the regulatory microscope of the Housing Corporation for several years. Three chief executives had been recruited only to leave the organisation in quick succession, a former senior director had won an employment tribunal for wrongful dismissal, and accounts were not approved. These were significant warning signals but the Housing Corporation did not intervene until there was a real risk of loans not being paid and tenants being in jeopardy (Housing Corporation, 2008).

Bringing the Ujima debacle into the wider discussion of race and housing leads to issues that concern us and are discussed herein. Some have accused the Housing Corporation of rushing into disposing of Ujima too quickly. Black housing organisations suggested that Ujima was not given sufficient time to organise a financial rescue that would have covered loans and provided a much needed financial injection (Inside Housing, 2009). Those taking this view suggest that the Housing Corporation acted with undue haste because it was concerned with governance rather than insolvency. Moreover, it should be noted that Ujima never defaulted on its loans although there was an unacceptable risk of this happening (Inside Housing, 2008). Nevertheless, the Housing Corporation used its statutory powers to place its appointees on the Ujima board and directed a takeover by London and Quadrant Housing Association (L&Q) which is a large, mainstream housing association. It was at this point that Ujima was dismantled and that fears about the loss of the community based black brand were raised. This was curious considering that Ujima had moved some distance from the community based organisation that was founded by black activists some 30 years before. Indeed the ill-fated Project Jerusalem would have moved the organisation even further from its brand towards a generalist housing association not dissimilar in ethos to L&Q. In reality, the larger black led housing associations such as Ujima were attempting to replicate the organisational culture of their larger mainstream peers. Salary levels for senior executives, large headquarter offices and even corporate boxes were symptomatic of the distance that had been travelled by such housing associations. In practice, the Ujima brand had been diluted by the rapid expansion related to the Housing Corporation Black and Minority Ethnic Housing Strategy.

There has been relatively little discussion about race as a factor in the handling of the break up and Ujima's transfer to L&Q by the Housing Corporation. There may be several reasons for this. First, as discussed previously, Ujima had expanded into a housing association of a significant size, which may have disconnected it from its radical beginnings. Regulators do not treat housing associations differently because of ethnicity (although some activists would take issue with this). Second, one of the key contentions in this chapter is the declining significance of race and housing. To a large extent, the social housing sector has seen race specific strategies that guided the development of the black led housing sector replaced with more generic policies concerned with equality. The emergence of community cohesion helped in the cleansing of race from housing debates. The government concept was focused on creating common norms and integrated spaces. In this view, black led housing associations seemed problematic with a specific identity, separate funding programmes and culturally specific services. Third, it could be stated that black professionals had made a breakthrough into senior jobs in the mainstream sector. Indeed this reached an epoch with the appointment of a black person as the Housing Corporation's final chief executive. In short, regulatory pressures on equality allied to specific programmes on black led housing associations had increased the number of black employees and black led housing associations resulting in the attainment of the two aims of the FBHO.

It should be noted that the failure of Ujima Housing Association, the largest black and minority ethnic housing association, was closely followed by the Housing Corporation using its powers to make statutory appointments to the board of the second largest black led housing association, Presentation in 2008 (Inside Housing, 2008). The reasons were associated with governance and concerns about income covering loan payments. Rather than collapsing as Ujima did, Presentation lost its chief executive and merged with the large mainstream housing provider, Notting Hill Housing Trust (Inside Housing, 2009). This meant that Notting Hill had taken over three formerly independent black led housing associations in 12 months, increasing its size by 25% in the process and increasing its inventory from 25 000 to more than 30 000 homes. This provides an example of the decline of black led housing associations since the 1980s. Indeed the Notting Hill example suggests that whilst there is a need for black led housing associations they do not have the financial or management capacity to address regulatory pressures. In addition, they do not generally have a leadership vision to meet the needs of new types of communities (Notting Hill Housing Trust, 2009). The new organisational form will maintain black led housing associations in order to meet a cul- turally sensitive need amongst different minority communities, but under the guidance of the larger mainstream housing association or parent. Mindful of the paternalistic tone of the parent and child relationship, Notting Hill's position was conciliatory and respectful: 'Despite the term "parent" being the correct jargon, the parent will value and learn from the subsidiary BME association, operating as an effective partner. We will guard against the relationship becoming, or appearing to be, a paternalis- tic one.' (Notting Hill Housing Trust, 2009: 6).

The collapse of Ujima, the merger of Presentation and the decline of FBHO could be viewed collectively as a metaphor for race and housing in the country. Changing macro policies and priorities, economic recession and organisational failure created a heady mix which has been devoid of race analysis. This seems strange given that we are discussing the largest black led housing association and the representative organisation for the sector. Race should be viewed as an important part of the analysis. In the case of Ujima, the problems were associated with governance which has often been a proxy for the assertion that black members could not run their own organisations (Black Housing, 1998). It has been discussed elsewhere that the drift from policies associated with race equality to those associated with community cohesion could be framed in the transition from social justice to the primacy of cultural analysis. This then leads to the import of normative cultural characteristics and collectivised behaviours to communities and organisations. Thus concerns about governance in black led housing associations need to be linked with changing policy priorities. It could be argued that there has been a slippage of the language on race that takes us back to the discredited debates that described black communities during the post-war period. (Worley, 2005). Similarly the decline of FBHO seems to parallel the trajectory from race equality to community cohesion. It could be argued that organisational leadership failed to grasp the challenge of the paradigm shift and continued to try and shape the race and housing agenda from an outmoded framework.

Declining interest in race and housing: the problem with regulation and representation

It would be easy to blame the policy shift from Macpherson to Cohesion as the basis for the declining interest in race and housing. It would also be inaccurate and simplistic. There is a need to focus on the way that housing associations were regulated by the Housing Corporation and also with the concept of representation in relation to race.

There are a number of problems with regulating on housing and race that follow from the policy discussion above. The first is simply the machinery used to analyse race equality. Regulators have moved to accommodate race within the much wider prism of equality and or diversity. This shadows the direction from Race Relations to Community Cohesion and the 1976 Race Relations Act to the 2010 Equality Act. It could be argued that the movement to accommodating race within the much wider lens of equalities is a signal that addressing racism is no longer important as a policy priority. Indeed, this has driven the complaints by many black organisations against the all-embracing Equalities and Human Rights Commission that replaced the Commission for Racial Equality when it was established in 2007. We are seeing a similar trend in the housing sector with more resources and priority being afforded to non-race equality areas by both the Housing Corporation and Audit Commission. For example, the Housing Corporation published a new Good Practice Note 8 on Equalities and Diversity that stressed the importance of housing associations dealing with wider issues other than race such as disability and sexuality (Housing Corporation, 2004b). This followed an internal publication that significantly embraced the wider equality agenda. Race is not mentioned specifically but seen within the context of other levels of disadvantage.

> The Housing Corporation leads a sector which provides services to the most disadvantaged sections of the community ... The main groups include: people from black and minority ethnic (BME) communities; lesbians, gay men, bi-sexual people and people who identify as transgender; households headed by women (especially lone parents); people with disabilities; older people; people with HIV/AIDS; people with learning difficulties; people with mental health issues; people suffering from alcohol or substance abuse; ex-offenders; people in contact with criminal justice services; those experiencing domestic violence or sexual abuse. (The Housing Corporation, 2003)

The proliferation of different groups will necessarily result in less time and fewer resources being invested in race equality issues. This was after all a government organisation that devised and implemented three five-year strategies specifically addressing race equality issues from 1986 to 2003. The contention is that race, in a way that closely resembles its national diminution, has been similarly shrunk in the housing sector.

Policy crowding out together with reduced priority sends a clear message to housing associations. Equality debates have moved ahead at a rapid pace. A decade after Macpherson, it could be argued that the policy and regulatory regimes are challenging housing organisations less on race equality and more on the priorities championed by community cohesion. The focus is not so much about regulation that addresses racism but one that delivers ethnically mixed neighbourhoods.

The inference is that race equality should not be seen as an end itself but merely as part of the wider landscape that helps to address the problems identified by the Community Cohesion Report (Home Office, 2001). Housing regulation has become all embracing and less nuanced at a time when society in the UK is becoming more diverse and fragmented. The need is for specific regulatory interventions on minority housing issues and yet relatively little has been said about the needs and aspirations of new migrants and how their voices will be heard by housing organisations, local authorities and government as a whole. These are after all the groups who have the greatest needs in terms of housing. Recent migration from Eastern Europe, Africa and the Middle East has changed the landscape for housing, race and representational policy in England. Many 'new' black and minority ethnic communities have very little in common with 'old' BME communities from the Caribbean, India and Pakistan (Beider, 2005).

There are a number of problems that need to be considered in adapting the framework for race and representation to respond to these societal changes. First, representation should take account of new barriers to involvement including language, expectations and awareness of institutions amongst newcomer communities. For new communities discussions and debates that are couched in English and with an assumed housing jargon will present considerable barriers in joining debates and housing partnerships designed to address needs. New groups may be excluded from being represented within housing institutions because of these basic barriers. Second, there should be explicit acknowledgement of the impact of change on 'old minorities' in the jostling for power and general community politics. The perception that hard won influence and resources will be diverted to 'new minorities' requires careful response. Research has shown that some old communities (i.e. established minority groups) are resistant to new communities (i.e. refugees and asylum seekers) from accessing political networks and representation on local area based committees (Beider, 2005). In some instances this could be viewed as 'recycled racism'. Old minorities are couching new minorities as a problem in terms of the link with neighbourhood decline and also placing pressures on public resources such as a larger family housing. This was very much the way that racism was espoused towards migrants from the Caribbean and Indian sub-continent during the 1950s and 1960s. It could be argued that new groups are perceived as the undeserving poor. There is a sense in some communities that old minorities had to organise and campaign for housing rights within the context of ant-racist struggles. New minorities are perceived to have accessed housing without the hardship endured by older and well-established groups. Housing regulation and policy discussion is reluctant to acknowledge and indeed understand these complex power related conflicts. The focus on representation at one end and building cohesive communities at the other misses important drivers for community change. There is no indication that the generic levels of policy analysis will address this shortfall in the future. Thirdly, the expectations placed on 'BME delegates' in representative models of involvement require reassessment. A singular representative cannot represent fragmented and complex communities from minority groups. Yet there is an implicit assumption with the housing regulatory literature that housing organisations should have a representative management committee and senior staff (Housing Corporation 2002; 2004b). Housing organisations simply need to recruit individuals from minority communities to satisfy this important requirement. No thought is given to quality and the problems of vesting power and influence on disparate groups of individuals who are recruited onto management committees. This could lead to tokenism of the worst type where housing associations simply use their networks to identify an appropriate person from a minority group and tick the box marked diverse representation. Moreover, empowering individuals rather than addressing racism and social justice leads to debates peppered with the terms of 'leaders' and 'community leaders.' These are often people who have been identified and selected by institutions to speak on behalf of communities. There are significant problems associated with such an approach. At a basic level it is short circuit consultation for housing associations speaking to a few individuals rather than fully engaging with communities. At an intermediate level there are problems about whether 'leaders' really represent the diverse groups that compose any community of interest (Mullins et al., 2004). These individuals may be out of touch with young people or women but are requested to speak on their behalf. Accessing minorities within minorities means that housing organisations are beginning to understand complexities. At an advanced level the discussion about community leaders is racialised. There is seldom any discussion about 'community leaders' applying to discussion in white communities. Its application to debates on race and community hark back to imperialist terminology associated links with leaders within Indian communities who helped the British to manage the Raj. Sixty years has elapsed since Indian de-colonisation and yet we still have not taken debates forward.

Finally, the increase in new economic migrants, refugees from political persecution following the enlargement of the European Union in 2004,, has significant implications for existing models of representation. It seems unlikely in this context that any single model for representation will be sufficient to develop effective housing policies and responsive housing services. However, there is no indication that housing regulators take these wider factors into consideration.

At the same time as these changes in policy and society occur, the social housing sector has also been changing in ways that make the task of building accountability with new minorities more challenging. The social housing sector is being transformed by a process of rationalisation, merger and group structure. There is a strong trend towards streamlining, reducing the size and number of committees and limiting formal local accountability arrangements. It is widely recognised that traditional forms of representation and governance are no longer fit for purpose and larger associations are actively seeking new models for accountability and involvement (Future Shape of the Sector Commission, 2006). The move towards rationalisation has meant that many smaller associations join larger groups. This is especially evident within the specialist BME housing association sector, with very few continuing to exist as independent organisations. They are becoming part of larger housing associations resulting in concerns about representation and engagement of minority groups; formal independence has been traded for the promise of wider influence, but the impact on accountability to minority communities is unresolved. Recently the largest BME housing association has collapsed because of governance and financial problems which have shaken the confidence in this sub-sector (see Inside Housing, 2009).

Rationalisation may mark the end of the BME housing sector but the decline has been evident for some time. The advent of private finance and increased regulation meant that many BME housing associations had to adapt to a business model of operating that was in some cases at odds with community mobilisation and advocacy roots. The need to demonstrate management control may have led to a shedding of radical origins. Though the rhetoric may continue to be about fighting community struggles, in reality even the smallest registered BME housing association is a multi-million pound organisation with the cultural symbolism that this brings. Policy shifts from race equality to community cohesion has already been discussed as reducing the rationale and influence of specialist black-led housing organisations. It could be argued that race equality was the dominant driver in equality and housing debates but this is no longer the case. Conversely it could be argued that the Housing Corporation has driven race equality policies from 1986 to 2003 into mainstream discussions amongst the wider social housing sector. Mainstream or white led housing associations house far more black and minority ethnic tenants and employ black and minority staff. This apparent commitment to race equality and changing organisational culture leads to questions on the need, identity and sustainability of BME housing associations (Beider, 2006). These have been accelerated with the demise of the largest BME housing association and also the closure of the Federation of Black Housing Organisations which had represented race and housing issues since 1986 (see Inside Housing, 2009).

Finally, in this new institutional landscape there are few opportunities for new organisations to form, and it is clear that there will not be a new generation of registered associations to respond to new waves of migration and meet the needs of Asylum seekers, refugees and new economic migrants. The Housing Corporation expected mainstream housing providers operating within a highly regulated and oligarchic market place to develop local services to address new needs. This should be contrasted with very different responses to the needs of black and minority ethnic communities. Previous policy drivers led to a framework for the emergence of over 60 BME housing associations and capital investment of over £500 million during the 1990s (Beider, 2007b).

Despite concerns about the performance of some black led housing associations, there is clear evidence that specialist support led to the emergence of new and important organisations that met the needs of black and minority ethnic communities and helped the social housing sector as a whole to improve its performance (Lupton and Perry, 2004). Moreover, the knowledge and professional skills were enhanced by black and minority housing professionals who inculcated the wider housing sector leading to greater cultural awareness and opportunities for leadership in mainstream housing associations. This level of support will not be afforded to new groups when there is evidence to suggest that housing needs are not being met by housing associations. Problems in awareness, understanding and engagement of new communities as well as the increasing number of older people from established minority communities may not be easily resolved by housing associations (Markkanen, 2009).

A recovery of the black and minority ethnic housing sector?

The preceding discussion can be summarised as the decline and fall of the black led housing sector. This has paralleled changes in public policy from Macpherson to the much less positive community cohesion. The nadir of the sector was the insolvency of FBHO in 2008. This, along with the demise of two of the largest black led housing associations, seemed to indicate that the race and housing would forever remain frozen in a specific time period. The Housing Corporation BME Policies had served to inculcate an awareness of race equality in the sector and minority staff had advanced into position of power and influence. Housing had moved beyond race.

As a representative body FBHO has succeeded in representing different and diverse interests. Its collapse in 1998 created opportunities for new organisations to fill the gap. Amongst these was BME National which emerged in 2009 (Inside Housing, 2009). Supported by the National Housing Federation (NHF) the organisation sees itself as helping to represent the interests of black led housing associations together with influencing policy within the NHF (BME National website: http://blog. bmenational.org.uk/). The strap line of *Empowering Communities, Integration Lives* may be viewed as an attempt to recapture the spirit of FBHO policies on positive action whilst being pragmatic on the shift to new policy framework. Membership is open to any organisation who views itself as black and minority led which is a distance removed of a black and minority led housing association used above. Moreover BME National is focused on supporting minority employees in the social housing sector. It is too early to predict whether this new representative organisation could mark a renaissance of black and minority ethnic housing.

Creating a space for a representative voice for the black led housing sector may be difficult. In Chapter 2 the new policy of integration was outlined which seemed to suggest a tougher stance on integration rather than promoting difference. In 2005 the then leader of the Conservative Party, David Cameron apportioned ethnic division in the country on multiculturalism and housing policy: 'Multiculturalism has come to mean an approach which focused on what divides us rather than what brings us together ... It often treats ethnic or faith communities as monolithic blocks, rather than individual British citizens. *It leads to public housing being allocated along ethnic lines.*' (Inside Housing, 2007: authors' emphasis).

This could be viewed as a rejection of not only multiculturalism but also black led housing associations. Indeed this Prime Minister seems to be coming back to some of these issues in his speech on security in Munich in February 2011 (Cameron, 2011). In contrast to the 1980s the policy environment appears to be unsupportive of single issue (see CIC, 2007) of themed organisations that speak for a collective perspective.

Alongside this are findings that demonstrate that minority communities are impacted disproportionately by disadvantage across a range of public policy areas (EHRC, 2010). Policy and practice seem to be pointing in different directions. A new start of the black and minority ethnic housing sector should be welcomed but needs to be cognisant of the policy challenges, meeting the needs of new and different communities who may not perceive themselves to be either black or minority and devising a practical programme of action.

Conclusion

During this chapter we have discussed the rise and decline of the black led housing sector in parallel to macro policy intervention. These have crystallised the role of the Housing Corporation's Black and Minority Ethnic Housing Policies from 1986 to 2003, the publication and positive impact of the Macpherson Report in 1999 and finally the emergence of community cohesion following the riots in 2001. Given the impact that these three policy interventions have had on wider debates on race, housing and public policy, the trajectory of the black led housing sector has been clearly influenced. The Housing Corporation played a pivotal role in creating a plan and providing dedicated funding for fledgling black led housing associations in 1986 for the first five-year plan. Two further five-year strategies that followed, whilst less generous, consolidated growth and provided a progressive framework to discuss race and housing issues. In this way, it could be argued that the State acted in a benevolent way towards disadvantage groups and communities. The notion of a flexible State is one which we will return to in the concluding chapter. Earlier on in the book we considered in detail the impact of the Macpherson Report on race and housing. It was argued that this could be considered the highpoint of race relations in the post war period. The report defined new terms such as institutional racism and a racist incident, led to legislative changes on race relations and also importantly provided a symbolic rallying point for black led organisations. In the context of housing, Macpherson, in practical terms, helped to initiate a new inquiry on race and housing and resulted in acknowledgement, if not additional investment, to the black led housing sector. Addressing discrimination, mobilising for change and celebrating the contribution of black led housing organisations reached an epoch immediately after 1999. Both the Housing Corporation and Macpherson, for different reasons, played a role in the growth and consolidation of the black led housing sector. This contrasts sharply with the ascent of community cohesion following the disturbances in Burnley, Oldham and Bradford in 2001. The concept underpinned much of the New Labour approach to race up to the 2010 General Election. As discussed in Chapter 2, community cohesion has contributed to a period of stagnation and decline for the black led housing sector. A rigid determination to focus on similarities between communities, an emphasis on common norms and shared public spaces inevitably raised concerns about the value of housing associations which were not only described themselves as black but were rooted in the anti-racist struggles of the past. At a stroke, black led housing organisations became out of step with mainstream policy. They began to look dated. It could be argued that black led housing organisations were either unwilling or unable to respond to community cohesion policies and that this contributed to the reduction in scale, size and importance of the sector.

Macro policy has played an important role in the development and decline of the black led housing sector. However, it would be remiss to fault this alone and not evaluate the role of the black led housing sector as a movement for mobilisation and change. As we have seen in this chapter, black activists had a critical role in highlighting overcrowding and poor housing conditions, problems in accessing public sector housing, and the barriers that prevented people from taking up employment in the social housing sector. Indeed the theme of housing and race was raised as a contributing factor to the 1981 urban riots which heralded new investment in inner city areas and later the first five-year strategy by the Housing Corporation. Thus community activists and organisations should be viewed as not passive recipients of housing policy but as helping to shape the terms of reference that led to more than 60 registered black led housing associations and the emergence of the Federation of Black Housing Organisations. It could be argued that the story of black political struggle has never been given full credit in the narratives on race and housing. This is part of the missing history of social housing in the UK. However, it has also been argued that the decline of the black led housing sector cannot simply be blamed on the Housing Corporation or the Homes and Communities Agency or the problematic nature of community cohesion policy. We have suggested here that black led housing organisations became complacent and dependent on the Housing Corporation. Increased levels of professionalisation demanded by regulators placed a strain on the community activist roots of many of these organisations. In short the dynamism and energy that had propelled the black housing sector became dissipated when the reality of running large and complex organisations was experienced. It could be argued that the radical roots of the black led housing sector became compromised. More than this, these organisations became dependent on the State for investment, jobs and patronage. As policy shifted to community cohesion many black housing organisations had not moved their thinking. The pronouncements were about the HCA continuing to support these organisations, partly because of identity when the pressing need was on delivering integrated and sustainable neighbourhoods. In short, black housing activists were accused of not moving beyond the rhetoric of Macpherson. Importantly, black led housing organisations also had not responded to the needs of migrant workers following the expansion of the European Union in 2004. This people flow was the largest seen in post-war Britain and workers were living in marginal conditions in the private and later in the public sector. Given the changes in policy and organisational flaws, there should be little surprise that the black led housing sector is in decline with the symbolic failure of its largest two organisations – Ujima and Presentation – together with the demise of the Federation of Black Housing Organisations, all of which has lead to a policy and practice vacuum in race and housing.

In retrospect, the decision by the Housing Corporation in 1986 to develop a policy to support the development of BME housing associations should be seen as one of the most radical interventions on race relations during the last 25 years. However it also marked the start of a declining significance of race in housing policy and practice which were variously due to: a changing climate for investment in social housing following the 1988 Housing Act; shifting policy priority from race to housing as seen from the transition from Macpherson to Cohesion to Equality; and the parochialism in the social housing sector and its regulatory framework that focused on fixed notions of representation which became redundant as a result of new types of immigration. In taking the debate forward, there is a need to reconfigure housing policy and practice. Social justice and equality of opportunity need to be emphasised in macro policy interventions rather than norms and culture. There is also a need for the HCA to reflect on the success of BME housing associations, understand the reasons for decline and consider the role for a network of progressive community based housing associations which work across policy and ethnic boundaries and act as the catalyst of neighbourhood renewal and change. In doing this we are not advocating returning to 1986 but supporting the need for advocacy, social justice and inequality that seems to have dropped off the social housing agenda.

There may be room for optimism for community based organisations in general and black led housing associations specifically. The 2007 economic recession has reduced the size and remit of government and the State. Indeed the mantra of the Conservative led government elected at the May 2010 election has become fixed on local solutions to local challenges. This pincer movement of a smaller State and localism could lead to opportunities for dynamic black led housing associations to broaden out from housing to community interventions in employment, regeneration and educational markets. This is almost a reversion to the roots of black and minority ethnic housing associations before the first Housing Corporation Policy in 1986. We shall return to the impact of new policies and government in Chapter 6 of this book.

5

Housing, Communities and 'Recycled Racism'

Introduction

In this book we have attempted to explore new ideas and themes on housing, communities and cohesion. This includes reflecting on how black and minority led housing associations have been framed by changing policy priorities in Chapter 4, the gap in cohesion and housing literature on meeting the needs of white working class communities in Chapter 3, and exploring new ideas and frameworks in the concluding chapter. New ideas and themes are needed in connection to housing and cohesion to take debates at policy and academic levels forward. To this end this chapter will explore how the changing demographic base of the UK may lead to conflict and tension over social housing. Debates on race and housing have tended to focus on white and minority communities and generated copious amounts of publications from the 1950s. Some of these have been highlighted in earlier chapters. The problem with the race and housing research is that, for the most part, the analysis has remained fixated as if we are still living in the 1950s. Of course, Britain has changed significantly in policy on race, integration and immigration. However, the most dramatic changes have been related to population. Specifically, Britain has entered the period of not simply diversity but 'super-diversity'.

Race, Housing & Community: Perspectives on Policy & Practice, First Edition.
Harris Beider.
© 2012 Harris Beider. Published 2012 by Blackwell Publishing Ltd.

This chapter has three objectives. First exploring the concept of super-diversity. Second, relating increased diversity to conflict and tensions in the domain of housing. Here we will suggest that the conflict between established minority and emerging communities could be framed as 'recycled racism'. Third, is putting forward policy recommendations in addressing intra ethnic conflict on social housing. The chapter should be viewed as explorative in introducing new ideas and themes. There is a need for evidence to explore, for example, the extent of the nature of relationships between different minority communities. This has been absent from academic and policy debates.

The emergence of super-diversity in the UK

Britain has attracted people from across the world for many centuries. These flows and their impact on society, cities and neighbourhoods have been explored by many researchers, notably Fryer (1984). More recently the historical nature of difference, diversity and place has been explored in the context of London (GLA, 2005; Dench et al., 2006). The concept of super-diversity should not be viewed as being entirely new or as a simple continuity. Contextualised in a country that has seen a significant influx of immigrants, we need to be clear about the definition presented on super-diversity. Vertovec states that the term can best be described as a complex mesh of circumstances:

> 'Super-diversity' is distinguished by a dynamic interplay of variables, including: country of origin (comprising a variety of possible subset traits such as ethnicity, language[s], religious tradition, regional and local identities, cultural values and practices), migration channel (often related to highly gendered flows, specific social networks and particular labour market niches), and legal status (including myriad categories determining a hierarchy of entitlements and restrictions). (Vertovec, 2007: 3)

The scope of the concept needs to be explored further. Certainly the extent and types of migration flows have changed in size and complexity. After 1945 a strong theme of immigration was the link with former colonies in the Caribbean and Indian sub-continent. People who came to work and eventually live in Britain were connected to the country through colonial experiences and citizenship as British subjects. Consistent levels of immigration, connectivity through legal status and links to places led to the emergence of communities in towns and cities across the country but largely in cities such as London, Birmingham and Manchester. Of course these communities were also complex in terms of class, gender, ethnicity but the analysis points to a straightforward analysis of race and immigration focusing on 'Caribbean' and 'Asian' communities. As we have seen in earlier chapters on policy and practice this led to concept of multiculturalism, integration and community cohesion designed to manage and promote co-existence between the majority and minority.

Super-diversity presents an altogether different vision. An unprecedented phase of migration during the last 20 years has led to the emergence of new groups in the UK. Many have no special allegiance to the country and have not been bestowed with citizenship rights. Some have moved to cities and towns that have had relatively little experience with the immigration of the 1950s and 1960s (see Kyambi, 2005; Vertovec, 2007). Much of this has resulted from the enlargement of the European Union in May 2004. More than 800 000 people have arrived in the UK to live and work (ONS, 2005). These were relatively young migrants who were citizens of the EU and for the most part worked in specific sectors of the economy that were suffering a labour shortage. There was no political or spiritual connection with the UK. It could be stated that they were migrant workers in the same way that Turks initially moved to Germany in the 1960s. It was a contractual relationship that did not confer full rights in terms of citizenship or access to welfare such as social housing (Audit Commission, 2007; Robinson and Reeve, 2006). Importantly it should be noted that the flow of migrants in 2004 was largely white in stark contrast to the post-1945 migration. Competition and conflict continued to be characteristic of neighbourhoods and communities receiving new migrants. Yet debates on community cohesion have been largely fixed in the relationship between established white communities and established minority (especially British Muslim) communities (Beider, 2011). Government policy has not kept pace with neighbourhood changes.

Migrants from Eastern Europe have composed a large part of the people flow to the UK. In addition, in the last 20 years people from around the world have migrated to the country. Many have been the result of conflict in countries such as the Balkans, Iraq and Somalia. The situation is more complex as seen in the stepped migration by some of these groups. For example, Somali communities exist in many countries in Europe such as the Netherlands and Sweden. Groups may already be EU citizens before they arrive in the UK whilst for others the situation regarding citizenship and rights is much more complex.

Super-diversity measured in migration scale and composition can be stated by the statistical evidence. In 1996, foreign born nationals accounted for 3.5% of the workforce but within ten years that figure had almost doubled to 6% (Audit Commission, 2007). According to the Home Office, there were more than 600 000 National Insurance numbers (Ninos; sometimes used as an indication of EU migration since the 2004 enlargement) (Home Office, 2007). In 1971 immigration from Commonwealth countries composed 62% of the total; this had reduced to 37% in 2002 (cited in Vertovec, 2007).

During the early 1990s the pattern of migration flow had changed. Though people were still coming from the New Commonwealth there were now more people from a range of countries. Proponents of this view point to the figures. After 1994, net inflows of immigrants reached a peak of approximately 237 000 in 2007 (Office of National Statistics – ONS). Though this figure decreased because of the economic downturn in 2008, the Government still predicted net annual inflow as being about 190 000 each year to 2020 (ONS, 2009). In contrast with much of the migration post-1945, the term 'new migration' has been used to describe movement to the UK from the 1990s (Kyambi, 2005; Vertovec, 2007). Countries as diverse as Poland, Kosovo, Iraq, Somalia, Congo and Kenya have contributed significantly to net inflow. For example, in 2008 it was reported that 522 000 Polish citizens were living in the UK (ONS, 2009). This was largely the result of the decision by the British government to allow entry with no restriction to nationals from the eight new member states that joined the European Union in 2004. The then booming economy, poor prospects in the newly emergent countries and good exchange rates provided the appropriate conditions to fuel this new immigration. Poland was the principal sender country. Indeed, recent analysis shows that Poland ranked only behind India as the top sender country to the UK in 2009 (CEP, 2010). Since 2004 the expansion of the EU led to the most important migration since the 1950s. Unlike Commonwealth immigration from the Caribbean and Indian sub-continent, these new migrants were white, transient and did not have the cultural, family and economic links to the UK.

The 2004 enlargement did not bestow citizenship rights and access to welfare services such as housing. This was restricted to those who could demonstrate a 'settled residency' which normally equates to 12 months' continuous employment (Rutter and Latorre, 2009). However, once residency had been proven migrants were allowed to apply for a range of benefits including social housing.

It could be argued that asylum seekers and refugees were the second reason for super-diversity. Conflict and persecution across the world meant that those seeking asylum in the UK reached a high of 103 100 in 2002 (Vertovec, 2007). The principal flow came from Iraq, Zimbabwe, Somalia and Afghanistan (Somerville et al., 2009). According to the United Nations, Britain received 15.5% of worldwide asylum applications in 2002, more than any other country (Somerville et al., 2010). The government policy of 'dispersal' meant that asylum seekers were forced to locate outside London and in many cases in local authorities that had a surplus of social housing (Phillimore and Goodson, 2008). It is estimated that about a quarter of people seeking asylum are granted permission to stay in the UK and, with this, an opportunity to access social housing and other welfare benefits (Salt, 2004).

Taken together, immigration and asylum help to shape the contours of a new super-diversity that in scope and composition is very different to the new commonwealth migration in the 1950s and 1960s. Directing communities under work permits (EU migrants) and dispersal (asylum seekers) channels communities into areas that previously had very little experience managing diversity and difference, for example, East Anglia and the South West of England. This being said, London still accounts for the majority of new immigration. Indeed the overall pattern of spatial settlement has changed little since 1985 (CEP, 2010). However, new immigration has occupied neighbourhoods which provide access to social housing or low cost rental housing. These are primarily located in receptive housing markets that continue to have high concentrations of established migrants. This is important because it provides the basis to explore housing and recycled racism which we will focus on later in this chapter.

Before discussing recycled racism we need to critically analyse the extent of super-diversity. There are several issues that need to be explored. First, commentary on the emergence of super-diversity seems to be located largely on demographic changes in London (Vertovec, 2007). This has been extensively documented by local government organisations (see GLA, 2005). Historically, the capital and the south east region have pulled migrants because of their preeminent position as the economic engine room of the British economy. Recently it has been put forward that all but two of the 15 districts with more than 30% minority populations are located in London (Hamnett and Butler, 2010). Furthermore, immigrants compose just under 40% of its population (CEP, 2010). Indeed, the focus of super-diversity to London has been commented on by some of its leading proponents (Kyambi, 2005; Vertovec, 2007).

Admittedly recent immigration, and especially economic migrants since 2004 together with asylum seekers and refugees, has been pushed by the market and government policy away from the capital. However, and predictably, London, given its role as a point of entry and its importance to the economy of the UK, has become the capital of these super-diversity flows. Thus, the city has clusters of 10 000 people or more from 42 different countries (GLA, 2005). Difference and diversity has been used in a positive way to attract investment and global interest (Newman, 2007).

The pace and scale of migration suggests a new level of diversity beginning in the 1990s. Britain has changed considerably and attracted new groups to add to those who came as part the established immigration patterns of the 1950s. Diversity has been welcomed and celebrated in cities (London) and through key events (2012 Olympics). Less attention has been given to the implications of super-diversity on public policy and especially housing.

Increased diversity has challenged the vexed question of identity in the context of race and housing. Policy making has been shaped by meeting the needs of black and minority groups. Initially the focus of Housing Corporation Policy was on supporting community organisations that could advocate on behalf of these groups. This led to the emergence of the black led housing sector composed of Caribbean and Asian led housing associations (see Harrison, 2005; Beider, 2007a; Netto and Beider, 2011). Indeed, Chapter 4 of this book suggests that policies on race and housing led to these housing associations occupying a role and status that the new groups would find much more difficult to gain (see also Phillimore and Goodson, 2006).

Increasing super-diversity has also challenged assumptions of 'black' as a generic term. This term, along with black and minority ethnic, was the concept that guided the Housing Corporation and other public policy interventions since 1986. As we have stated, a substantial proportion of immigrants to the UK since the 1990s may find it difficult to be accommodated under such an all encompassing term. For the most part, migrant workers from Eastern Europe would view themselves as white but may have similar or greater housing needs than established minority groups (Robinson and Reeve, 2006; Audit Commission, 2007). Similarly, black and minority ethnic housing policies could prove difficult in relating experiences of refugee communities escaping conflicts in different parts of the world. Yet the evidence suggests that new immigrants, irrespective of legal status, have encountered a range of challenges in terms of housing.

This includes a lack of representation and advocacy (Mullins et al., 2007), high levels of overcrowding (Gryszel-Fieldsned and Reeve, 2007), unsafe housing (Koscielak, 2007) and related health problems (Phillips, 2006). A range of pressing and persistent housing challenges may not be best addressed though the term of black and minority housing. The complexity of groups and individuals may be masked by policy which uses broad categorisations as a point of simple convenience. Policy makers and established minority based housing organisations have been slow in meeting the needs of super-diversity.

Taking this further, some have argued that 'black' in terms of public policy has been rendered meaningless. Fanshawe and Sriskandarajah have suggested that simple categorisations conveniently ignore differences within and between groups. Conversely they may also compound differences between people when many have similar concerns and challenges (Fanshawe and Sriskandarajah, 2010). The incidence of super-diversity and those calling for new types of policy discussions beyond 'black' housing my not entirely coincide. However, the rationale needs to be considered. Discussion and debate in public policy areas such as housing have been too simplistic and categorised on the black- white spectrum when, in fact, communities and groups have shifting and multiple identities. For example, Poles came from being the thirteenth largest foreign born group in the UK in 2004 to being the largest in 2008 (Pollard et al., 2008). Discrimination to this white minority in housing and related areas has been shown to be extensive (Spencer et al., 2007).

The politics on black and minority communities may have helped to exclude the issues and concerns of new groups. This is not to blame black and minority housing organisations; rather the process of policy making and framing that creates a limited space to consider different perspectives. Indeed the terms themselves seem redundant to the complexities and opportunities offered by difference and super-diversity. The reduced importance given by the Housing Corporation and then its successor, the Homes and Communities Agency, to issues of race equality do not bode well to support the housing demands of new groups. Reduced housing investment and the move towards larger housing organisations to achieve economies of scale combine to prevent the emergence of new types of housing organisations (Pawson and Mullins, 2010). Black and minority ethnic housing associations have reduced in number because of increased regulatory demands and the focus on low rents, efficiency and governance. Many have been forced to consider partnership arrangements with larger housing organisations which reduce the voice of the sector as whole

(Beider, 2007b). In short, there is no indication from the Homes and Communities Agency that investment and encouragement will be given to new groups and communities to develop housing organisations that will represent specific needs as seen with the emergence of the black and minority ethnic sector.

Related to housing economics and governance is the emergence of community cohesion. This was perceived to be a critical response to the emergence of multiculturalism and support for minority organisations. Hence the focus on common norms and values may weaken demand for new housing organisations. Single group funding has been criticised in the report by the Commission on Integration and Cohesion (CIC, 2007). It led to imbedding difference when the focus should have been on integration and similarities. More recently, the Coalition Government has announced that a much more aggressive approach to integration should be developed emphasising similarities over difference (Cameron, 2011). Housing needs of new communities seem to have been squeezed by policy priorities and economic constraints.

Notions of super-diversity are important in shaping discussions on key public policy areas such as housing. The conventional wisdom on housing and race has emphasised the importance of groups and communities from the Caribbean and Indian sub-continent. Indeed policy and, to a lesser extent, academic literature shows research gravitating to these groups. Examples of this include: the Housing Corporation approach from the first Black and Minority Ethnic Housing Policy in 1986 (Harrison, 1995 and see also the review of policies, Hann and Bowes, 2004); debates on housing conducted by representative organisations (NHF, 2001); and academic perspectives (Harrison et al., 2005). Reification of these groups have ignored complexities and also excluded new and emerging communities. Caribbean and Asian housing organisations have benefited from housing investment, advocacy and networks. Of course, we should also be reminded of public interventions on race such as how the Macpherson Report (Home Office, 1999) helped to consolidate the view that race needed to be played within the parameters of the binary analysis of black and white. Given this, there was relatively little space for new and different groups to voice concerns on housing and get their issues onto the political agenda.

It is not surprising that debates on race and public policy have been rooted in the collective experiences of Caribbean and Asian migrants. These were the groups that were subject to racism and exclusion in the UK (Daniel, 1968). In response, organisations embedded within these communities were developed to undertake campaigns using cultural identity as an active agent (Sivanandan, 1982; CCCS, 1982). It should be noted that the rich data still needs to be mined to record and celebrate this history of black resistance in Britain. This is even more important given that the recent government policy on community cohesion has been configured on shared norms, which could be seen as a critique of difference and multiculturalism (Burnett, 2004). The legacy and influence of Caribbean and Asian communities on public policy should be seen as a positive achievement. Campaigning and community mobilisation led to significant legislative changes such as the 1976 Race Relations Act, the urban renewal following 1981 riots, and, of course, the race equality measures in housing from 1986.

Collectivised identity made it easier to lobby the State and its institutions to improve performance on race equality. Reification was and continues to be a problem that super-diversity has helped to deconstruct. Transforming different communities into a single group may have been the result of these anti-racist initiatives. However, it could be argued that race relations research combined with the response of government cemented a singular identity of the diverse experiences. As we have seen in the opening chapter of this book, a consistent feature of some publications in this area has been the tendency to apply a coat of pathological paint to minority experiences (see for example, Patterson, 1963; Rex and Tomlinson, 1979; Cantle, 2008). In part, research has influenced government responses on race and the establishment of a binary analysis of black and white. Not only has this been inaccurate in terms of ethnicity but has also considerably downplayed the significance of income, gender, disability, age and sexual orientation in these communities. Simplistic black and white categorisation has enabled the State to develop sometime simplistic responses to complex issues. Apart from nullifying difference, this simplistic analysis on race allowed representatives from different communities to position themselves as gate-keepers to communities and allowed for the rise of the vexed term 'community leaders'.

A triple lock develops that freezes analysis despite the changing nature of immigration, politics and communities. Community mobilisation helped initially to address the challenges of racism. Research pathologised groups into collectivised behaviours based on a social and racist construction. Dividing race into two or three groups that could liaise with the State on resources and representation made the job of government relatively simple. In this context, super-diversity helps to move analysis into taking difference into account.

There is more that needs to be done. Super-diversity has shown a compelling vision of a new type of Britain that is very different to the 1950s. New groups and communities have emerged, especially in larger cities, which add to the richness of the country as whole. We have also noted that governance generally has failed to keep pace with changes, with a rigid adherence to a categorisation of groups that may have no bearing on the reality within society. Now there is a need to explore how super-diversity plays out in neighbourhoods and in the context of housing. In the next section, research will be used from recent studies in Birmingham to explore public policy implications of difference and resources. Difference and diversity should rightly be celebrated as enriching the country and cities but it may also lead to conflict and resentment manifesting in racism and racialised language. This is not necessarily framed in the analysis of community relations that has developed in this country in the post war period but rather the conflict, cohesion and integration of established minority groups and new communities.

Recycled racism

The problem with choice constraint analysis was discussed in Chapter 1. Much of the analysis on race and housing comes from the perspective that minority housing preferences are the result of preference towards ethnic clustering and access to support networks (Dayha, 1974). They exercise a choice. In contrast, the constraint perspective emphasises discrimination by housing officers (Rex and Moore, 1967) and the housing system (Henderson and Karn, 1987). This prevents minority groups from moving to certain neighbourhoods and leads to segregated neighbourhoods. Ratcliffe (2009) summarised the limitations of this approach. These include not recognising a change in housing and neighbourhood preferences. Thus the conflict between different groups in gaining access to public sector housing may have been sharper during the 1960s because this tenure was seen as being preferable to other options such as private renting. However, given the reductions in housing investment and move towards owner occupation, public or social housing may not have such a preferential position. In short, choice and constraint are fixed in time. Structuration theory developed by Giddens (1976) and applied by Sarre et al. (1989) to race and housing showed that structure and agency could be interdependent and dynamic.

Super-diversity needs to be considered in the context of both choice and constraint and also structuration theory. New and different types of migration since the 1990s could lead to new forms of conflict. This needs to go beyond the reification present in the development of policy and practice in race and housing seen in the Housing Corporation and Homes and Communities Agency. As noted, race and housing is related to black and minority ethnic groups. In reality, much of the discussion is focused on Caribbean and Asian British communities. Furthermore, discussions on super-diversity have not put forward a substantial analysis of the conflict and tensions between different groups living in the same neighbourhood. The reality of competition for public resources such as housing or indeed neighbourhood may lead to new forms of conflict in addition to new forms of demography.

The emergence of different communities since the 1990s has run parallel to the decline of multiculturalism and move towards community cohesion. At national and local level it could be argued that difference is not so much celebrated but regarded as being problematic. Indeed it was suggested in Chapter 2 that there has been a slippage in language and policy away from multiculturalism towards integration and assimilation. Since the Macpherson Report was published (Home Office, 1999), leading to changes in the Race Relations Act, much of the focus has been on supporting new communities to espouse shared and common values (CIC, 2007). Super-diversity and super-difference between communities has coincided with a move from social justice and race equality towards 'a muscular liberalism' (Cameron, 2011). Different communities must not be allowed to cling on to different value sets that run counter to 'British values':

> Under the doctrine of state multiculturalism, we have encouraged different cultures to live separate lives, apart from each other and apart from the mainstream. We've failed to provide a vision of society to which they feel they want to belong. (Cameron, 2011)

The policy and political language suggests super-diversity is seen as much as a liability as asset to the UK. In this context, new immigrants may be viewed as problematic by existing residents whose parents and grandparents arrived to the country as part of the post-1945 immigration from the Caribbean and Indian sub-continent. The conflict points may be associated with neighbourhood change, pressure on social services and, importantly, competition for housing in the private and public sectors.

This may be manifested in racialised language by established minority groups towards new minority groups, language that is not dissimilar to that used towards previous migrants in the 1950s and 1960s. Super-diversity could lead to recycled racism that goes beyond the dualism of black and white. Conflict and tensions may encompass a variety of forms.

A case study of Birmingham

Birmingham has been described as 'one of the most ethnically mixed cities in the UK' (Fenton et al., 2010: 37). The population of the city has been layered by different phases of migration, commencing from the mid-nineteenth century from Ireland, to the post-1945 immigration from the Caribbean and Indian sub-continent, and more recently by groups coming from Eastern Europe, Africa and the Middle East. The concepts of super-diversity and recycled racism will be discussed in relation to research completed by the author in Birmingham. This may help to relate concepts to reality but of course there are limitations, including a relatively small sample and a basis in one city. Nevertheless, the findings shed light on certain ideas and themes that help to move the dialogue forward.

Established minority communities are those migrants who arrived in the UK after 1945 from the Caribbean and Indian sub-continent. They settled in cities such as Birmingham to support essential sectors such as transport and health and also found work in factories and foundries. Indeed it could be argued that these minority groups helped Birmingham to sustain economic growth and expansion, making the city a symbol of success (Newton, 1976). Even though established minority groups were an engine for economic growth they quickly became settled in poorer housing markets clustered around the city centre. This was a result of discrimination in public and private sector housing markets (Rex and Moore, 1967; Ratcliffe, 1981; Henderson and Karn, 1987). Indeed, research demonstrates the extent of concentration when in some areas two out of every three people come from a Pakistani background (Bibby, 2005) and Birmingham is likely to become the first city in the UK by 2026 where no single group has a majority population (Fenton et al., 2010). Regulations on the flow of immigration since the 1960s have not prevented the increase of the minority population in Birmingham. This is principally the result of the more youthful profile of such groups and increased fertility rates. Post-war immigration has created established minority groups and residential patterns as well as a social and community infrastructure to support groups.

In contrast, emerging minority communities have moved to Birmingham since the 1990s from a much greater range of countries in sub- Saharan Africa, Asia and Europe. During the last five years and since the establishment of NASS (National Asylum Support Service) a significant number of asylum seekers have arrived in the city. Many have received leave to remain and decided to stay in Birmingham. Indeed, the inner urban areas have served as a dispersal area for the city as a whole (Phillimore and Goodson, 2008). As stated by Vertovec (2007) these groups have different levels of legal status that impacts on safety, security and permanence. Again, the contrast with established minority groups in an embedded community structure is stark. In addition to refugees and asylum seekers, which may now account for 6% of some wards (Phillimore, 2010), Birmingham and the West Midlands has also attracted migrant workers from Eastern Europe. According to a recent report, more than 120 000 came to the region (ONS, 2009).

New migrants have largely settled in neighbourhoods previously populated by established migrant communities located in inner urban areas. Housing based discrimination combined with clustering leads to an uneven distribution of communities in Birmingham (Fenton et al., 2010). Hence, diversity is increasing and challenging assumptions on mediating relations between a small number of groups. Indeed, it could be argued that our understanding of diverse neighbourhoods in fact is associated with areas that have largely established minority populations composed of people who came to Birmingham in the post war period from Pakistan, Bangladesh and the Caribbean together with emerging communities from Eastern Europe, Africa and Asia. The common denominator is the small and declining white population (Goodson and Beider, 2005; Beider, 2011).

It is helpful to distinguish different types of groups before discussing the concept of recycled racism and the extent to which it is happening in a city such as Birmingham.

Given the different phases of migration, settlement and legal status of movement, the commonly held notions of race and community need to be challenged. As noted earlier race, cohesion and integration cannot be fully discussed within the bounded perspective of black and white. A mosaic of different groups and communities now reside in Birmingham and may have differing needs and aspirations. Many cannot be described by the label of 'black' as it applied in the debates on social housing. The situation is much more complex with differences on language, faith, legal status and tradition all being important in shaping understanding of identity. For example, Polish communities have now clustered in different parts of Birmingham (Fenton et al., 2010) and did not have immediate access as migrant workers to social housing. These groups may take umbrage at being categorised as either black or minority ethnic given they are residents of the European Union. Recognition of difference is important to develop policies and interventions for different groups.

Resident patterns for new and established groups show a correlation with deprivation. The prospect is for super-diversity to increase in those neighbourhoods most at risk from poor housing, health and educational outcomes and joblessness: 'Given the age structure of these populations, and the indicators of recent population composition in Birmingham's most deprived areas has grown even more diverse over the past eight years.' (Fenton et al., 2010: 39). In these circumstances there is a need to critically review power, conflict and co-existence between established and emerging communities. Resources will be limited and groups do not start from the same position in terms of political networks, relationships to institutions and levels of information and awareness. It is not surprising that conflict may arise between established and emerging communities. In contrast to studies on the phenomena of super-diversity relatively little has been discussed on how conflict is structured (Mullins et al., 2004).

Importantly governance in Birmingham and in domains such as housing may be problematic in meeting the needs of different groups. Representation in politics, housing associations and regeneration boards is often based on the size of local groups. It has been noted that governance on black and minority ethnic housing associations is related to the number of Caribbean and Asian representatives on the management committee. This defines whether the organisation is considered a BME housing association. Similarly, established minority communities in Birmingham have successfully mobilised to secure representation at the local authority. For example, Pakistani communities have successfully secured representation at parliamentary, local government and voluntary sector levels since the 1980s. Two MPs of Pakistani descent were elected at the 2001 and 2010 general elections in Perry Barr and Ladywood respectively; 12 councillors of Pakistani descent are currently on Birmingham City Council from 120 councillors; a number of community and voluntary sector organisations have been supported by the local authority and are based in neighbourhoods that meet the social and cultural needs of these communities. The level and scope of representation should be celebrated. After all, some supporters of social capital would view this as evidence of engagement in civic institutions in the city (Putnam, 2000). It is also not surprising given that these groups have been living in Birmingham for at least 50 years. Moreover, though the Pakistani population account for 10.6% of the population across the city they compose 77.2% of those living in the most deprived areas (see Fenton et al., 2010). This has transformed into political mobilisation, votes and representation.

Yet there is a need to also discuss how power and representation may be used to exclude other groups, both established minority and emerging communities. First, the process that led to the influential position of British Pakistanis has been subject to debate and scrutiny. In short, it is how 'patron-client' politics has been used by mainstream political parties to broker deals with communities (Solomos and Back, 1995). It is contended by some that politics has been disfigured by political organisations using relationships with so called 'community leaders' to deliver a block vote that could be decisive in the outcome of elections (Mullins et al., 2004; Beider, 2007b). The process of politics based on numerical strength, block votes and 'backroom' deals is mired in risk. As much was revealed in the judgement of a specially convened Electoral Court in 2005. This was convened after petitions were served against the election of councillors in two inner urban wards in 2004. Significant fraud was revealed relating to postal votes which led to the elections being declared null and void (Stewart, 2006). The report suggested that corrupt practices by 'community leaders' had played a part in the fraud. Such actions only serve to decrease trust between people and institutions. Combined with electoral dominance of a single group it may prevent the emergence of young people, women and other underrepresented groups from having a political voice in local government. In the local politics of race, super-diversity had only deepened the sense of winners and losers. This does not increase belonging but may lead to rising tensions between different groups.

There is also a perception held amongst some African Caribbean community groups that I have spoken to 'off the record' some ethnic minority communities have benefited more because they have been more successful at playing this game ... the fact that some minority groups feel that there is a segregation of resources based on the political activism of some groups more than others who do not engage but have similar or greater needs is something that politicians, policy makers and communities need to address and challenge. (Local government officer cited in Goodson and Beider, 2005)

Established groups may be reluctant to share political resources and power with those who have newly arrived. This is not surprising given that mobilisation has led to political representation and a powerful infrastructure that may provide access to decision-makers at a local level. A concentration of capital and knowledge may be used to defend interests and exclude groups (Bourdieu, 1986). In these circumstances it will be difficult for super-diversity to be replicated as a distribution of power. New and emerging groups in cities such as Birmingham are still trying to establish themselves in local politics. Some have started to form groups and organisations to try and mobilise and influence local agencies but many are still at an embryonic level (Mullins et al., 2007). Policy changes away from multiculturalism towards integration have made securing funding more difficult than in the past. The onus is more on interacting with different groups and developing shared vision and values for a neighbourhood or a city and less on meeting specific minority needs. Alongside the shift on social policy are tight financial circumstances since the 2008 recession. There has been a significant impact in Birmingham which is the largest local authority in the UK. It has been predicted that 7000 jobs will have to be cut (out of 18 500 full time employees) by 2020 to maintain financial stability. New and emerging communities who have arrived since the 1990s need to pool resources with groups that may have little in common or actively exclude participation.

In short, the position of emerging groups compares unfavourably with established groups in a city such as Birmingham. It could be argued that they have missed out at a time when public policy was supportive to meeting specific needs such as the Housing Corporation Black and Minority Ethnic Housing Policy (1986–2003) and Macpherson Report (Home Office, 1999). Instead they are trying to establish themselves and secure resources during a period when public policy has become much more restrictive on immigration and has also moved away from multiculturalism. This has been symbolised by the evolution of community cohesion into a harder form of integration (Cameron, 2011). Moreover emerging communities do not have the numerical strength in terms of population to mobilise and secure political representation on the local authority and regeneration bodies or the networks to influence housing associations.

Despite the disparity of power and representation, established groups perceive that new and emerging groups are gaining a disproportionate amount of support and funding from local authorities and housing associations. There are two aspects to consider. First, there is the sharp competition for public resources. This may be keenly felt in housing resources, especially larger family dwellings, but also in access to schools and health services. The importance of meeting housing needs and a points based allocation system results in new and emerging groups accessing larger family houses in inner urban areas in direct competition with Pakistani and Bangladeshi families. Second, new and emerging communities may lead to deeper concerns about the transformation of urban spaces that had previously being identified as being predominantly Pakistani, Caribbean or Indian. Concerns about neighbourhood change may be conflated with perceptions that new and emerging groups are responsible for increased crime and anti-social behaviour in the area. A sense of decline and blame becomes woven in narratives between established and emerging groups. It could be argued that established groups are framing new communities as a distinct 'other'. The process has been described as where culture and taste can be used to distance groups in society from mainstream norms (Skeggs, 2009).

The increased competition for resources can be viewed as destabilising the relationship between established groups and the local authority. Networks, political representation and knowledge may be weakened by increased super-diversity. For example, in some parts of Birmingham the established Pakistani and emerging Somali communities are in direct competition for larger family social housing. This is a scarce resource and demand exceeds supply. The process of allocation and letting is determined by meeting those families with the most acute housing need which in some cases leads to allocation being made to emerging groups. Emerging groups miss out but more importantly neighbourhoods start to become associated with emerging communities. Of course, concerns about changing character of neighbourhoods is not so dissimilar to debates across the country in response to Commonwealth immigration from the Caribbean and Indian sub-continent during the 1950s and 1960s. Here, established white residents and community organisations mobilised against the presence of new immigrants. Complaints were about access to housing, employment and association with increased crime (Patterson, 1963). These were based on racism and were linked to growing public policy concern about immigration. It is argued here that the portents are similar to the modern context of increased immigration in the 1990s and the emergence of super-diversity. Racism is being recycled by established minority communities to come to 'common sense' assumptions about new communities. The narrative, conflict and imagery show a strong similarity to the debates in the 1950s and 1960s.

Recycled racism: culture, competition and conflict

The premise regarding recycled racism needs to be developed further. It could be argued that the increased diversity and residence in poor neighbourhoods in Birmingham will inevitably lead to tensions and possible conflict. This is largely because of completion for scarce resources. The source is economic rather than cultural. However, this type of economic reductionism diminishes how conflicts are racialised by different groups to maintain a position of dominance and hierarchy in a city (Bourdieu, 1986).

The assumption of fixed identities ascribing collective behaviour is flawed in both practice and theory (see Patterson, 1963 as a classic example of this work). Minority groups have shifting identities that are shaped by different contexts and locations. For example, in the family home a minority identity may be pronounced in say communication and language; identity changes towards organisational, school or university in these circumstances and also when people follow sporting teams. Minorities are multi-layered and faceted and not the one dimensional groups that researchers sometimes imply. Religion and faith pull people together of course and this has been seen vividly in the role of Islam. For the most part communities have shifting identities shaped by differential contexts.

The problem with housing has been ascribing fixed labels to complex issues. It is suggested that some academics and policy makers have preferred a simplistic representational route and did not realise that some groups could be excluded when society changes. Super-diversity and increased and different types of migration flows may result in a representational model being redundant. For example, the housing needs of refugee communities are not being met by the creation of a new generation of housing associations despite the evidence showing there is a need for housing agencies to invest in capacity building and supported housing. (Mullins et al., 2007).

Recent research in Birmingham shows that tension may exist between communities. (Beider, 2005). Again established groups are those migrants who arrived in the UK after the 1950s and 1960s. These were generally people from the Indian sub-continent and the Caribbean who were employed in manufacturing, foundry work, transport and the health service in Birmingham and indeed across the country. Economic sectors that were short of unskilled and semi-skilled labour but essential to the well being of both the local and national economies. These were essentially economic migrants. Established communities clustered in inner urban areas of Birmingham such as Sparkbrook, Handsworth and Aston. Initially family and social networks were consolidated for mutual support and safety. The changing nature of these neighbourhoods resulted in more concentration of established groups and also the decline of the white population. Indeed, parts of East Birmingham such as Sparkbrook, Alum Rock and Sparkhill became synonymous with Pakistani and later Bangladeshi communities (Rex and Moore, 1967).

These groups aspired to get their issues related to housing, social services and educational needs onto the local political agenda in Birmingham. Initially communities formed voluntary sector and quasi-political organisations to provide self-help opportunities and influence policy agendas (Rex and Tomlinson, 1979). Later, many organisations were co-opted by local government and mainstream organisations. This can be seen in the work of political organisations such as the Labour Party and Trade Unions. In the former, increasing local numerical strength led to the election of local officers and eventually elected local council-lors (see Solomos and Back, 1995).

Emerging groups have had a presence in Birmingham since the 1990s. These groups are drawn from countries that have seen significant conflict such as Somalia, Afghanistan, Iraq and the Balkans. Political reasons may have been just as important as economic reasons for coming to the UK. Following the establishment of National Asylum Support Service (NASS), there has been significant numbers of asylum seekers and new communi-ties arriving to Birmingham (Phillimore and Goodson, 2006). Over this period, and particularly since the increased speed of asylum claim processing in 2003, many of the asylum seekers dispersed to Birmingham have received leave to remain in the UK and decided to settle in the region.

Parts of East Birmingham have served as a dispersal area for the region with a significant asylum seeker population in Sparkbrook/Sparkhill, Small Heath and Nechells. Research indicates that many of these newcomers intend to remain in Birmingham and thus it is necessary to ensure that future plans take into account their needs and aspirations. They have been drawn from a variety of countries that have seen some form of conflict or instability. In Birmingham there are emerging groups of Somalis, Kurds, Bosnians, Iraqis and Congolese (Goodson and Beider, 2005). Some of these new communities have started to form groups and organisations but many are still at an embryonic level (Mullins et al., 2007). Political representation in the form of elected councillors is non-existent in contrast to established groups discussed earlier. Many new communities are not represented at key forums that decide housing and voluntary sector investment (Goodson and Beider, 2005). This may be a result of exclusion because of the actions of more powerful organisations or simply because of lack of information and knowledge.

Whilst there has been a small concentration of NASS placements in North Solihull, the main concentrations have been in neighbourhoods that have large, established minority communities. Spatial concentration of new communities, especially the growth of the Somalis, has been the most significant change in Sparkbrook during the last ten years. Changing population patterns may appear to be more dramatic given local residents' perceptions not only of 'white flight' but also 'brown flight', the latter of which refers to the movement of Pakistanis away from the inner ring. This, taken together with the growth of Somali social and political infrastructure, confirms that parts of Sparkbrook are becoming predominantly Somali neighbourhoods. The symbolism of change attracts further Somali communities as a place of security and residence but may also lead to displacement of established groups.

The relationship in East Birmingham may be conceptualised as a process of conflict and integration. There was a sense that new communities place additional burdens on public services in areas that are already stretched because of limited resources, addressing disadvantage and also increased super-diversity. For example, there were fears that funding and support would be disproportionately apportioned to new communities rather than other disadvantaged groups in the area. Of course, this could also be understood as established groups protecting their vested interests with local government and housing providers. They do not want to share power and capital accumulated since the 1960s. As discussed, housing in Birmingham may be a source of conflict because of larger family groups in the Pakistani, Bangladeshi and Somali communities and a restricted supply of social housing in the inner city. New communities who have been placed in larger housing may be viewed as circumventing the process. Research with established residents showed that Somalis and other new and emerging groups were deemed to be undeserving of these types of public resources. There were real and palpable tensions between different groups. It was felt that relations could be improved if there were some assurances that newcomers would not get 'more favours' than established groups (Goodson and Beider, 2005).

In Birmingham, research has shown that concerns about increased competition for resources such as social hosing may be racialised.

Perspectives on new communities and neighbourhood impact echo the racist discourse surrounding the first wave of migration during the 1950s and 1960s. In some case the images of new communities were based on prejudices whipped up the media.

> I have heard that some of the Pakistani communities are saying that we are taking houses that's in the areas and that there isn't anything else left for them and why are we still moving into the area?. (cited in Goodson and Beider, 2005)

New groups were concerned about the lack of access to political resources. One respondent believed that the Pakistani community was in an advantageous position given its political and institutional links to the Council as well as the large number of local authority funded community and voluntary organisations that represent the Pakistani community. Another respondent believed that new communities 'are not normally getting the space to articulate issues in mainstream BME liaison groups.'

In these circumstances, new and emerging groups develop a process to get issues to decision makers outside of formal and established methods. This includes direct conversations with leading directors of housing organisations or senior councillors. In this way, new migrants may be better organised at raising key issues with policy makers than previous BME communities. Housing providers not only need to invest resources to access new migrants and manage established communities but also to deal with local community politics in the context of declining local resources.

New and established communities in Birmingham may also have points of similarity. There is evidence of co-existence between Somali and Pakistani communities in terms of faith and also economic renewal. Both groups follow the Islamic faith and this identity is important in building common interests. In addition, established groups recognise the role of emerging communities in the economic regeneration of previously desolate areas.

Islam has become an iconic as well as a religious symbol for many Muslims in East Birmingham. It has become a form of cultural and political resistance enabling communities to become mobilised on issues ranging from the need for single sex schools in Sparkbrook to making sense of international politics. In the study, there was evidence that levels of harassment increased after September 11 and the Iraq War. Global politics shaped local perceptions and experiences of racism in the Alum

Rock neighbourhood located in East Birmingham. The September 11 attacks and the Iraq War have led to tension between communities in the Eastern Corridor and across Birmingham. Some commented that young Pakistanis are being scrutinised by the Police. Others suggested that symbols such as the headscarf and veil help white people to categorise all Muslims as terrorists.

> Personally I've found I've got racism in public places. Mainly 'cause I wear a headscarf I've found that after September 11th I get a lot of very strange looks – yeah, I've had loads of incidents. (cited in Goodson and Beider, 2005)

A shared Islamic identity helps to make sense and get through day-to-day living in a secular and sometimes hostile environment. Some people felt Islamic identity brought together emerging and established groups and may develop solutions to overcome conflicts around housing and public services. It was felt that Islamic principles and places of worship such as mosques and madrassahs could help to bring these disparate communities together.

> We mix because we have the same culture and the same religion. When we have religious festivals we will give food to each others houses, we will go to the mosque together and embrace each other, so it is good between us. (cited in Goodson and Beider, 2005)

New communities were also viewed as playing a pivotal role in regenerating previously run down parts of the Eastern Corridor. Participants were positive about the role of the growing Somali communities in this renewal. Some commented on how the Somalis had transformed Stratford Road in Sparkbrook by creating new businesses, restaurants and clubs. Previously it had been akin to a 'ghost town'. The impact helped to confirm Birmingham as a positive and diverse city.

> There have been some big changes, like I said, I remember there being a big white population here but that's going back a long time. There are a lot more refugees and asylum seekers now, close to where Stratford Road starts. They've opened up a lot of shops and restaurants which is nice for that area. (cited in Goodson and Beider, 2005)

The combination of religious identity and social entrepreneurialism provide a common ground between established and new groups in East Birmingham. This helps to generate community cohesion and stable communities. The commonality between emerging and established residents does not resolve the challenges of super-diversity, conflict and cohesion. Rather coalescence on faith may not arguably lead to increased diversity. Instead it could simply result in neighbourhoods such as Sparkbrook being identified as segregated enclaves of minority and Muslim communities. Some emerging groups such as Eastern European migrants may not share the cohesive force of religion. To them Somali and Pakistani unity on Islam may simply reinforce division and difference and make the prospect of community cohesion much more difficult to achieve.

The sum of super-diversity is more than simply emerging Somali communities living alongside established Pakistani groups in East Birmingham. Conflict may be multi-dimensional to reflect the disparate nature of new groups. Thus, it could involve tensions between two established groups in Birmingham such as the Lozells Riots in 2005 (Black Radley, 2006). The reasons behind the street violence are complex. These started with rumours about an alleged rape of a Caribbean woman by Asian men and were spread by community radio stations. The resulting violence led to shops and cars being attacked and one person being murdered. Community activists suggest that the Lozells riots happened because the area had been transformed from a Caribbean to an Asian neighbourhood with local shops, amenities and networks reflecting this change. 'The reality is that there's an apartheid situation. We live in a society where you've got white on top, Asians in the middle and then black at the bottom, particularly in economic terms.' (BBC, 2006).

Community cohesion has been based on a framework of increasing interaction and contacts between white and minority communities. Riots between minority communities such as Lozells or tensions between established and emerging communities are much more difficult to address. Cities such as Birmingham have been attempting to manage complex relationships between groups using outmoded models of representation or community cohesion. The focus on collective action, and analysis of race in terms of generic groups, has prevented a discussion of tension, conflict and consensus amongst different minority groups. Minority neighbourhoods have relatively few numbers of white people so the real conflicts are not black/white but minorities and other minorities, that is Pakistanis and Somalis or Indians and Caribbean groups. These tensions may lead dominant or established minority groups to complain about the detrimental impact of smaller or new minority groups on a neighbourhood. Further, established minority groups may resent increased competition from new migrants for scarce resources such as housing, schools and jobs. In practice, this is recycled racism; established minority groups using the same 'common sense' racist explanations that were employed to rationalise racist behaviour to minority migrants during the 1950s and 1960s. Power, conflict and competition for resources may be a growing feature of minority- minority relations in the future and is an area that has not been discussed in the 'race' and housing literature.

The discussion in this chapter has focused on super-diversity and shown that it may lead to richness but also conflict between different groups. Recycled racism has been posited as concept to explain tension based on research conducted in Birmingham. There is a need to consider how super-diversity and recycled racism could be addressed given that representational models of governance together with community cohesion may not be appropriate frameworks to increase tolerance and understanding.

As a first step, a policy of positive action should be developed to support new and emerging communities. Power and resources are not evenly distributed and established groups may operate in a way to exclude new communities. Hence practical intervention is needed to meet the growing housing, educational and support needs of these groups. This may prove to be difficult given the policy changes since 1999. However legislation exists in the Race Relations Act to mobilise resources and support specific interventions for groups. Secondly, capacity building and support should be part of this process to invest in community organisations and groups. In new communities, the objective is to develop robust organisations that could help to lobby and influence for change. In established groups, a campaign to raise awareness and knowledge has to be implemented identifying the social and economic issues at stake together with the reasons why new groups needed investment. Cross issue and neighbourhood working may ease tensions based on ethnicity and racism. This requires groups to share functions and ideas which may not have been possible in the past. However, in the current financial climate with local authorities cutting back on community investment, different organisations will be compelled to consider ideas to deliver more efficient working practices. Thirdly, protocols for voluntary sector engagement could be developed to support organisations that seek to demonstrably tackle the problems of recycled racism. One example would be developing a clear policy of cross community working and reaching out to new groups. In this way a progressive and new type of leadership could be developed not tied to vested interests but a new and different version of co-existence in the era of super-diversity.

Conclusion

This chapter has attempted to develop new ideas and frameworks to understand the relationships between different communities. Super-diversity has been explored. It is clear that the scale, status and range of new communities coming to the UK since the 1990s have been different to previous cycles of immigration. This is especially the case for immigration from the Caribbean and Indian sub-continent in the 1950s and 1960s. For the most part the super-diversity has been layered in cities and neighbourhoods that were identified with minority communities. In addition there is a strong correlation with area disadvantage. Yet there has been relatively little discussion on how super-diversity may lead to increased conflict and tension between established and emerging groups. Models of representation and community cohesion that have been used in public policy and housing specifically are contextualised in a society that has changed substantially. Thus the focus has been mediating conflict between black and minority ethnic communities, white communities and the State. The Housing Corporation approach to race and housing policy is a classic example of framing the problem into meeting the needs of collectivised groups rather than considering societal change and nuances between communities. The causes of tensions have been explored but largely from a non-academic perspective. Recycled racism has been introduced as a possible frame of reference to make sense of increasingly diverse and complex communities. Conflict over public resources such as socialised housing may lead to an increase in racialised narrative not simply from white communities. In reality, racism could be recycled by established minority groups towards new and emerging communities. In this way language is appropriated from how established groups were treated by white communities in the 1950s and 1960s. Indeed, the research from Birmingham suggests that neighbourhood loss, competition for resources and access to the local authority are developed as common sense responses to new groups. Racialisation and 'othering' separates different communities from developing common values and shared spaces. This has helped to fill debate with normative assumptions about communities. Recycled racism will be much more difficult to address. There is less funding available to support grassroots interventions to bring different groups together. Also, the direction of policy has moved away from multiculturalism to cohesion and integration. In short, a very real risk exists of increased super-diversity being coupled with new and different types of conflict. There is a need for a much more nuanced approach to cohesion and housing. Rather than adopting rigid models of intervention, community cohesion needs to start operating at a micro level addressing localised challenges and opportunity of super-diversity. Social housing needs to consider different models of race and representation. These could be based on social justice, equality of opportunity and housing need. The intention of the chapter is not to arrive at a solution but simply to move to different and diverse interpretations of housing in the era of super-diversity. This will help to move forward our conceptual understanding and practical application to housing and related areas, which can lead to at least a part of the solution.

6

New Frameworks for Race, Housing and Community

Introduction

A final chapter should be more than the summary of the preceding discussion. To this end we would like to suggest new ideas on how race, housing and community could be developed. First, we will review some of the key themes discussed in previous chapters. Our overall contention is that there has been a decline in the significance of race and housing as a subject in its own right. The drivers may be sourced from changing macro policy direction and especially the rise of community cohesion. However, the reduced importance on race and housing cannot solely be placed on changing policy. Recent global migration to Britain has generated discussion on the appropriateness of housing organisations that were established to meet the needs of migrants from the Caribbean and Indian sub-continent. Conflict for scarce housing resources could not simply be reduced to the 'black-white' paradigm but needed to consider the sometimes vexed relationships between established and emerging communities who lived in the same housing market. This was labelled 'recycled racism' in a previous chapter. The final theme which emerges from discussion is how race and housing have moved from the collective (i.e. black led housing associations, black and minority ethnic housing

Race, Housing & Community: Perspectives on Policy & Practice, First Edition.
Harris Beider.
© 2012 Harris Beider. Published 2012 by Blackwell Publishing Ltd.

policies, community cohesion) to the individual (diverse housing responses from different organisations, race and equality policies, and diversity). Reductionism to labels and overarching policies has become more difficult in a fluid society composed of communities with different needs and interests on housing and related matters.

Second, we will assess the impact of themes on housing organisations, especially black led housing associations, which were the focus of Chapter 4. It has been argued that these organisations have been diluted in their importance because of the increased influence of generic policies such as community cohesion. In addition black led housing associations have been critiqued for not moving quickly enough to grasp the impact of new patterns of migration. In short, housing associations had not kept pace with changing demographic patterns in the country and could be considered to be outmoded. Similarly the regulation has changed on race and housing. There has been a shift away from race specific to equality generic scrutiny of the social housing sector. Moreover, the commitment of the Housing Corporation to race equality was raised following the decision to replace the Black and Minority Policy with an Equality Plan. Given the themes on race, housing and community as well as the changes to housing organisations, we must reconsider how these issues should be discussed.

In the final section of this chapter, we will conclude by suggesting that existing theory and practice continues to use outmoded models of analysis that are no longer appropriate in organising housing services. Fixed notions of race and representation need to be modernised and set within an increasingly dynamic and fragmented society. The new framework needs to recognise the limitations of centralised policy interventions such as community cohesion which were discussed in depth in Chapter 2. The discussion on race, housing and community need to take place in a society that has changed fundamentally because of policy, migration and the role of the State which can be both responsive and restrictive.

It has been stated that the high point of race and housing came with the publication and immediate aftermath of the Macpherson Report in February 1999 (Home Office, 1999). A slew of actions on race equality emerged including the 2001 Race Relations Amendment Act as well as new definitions for a racist incident and institutional racism. The housing sector reacted by conducting an inquiry into race and housing, creating a forum to debate the issues and committing to development funding for black led housing associations at around 9% of overall investment (Housing Corporation, 2004a).

Of course it should be noted that Macpherson was the culmination of a series of progressive interventions on race and housing commencing with the radical Black and Minority Ethnic Housing Policy in 1986 and the emergence of registered black led housing associations. Race and housing mattered in 1999 and were viewed as important drivers of policy within the sector. In retrospect, the declining significance of housing and race started with Macpherson and to a certain extent was inevitable. First, despite the real achievements of Housing Corporation policy the most influential legislation was arguably the 1988 Housing Act. This encouraged housing associations to secure investment from the private sector to support organisational growth. Given that the majority of black led housing associations had only been in existence for two years, it was difficult for them to pool resources to secure the most advantageous deals. Second, the majority of black tenants and employees were located in the mainstream housing sector. Meeting the needs of consumers and workers became the focus of the Housing Corporation from 1992 rather than supporting black led housing associations. Third, and related from the move away from producer to consumer, the role and remit of specific race and housing policies were debated more widely. The theme of policy and practice began to weighted against importance of race and difference led by senior figures in the Labour government. Thus Macpherson did have a considerable if short lived impact on race and housing. In reality economic and policy changes in the housing sector were already diminishing the importance of race in housing.

It is evident that 2001 was a catalytic year for discussions on race generally and housing specifically. An amendment was made to the Race Relations Act following the Macpherson Report, placing a positive duty on public authorities to promote race relations. In the same year serious disturbances occurred in Burnley, Oldham and Bradford within a relatively short period. Though the places were different in terms of history, politics and demographics, the Home Office Inquiry had been tasked to find out the causes of the disturbances. The problem was fragmented and divided communities compounded by a lack of common norms or cultural understanding. The concept of community cohesion was not formalised until after the Inquiry Report but it quickly became part of the new lexicon in discussing issues of race. The concept was to play a critical role in shaping discussions on race and housing issues. Community cohesion heralded a new language based on values, norms and culture which was very different to the Housing Corporation Policy or indeed the Macpherson Report, both of which focused on racism, advocacy and correcting disadvantage.

The very role of black led housing associations was questioned as community cohesion began to be regarded as unhelpfully propping up sectional interests rather than promoting cross cultural contact. Under these circumstances, it is not surprising that we have witnessed the declining significance of race and housing. Race was problematic, race equality only spoke to some communities, and race organisations hindered the development of common norms. The journey from Macpherson to Cantle was discussed in depth earlier in the book but could be described as moving from heady optimism to cold reality.

A key challenge for those interested in moving forward the agenda on race and housing is how to move from a one dimensional to multi-dimensional approach. Much of the discussion and analysis is still shaped by the experiences of migrants who came to the UK in the 1950s and 1960s. Yet the most rapid pace of immigration to the country has been since the 1990s with immigrants coming to the UK from a range of countries and for a variety of different reasons. Britain's apparent super-diversity has been explored with compelling evidence of change especially in the larger conurbations (Vertovec, 2007). This has been taken further by assessing the impact on neighbourhood and housing choice (Phillimore, 2010). However the conflict and racism that arises from new patterns of communities has been absent. We have termed this recycled racism. That is, how conflict between minority communities can be framed in racist or racialised discourse going back to the migrants of the 1950s and 1960s, who were subjected to racism by host communities. It could be argued that these established minority communities are using 'common sense' racism to frame their relationships with new migrant communities in terms of housing resources, demand and neighbourhood change. Typically the conflict in these housing reception markets is not between black and white communities but between different types of groups living in the area. Racism is not the preserve of white communities or indeed the State. In many cases the white community in these housing markets is in the minority and the State has developed a battery of anti-discriminatory legislation. Housing regulators have decided to operate within a black-white paradigm to frame policies and interventions. This does not take into account demographic change, new types of housing needs and the importance of empowering a range of different organisations, not simply black led housing associations. Racist discrimination may be practiced by different groups of organisations and communities. Housing and related areas of public policy such as schools, policing and the environment are places where tension could be located. Immigration and globalisation has led to a kind of super-diversity in many urban spaces. Policies, frameworks and interventions need to be cognisant of rapidly changing demographics and multi-national levels of tensions and conflict. Moving towards a nuanced analysis where housing discrimination may operate at different levels and contexts is required as part of the new framework on race and housing. Mediating conflict may not simply be about cultural contact as proposed by community cohesion but rather recasting the way which analysis on race is modernised to reflect society as it is now rather than what is was in the past.

A move towards a modern analysis on race and housing starts from a basis of taking a collectivised view of housing needs. As we have suggested, this type of analysis assumes a normative perspective. It becomes too easy to develop a socially constructed position on housing that is shaped by racist perceptions rather than real evidence. Again, the way in which regulation was conceived is partly to blame. On balance, there was far too much focus on a single and unified view of black housing needs, broken down only by the use of the terms 'black' and 'Asian'. There is very little discussion about diversity within diversity. For example, nuanced debates on class, gender and place may be as important in determining housing product and neighbourhood as is ethnicity. To this end, and just as we suggested in terms of conflict and recycled racism, the multi-dimensional argument could be deployed in moving from a collectivised to an individualised view. Increased immigration and the resultant super diversity suggest different types of housing interventions based on household rather than community needs.

The narrative shows that race and housing has been in decline since 1999. This has been largely the result of changes in policy direction which squeezed out discussion about race and replaced it with nebulous terms such as cohesion and diversity. We have also noted that increased immigration made a simple reductionism on race to black or white a faulty framework. These are external factors but what about the role of black led housing associations and the Housing Corporation and latterly the Homes and Communities Agency? There is little doubt that the black led housing sector has been one of the more significant developments in post war race relations. Disadvantaged households have been accommodated in good quality housing and in many cases being given a culturally sensitive service. Indeed the value of black led housing associations has been recognised by independent evaluation (MDA, 2004). Despite this, we have now come to a position where the once highly influential FBHO has closed down because of a lack of support. The number of black led housing associations have declined to levels seen in the late 1980s and the largest association of this type, Ujima, is in danger of becoming the first housing association to become insolvent, being 'rescued' only by merging with a large mainstream housing association.

It is suggested that the policy environment may have been a contributory factor to the decline of race and housing but organisational weaknesses need to be addressed as well. The black led housing sector was complacent in responding to changing policy priorities. For example, community cohesion could have been critiqued as being a centralised, cultural and accommodating response to problems that had their roots in poverty, disadvantage and racism. Instead the black housing sector was perceived as being part of the problem in supporting sectional housing interests (Cantle, 2008). Moreover, black led housing associations did not respond to fast changing demographic patterns across the country as a result of workers coming from Eastern Europe after 2004 or the growing economy attracting migrants to the UK from around the world. In the latter case especially, black led housing associations could have used their experience as grassroots organisations to work alongside community groups. Instead, this was the exception rather than the rule (Mullins et al., 2007). Given these points, it could be that there was a sense of complacency in responding to population and policy changes. The decline of black led housing associations could be seen as a metaphor for the decline of race and housing. Reduced investment, forced mergers and a considerably less supportive political environment does not make it easy to see a resurgence of the black led sector unless there is a radically different perspective.

Alongside the decline of the housing associations, we have also seen the eclipse of the Housing Corporation and its replacement by the HCA. We have repeatedly stated that some of the most radical moments in race and housing has been instigated by the Housing Corporation most notably the 1986 Black and Minority Ethnic Housing Policy, which led to new investment and a different type of housing offer for tenants and lenders. The regulatory approach embedded race equality into the framework of reporting for the social housing sector as a whole. However, the Housing Corporation was also the regulator, criticised by the independent inquiry into its handling of Ujima, retreating into the haze of debates on equality in its new guise as HCA. There is a sense that regulation became a blunt and inflexible instrument that was process rather than outcome driven. In the case of Ujima, this prevented early intervention that could have maintained the independence of the housing association. More widely, regulation on race was often reduced to a 'tick box' approach that measured numbers of black people represented on the board or management group rather than the ethos of the housing association. The same charge of complacency may be levelled against the Housing Corporation, as discussed above with reference to the black led housing sector. Its regulation was not sufficiently nimble to challenge housing associations to meet new and different types of housing needs. The Housing Corporation made way for the HCA and the commitment to race equality became framed as a wider commitment to diversity and equality. The organisation cannot be blamed for this as it is a creature of government. However, the legacy of the past should help to develop a future vision.

Table 6.1 summarises some of the key challenges on housing, communities and cohesion:

Table 6.1   Key challenges on housing, communities and cohesion.

Themes	Organisations
• The declining significance of race and housing	• A weakened black housing association
• Journey from Macpherson (high) to Cantle (low)	• Complacency in responding to changing priorities
• Recycled racism and mediating conflict	• Narrow options because of economic and politics
• Collective to the Individual	
Institutions	**New agenda?**
• Housing Corporation to HCA	• Dynamic notions of identity and space
• Beyond race and representation	• A responsive and restrictive State
• Blunt rather than nuanced regulation	• Diversity, atomisation and housing choice
• Specific to general accountability	• Power, conflict and social capital

Towards a new approach to race and housing

During this narrative we have critically appraised the debates on race and housing before reviewing the synergy and contribution of selected publications undertaken by the author. The final stage is to discuss ideas that could take some these crucial debates forward. Inevitably this will probably lead to more discussion and should be welcomed. The ideas for consideration are dynamic notions of identity and space; a responsive and restrictive State; diversity, atomisation and housing choice; power, conflict and social capital.

Dynamic notions of identity and space

A major limitation of the race and housing research has been the view that communities have fixed identities and are bounded within neighbourhoods. These are not simply associated with cultural theorists but include those who would claim to be Marxists. The focus is on collective action and behaviour within a rigid and stratified society. There are a number of weaknesses with this approach. First, fixed identity ascribes collective actions predicated on biological determinist models of behaviour. Grouping individuals together suggests that people are related by ethnicity (arguably this is on the continuum of biological determinism) and cannot escape from this perspective. Second, the idea of minorities living in bounded neighbourhoods has been an enduring characteristic of housing studies. Many have suggested that minorities have had very little choice to move away from traditional areas of settlement because of housing based discrimination. We are not for a moment suggesting that discrimination has not impacted on choice and shaped residential settlement across the country. However, minorities are active in deciding on their housing options and housing careers.

Housing and spatial context has moved on since the work of Rex and his associates. Our criticism of the models of race and housing was partly based on the fixed models of housing markets leading to minorities being concentrated in poor housing. Spatial development and housing has since progressed. In some cases, minorities are being viewed as key drivers for stability and growth in new types of neighbourhoods contiguous to traditional housing markets. In others, minority communities themselves have revived once derelict neighbourhoods through investing in shops, organisations and other types of infrastructure (Goodson and Beider, 2005). In both cases of institutional intervention and community action the emphasis is on dynamic neighbourhoods of opportunity rather than those where housing choice is limited.

We should have dynamic notions of identity and space. Minorities have different forms of identity that varies in different contextual situations such as the home, work or school and a social setting. The emphasis placed on race and identity should consider these different circumstances. Minorities are multi-layered and there should be further research that explores the impact of gender, class and age within these groups. From undertaking such an exercise, the non-reification of minorities will follow and mark a complete break from the normative labelling that has characterised race and housing.

A responsive and restrictive state

Research has focused on how the State has acted in a way that excludes minority communities in housing. It has been suggested that this has included restricted access, preventing people from being employed in housing organisations or becoming board members. These and other actions have led to minorities living in the worst housing conditions in the poorest neighbourhoods. However, we also need to understand that it is not too late for the State to respond and reform itself on race and housing. For example, direct discrimination has been outlawed (1976 Race Relations Act), the pervasive nature of institutional racism has been acknowledged (Macpherson: Home Office, 1999), and minority based housing organisations have been viewed as an example of black leadership (Housing Corporation, 1998).

The State has responded to external drivers for change. Access to decent housing services, gaining employment opportunities particularly at the most senior levels of management within housing organisations, and gaining support for housing activities remains a problem. Still, it is important to recognise that the State has evolved on minority issues in housing. Representation has been criticised in this narrative as a measure for success in housing but there has been clear progress in the increased number of minority senior managers in the sector as a whole combined with measures on race as part of regulation.

Macro policy on race has been contradictory for much of the post-war period. Restrictive policies to curb immigration, problematic labelling of minorities and State acculturation have been in an uneasy 'embrace' with measures against discrimination, supporting minority based housing providers and promoting positive action in housing. More recently there has been a contested debate about community cohesion and its applicability to the UK.

In the same way as identity is dynamic, we need to consider the capacity of the State to be both restrictive and expansive on race and housing. It should not be seen as a fixed repressive force but one which can adapt and change to meet different circumstances.

Diversity, atomisation and housing choice

Minorities are becoming increasingly fragmented and atomised as a result of renewed immigration, outflow of mobile minorities and community retrenchment. Labels such as 'black' or 'black and minority ethnic' are becoming much less relevant to our discussion of housing and yet these terms are used together and are interchangeable within policy and academic literature. Increased diversity and atomisation within the population suggests the need to discuss new terms of reference. However, this may be difficult. The reality on the ground is that groups are being defined by faith, geography and generation. Some African groups want to go beyond the 'Black African' category offered by regulatory forms. In these circumstances, it is important for minorities themselves, not the State, to shape their identity.

Diversity can also bring conflicts and competition over housing and neighbourhood, not just between 'white' and 'black' communities but Pakistanis and Somalis, or Somalis and Poles, or indeed different Somali groups. Fragmentation has an impact on access to resources and power that is being increasingly played out in urban areas across the country. Discussion and analysis on 'race' and housing needs to consider the debates about 'minorities within minorities' and how 'recycled racism' is used to exclude some groups over and beyond the conventional black-white framework.

Demographic change also has an impact on the delivery of housing services. Housing organisations need to develop diverse approaches for fragmented communities but the tendency has been to construct an analysis on broad categories which sometimes makes very little sense. Partly this has been the result of insufficient data for analysing smaller groups but also the continuing reification by researchers and institutions. Complex relationships between different minorities may result in residential patterns emerging that are very different to those that framed previous research discussed earlier.

Power, conflict and social capital

The race and housing literature has been characterised by different theoretical approaches. These have been analysed in an earlier section of this narrative. Though there has been considerable discussion about minorities, housing, and the local State, very few have discussed the role of power, conflict and social capital as key frameworks.

Power and its distribution should be at the centre of race and housing. Local politics is partly about the allocation of scarce resources. The analysis of power in race and housing also impacts on the discussion of different groups in a local area. Community power studies (Bachrach and Baratz, 1970; Crenson, 1971) developed an innovative approach to local studies to show how dominant groups acted in a way to prevent difficult issues from getting onto the agenda of local government. The debates on decisions, non-decisions and preventing public policy issues from getting on local agendas seem particularly relevant to race and housing politics. Increasing numbers of minority groups are competing to gain a fixed or diminishing amount of local resources to support local initiatives. In this context, power and conflict (as well as partnership) will inevitably shape relationships between different groups.

In the same way that power has not had a significant role in race and housing research, the same could be said about social capital (Putnam, 2000). However, there are problems with the social capital debate when linked to the issue of race. For example, minority communities are less likely to join organisations such as tenant associations because these are not perceived as relevant to their lives and aspirations. Formal and informal mechanisms such as black-led churches, mosques and carnivals provide a basis for building social capital.

Bourdieu goes much further than Putnam when labelling social capital as a selective resource that results in the dominance of elite groups in a society (Bourdieu, 1986). This is a far more radical approach than Putnam, where social capital is seen as delivering effective public services to reenergised communities. There appears to be considerable merit in optimising the work of Bourdieu to explain race and housing within an increasingly complex society.

The new agenda for race and housing should take into account how power, conflict and social capital can be used to ration resources, access to homes and neighbourhoods and produce dominant and competing elites. Conflict and competition in housing may open up an extremely interesting discussion about intra-group and inter-group power in relation to the State.

Looking ahead: a new agenda?

Recognising the weakness of community cohesion generally, as well as specifically when applied to housing, should not result in simply turning the clock back to 2000. Multiculturalism did advance representation, addressed specific needs and generated new ideas on race and housing. It could also be argued that the concept and organisations supporting key tenets did not sufficiently acknowledge the impact of new and different migration flows on housing needs and advocacy. The dominant domain was a binary analysis of race together with a resistance to working with the State, yet at the same time being the recipient of investment and support based on race. Resourcing models pitted communities against each other in a deficit sum theorem that inevitably led to disconnection and alienation from groups who were unsuccessful.

Discussion of race and indeed class in housing seems strangely sterile and fixed in the past. The assumptions on equalities and legislation need to be reviewed in the search for new models and ideas that can advance analysis. Community cohesion could be viewed as a response to multi-culturalism but also public management which focused on management processes which seem to embed disadvantage. Policies based solely on representative outputs will inevitably lead to a 'tick box' mentality. Minority organisations and individuals long had to fight implicit and explicit accusations of favouritism after successfully securing employ-ment or resources. In these circumstances, leadership should have connected interventions to address disadvantage. There remains a need to emphasise the diversity dividend on personal and organisational development. Instead, excluded individuals and organisations feel disconnected from the politics of race. In short, policies apply to the minority rather than the majority.

We should also resist calls for a simple class reductionism allied to a malevolent view of the State. Discussions on race have long argued the relative merits of class, race and the State (Miles, 1982; Sivanandan, 1982; CCCS, 1982). It could be argued that all were entrenched in fixed notions of class and the State and an alignment to a dualistic approach to housing that prevented discussion from moving forward. The dualism between choice and constraint and the relative importance of structure and agency is interesting but limiting. There is a danger of the race and housing debates leading to an intellectual cul-de-sac.

The seminal work of Giddens provided the basis for race and housing debates to move away from the dualism of structure and agency by suggesting that rather than being fixed and durable concepts they are both subject to change over a period of time. Individuals (agents) can influence the State (structure) and both are interdependent (Giddens, 1976). As he argues: 'Structures must not be conceptualised as simply placing constraints upon human agency, but as enabling.' (Giddens, 1976: 60).

Recent research on the subject has appeared to take a less rigid stance on choice and constraint. Harrison has suggested that policy debates on race and housing have inevitably been highly normative in suggesting that minority residential concentration is a problem (Harrison, 1995).

However, as Ratcliffe notes, the problem with these theories (and indeed much of the debate on race and housing in general) is that they provide very little room for taking on a dynamic approach to structure and agency (Ratcliffe, 2009). One of the more interesting attempts to take this debate forward with reference to race and housing was undertaken by Sarre and his colleagues (1989). The study of minorities in the small town of Bedford particularly focused on the Italian community. Advancing Giddens' structuration theory, they sought a model that would reconcile choice and constraints. To Giddens, the structures within society that limit the choice of housing available to minorities are not independent. They may be influenced and changed through the actions of individuals within society. For example, private lenders that prevented Italians from securing competitive loans to buy homes lost this business as it moved to more progressive organisations. This helped to change patterns of lending in Bedford (Sarre et al., 1989). More recent examples of changing behaviour in housing institutions can be seen with mainstream lenders such as HSBC offering Islamic mortgages in a specific appeal to the growing number of Muslims in the country (CIH, 2005). Similarly, a provider perspective is the role of housing associations in trying to work with refugees to renew neighbourhoods and communities in areas of economic decline (Mullins et al., 2007).

The value of structuration theory is that it brings dynamism to the debates. The interdependence between structure and agency may provide a positive way forward for future research. Community cohesion similar to many government generated concepts remains frozen in 2001.

Housing and spatial context has moved on since the work of Rex and his associates. Our criticism of the models of race and housing was partly based on the fixed models of housing markets leading to minorities being concentrated in poor housing. Spatial development and housing has since progressed. Housing markets are much more dynamic because of interventions such as Housing Market Renewal and the City-Region. In some cases, minorities are being viewed as a key driver for stability and growth in new types of neighbourhoods contiguous to traditional housing markets. In others, minority communities themselves have revived once derelict neighbourhoods through investing in shops, organisations and other types of infrastructure (Goodson and Beider, 2005). In both cases of institutional intervention and community action the emphasis is on dynamic neighbourhoods of opportunity rather than those where housing choice is limited.

We should have dynamic notions of identity and space. Minorities have different forms of identity that vary in different contextual situations such as the home, work or school and a social setting. The emphasis placed on race and identity should consider these different circumstances. Minorities are multi-layered and there should be further research that explores the impact of gender, class and age within these groups. From undertaking such an exercise, the non-reification of minorities will follow and mark a complete break from the normative labelling that has characterised race and housing.

Policy implications

In the UK, recent events and policy developments have served to highlight the importance of race, communities and housing issues at a national level. These include the concerns about race and segregation identified in the Home Office's Community Cohesion Report (2001), the Commission for Integration and Cohesion (2007) and the Connecting Communities Programme (Denham, 2009). Changing patterns of race and residence as well as new approaches to community involvement and empowerment are evident in both countries. There is an underlying debate about the convergence and divergence of policy and research agendas. Given this context, and the previous discussion, we will now focus on the implications for policy makers.

Housing products and neighbourhood choice

Minority communities in the UK are changing, spatially, educationally and also regarding preferences for neighbourhood choice and tenure (Vertovec, 2007; Ferrari and Lee, 2007). Much more qualitative work needs to be undertaken to understand the contours of change. As noted earlier, the speed of change is faster for some groups than others and the first step for public agencies is to map out existing communities, their preferences and aspirations before designing and building new housing and planning future services (Markkanen, 2009). These changes go beyond a binary debate between white and black communities and even new groupings such as white, African-Caribbean and Asian. Discussion on race must be placed in a context of valuing differences between 'new' and 'old' migrants, class, income and age which has flowed from demographic, economic, social and spatial change.

The task for housing organisations is to proactively respond to change. At a micro level, housing organisations will need to develop more diverse policies to meet the needs of increasingly heterogeneous communities. Importantly, housing organisations also need to extend the range of housing products and choice of neighbourhoods available to communities. Given demographic changes in minority communities, housing organisations need to consider attracting communities to new housing developments contiguous to previous areas of settlement. Moreover, housing preference for minority communities should be linked to a greater understanding of wider 'lifestyle' choices concerning schools, amenities and access to retail outlets as well as proximity to social networks and places of worship (Goodson and Beider, 2005; Markkanen, 2009).

There is a consensus within the academic and policy communities about the urgent need to break up concentrations of poverty and, to a lesser extent, racially segregated communities. A route out of high density, poor quality housing in the inner cities to better quality and low density housing in the suburbs is a policy that has been tried in the US. The results are mixed. However, a pathway out of poverty through increased housing choice could be reconsidered. Schemes such as vouchers, or subsidies, to access decent housing in neighbourhoods of choice may lead to housing change but also opposition by groups on the grounds of unfair allocation of housing goods. Enforcement of any scheme and the proactive selling of diversity are required to build sustainable and diverse neighbourhoods.

Just as interesting are the attempts to revive housing markets located within inner city neighbourhoods. Making the most of historic districts, waterfronts and easy access to the main employment core may attract middle and high income earners to these markets. In addition, housing mobility schemes operating in the public but especially the private sector could also lure key workers and young families. Local authorities in the UK could replicate (on a much smaller scale) the New York approach to buying derelict property and marketing this to communities whose incomes are likely to rise. This may also contribute to breaking up concentrations of poverty and racial segregation, increasing investment and encouraging diverse communities and improved neighbourhood trajectories.

Housing organisations need to develop projects and initiatives that are based on meeting the concerns of tenants in terms of a ladder to homeownership, increased quality of social housing and providing access to neighbourhoods of choice. Housing mobility schemes together with proactive intervention in declining housing markets may contribute to creating mixed communities in both the inner city and outer suburbs. Vested interests in both types of areas need to be addressed to ensure that policies can work in practice. In this way, access to new housing markets can be made much easier than is currently the case.

Connection to 'geographies of opportunity'

Communities in themselves cannot transform neighbourhoods. Connections need to be made with wider economic and public policy themes operating at regional and sub-regional levels. The task is to link disadvantaged minority communities to the wider 'geography of opportunity'. Sometimes there is a housing/jobs mismatch with an oversupply of poor, unemployed and under skilled people living in inner city housing markets and a surplus of middle to high skilled jobs in the wider region. This can be seen in the West Midlands where there is a need to support poor communities into new jobs. This cannot be achieved at a neighbourhood level. The challenge has to be taken up at regional and national levels. The regional task is to make both inner city and suburban housing markets work.

Conceiving race as part of a wider geography of opportunity in the UK could be problematic. The fact remains that minority communities (despite new population trajectories) reside in concentrated neighbourhoods in the conurbations of London, the Midlands, North West and West Yorkshire. There may be a reluctance to relocate for new jobs and housing. However, people first need to be made aware that there is a *choice* and then be given the *tools* to access opportunities. For example, large regeneration projects in Stratford and Docklands provide job opportunities for minority communities in Newham, Tower Hamlets and Hackney. Government has a key role to connect people with low incomes to jobs at a regional and local level.

The new lens, focusing on regions rather than neighbourhoods, is a radical shift for policy practitioners and politicians. It was not so long ago that housing and especially neighbourhoods were at the centre of discussion and debate. Urban policies such as task force, city challenge, single regeneration budget and social exclusion policies (recent UK initiatives) were being promoted by the policy and academic community as mechanisms to revitalise communities. Commentators now suggest that these well-intentioned relatively small-scale initiatives have done little to reduce poverty or polarisation of race and class.

Indeed, they may have been counterproductive, effectively stigmatising poverty and race still further (Katz, 2004).

Does this mean we can now discard the concept of neighbourhood? Community based organisations operating at local levels do have an important role in campaigning for new investment and better amenities. Indeed, Birmingham has seen two celebrated examples of community activism; residents in Balsall Heath (protesting against prostitution and crime) and Lee Bank (fighting declining housing and rising crime) activated change at both local and national level. These are exceptions rather than the rule. It should be noted that Balsall Heath could be viewed as conflict over space between two marginal groups – low income Pakistanis and prostitutes and their pimps. The conflict was not characterised by discussion and debate. It was akin on some occasions to 'hand to hand' combat as one group tried to reclaim a community. The results have been impressive in the form of neighbourhood development, housing popularity and reduced crime, but the prostitutes have simply decamped to the neighbouring area. The expectation is that neighbourhoods, politics and community development will be shaped by factors and decisions taken at regional, national and local level. The task for activists is to link into this new geography and economy of opportunity and ensure integration between neighbourhood and housing market renewal agendas to work for the benefit of local people.

Social capital and race

The debates on social capital have influenced much public policy making in UK. Social capital is associated with Putnam who defined it as 'connections among individuals – social networks and the norms of reciprocity and trustworthiness that arise from them' (Putnam, 2000). There are two further dimensions of the debate: *bonding* and *bridging* capital. Bonding gives people a sense of identity and purpose (such as ethnicity) and holds people together in groups. Bridging provides connections between people who may live in the same neighbourhood, city or country. Bridging capital can be conceptualised as the key towards building community cohesion and greater understanding between communities.

There are some problems with the social capital debate when linked to the issues of race. For example, minority communities are less likely to join organisations such as tenant associations because they are not perceived as relevant to their lives and aspirations (Mullins et al., 2004). Formal and informal mechanisms such as black-led churches, mosques and carnivals provide a basis for building social capital. Not all forms of social capital have positive consequences – for instance inner city gangs may have a corrosive impact on the wider community. As we have mentioned elsewhere, minorities may not wish to belong to integrated neighbourhoods that dilute capital.

There is a view that new policy drivers such as neighbourhood renewal and establishing consultative mechanisms neutralise debate and allow planned and market led displacement to take place. Justification is provided by social capital theorists who emphasise the lack of 'connections among individuals' (Putnam, 2000). The assumption is that poor and minority communities have a social capital deficit, which needs to be accumulated through the creation of new businesses and mixed neighbourhoods. Apart from the inherent dangers of developing pathologies on poor and minority communities, it negates the importance of social networks, the role of grassroots organisations and the important collectivist ideology within poor communities and families. Often this type of social capital holds communities together when local authority and other stakeholders have long exited from a community (Venkatesh, 2000).

Policy based on housing market change, either through demolition and the creation of mixed tenure communities, or the work of the market through gentrification, should consider the importance of building on the social capital, networks and culture existing in poor, minority neighbourhoods. The process of 'washing out' or emptying communities should be resisted. It is argued that 'gentrification' has left residents of low income neighbourhoods in a situation where, since they exert little control over either investment capital or their homes, they are facing the 'choices' of either continued disinvestments and the decline of the quality of their neighbourhood, or reinvestment that results in their displacement.

There is a danger that social capital may be associated with groups, households and spatial areas that are white, owner occupied revitalised city markets or suburban communities. Reducing diversification in terms of ethnicity and tenure may ultimately lead to neighbourhoods and communities that are devoid of ideas and tools required to meet the challenges of an increasingly complex world. The premise is that new communities can be built on existing social capital; organisations need to meet their obligations on representation of issues and there has to be a menu of housing choice and ownership for increasingly diverse communities. The implications for policy makers are that poor minority communities and inner city areas need investment and support to rebuild neighbourhoods. Demolition, displacement and replacement may erode social capital rather than help to create it.

Social capital is a useful tool to discuss the renewal of civic engagement. On its own it does not explain the problems of cities, segregation and sustainability. Complex relationships, ties and bonds within minority communities are sometimes simply not recognised and valued by policy makers and researchers. The task is to develop a much more inclusive social capital model.

Increased diversity, community cohesion and shifting identities

We have already noted that the UK is becoming increasingly diverse, fragmented and polarised (Vertovec, 2007). This is even more the case for communities residing in cities. Seismic social movements such as immigration and ageing combined with global economic change and technological advances are re-shaping countries, cities and neighbourhoods (Katz, 2004).

The discussion of race relations cannot be adequately referenced through binary analysis of 'black' and 'white'. Diverse societies need diverse solutions, which sometimes rests uneasily with equal opportunities legislation and fair housing policies. Census material in both countries shows that some minority groups have become less polarised and moved to outer suburbs from inner city locations. This may be as much to do with educational and income prosperity as with any policy interventions. Policy interventions must recognise the mosaic of different communities that make up many urban neighbourhoods. A variety of responses are required to ensure that all communities have access and choice to education, housing and welfare. This may have a resource implication. For example, it could be argued that much more should be done to support new migrants than established minority communities. Of course, the response from some minority organisations could be that new and old migrants still need help and support. However, a finite budget and infinite choices means hard decisions have to be made. Positive action becomes more complicated when the decision to appoint is not based on a white or black applicant but on a Pakistani or Somali person. For a society that has not resolved the binary problems on race equality, dealing with a much more complicated picture becomes highly problematic. Society as a whole has to deal with not only primary racism but also secondary racism as well.

Mediation on race and creation of stable communities has been a focus of community cohesion (Home Office, 2001). Across the Atlantic, in the US, directive policies restricting low-income housing, prescribed rights and responsibilities, and the reliance on housing vouchers are tools at the disposal of government. American identity is promoted and citizenship is enshrined in the Bill of Rights. As we have discussed above, the UK is struggling to come to terms with transforming itself to accommodate increasing ethnic diversity. Responses to the disturbances in Oldham, Bradford and Burnley in 2001 together with the negative debates on asylum and immigration could be seen as counter-productive to the goals of shared identity and citizenship. New and old migrants are less likely to feel any obligation to contribute to community cohesion when they are being identified as being part of the problem.

The fact remains that Britain has seen successive waves of migration into towns and cities. The difference in post-1945 migration is that newcomers are more visible and different. In reality, community cohesion based on a mix of communities, tenure and income is the exception rather than the rule. Social intervention is unlikely to speed up the process. Would it not be better to accept that the path to community be based on choice, celebrating differences and recognising that migrant communities, new and old, have stabilised communities rendered weak by 'white flight'? Connecting to neighbourhoods of choice, providing options for key public services such as education and health, and remodelling transport show another way to cohesion. Moreover, some neighbourhoods have benefited from the impact of new migration. For example, the Sparkbrook area of Birmingham had seen an outflow of whites, Irish and Pakistani communities and had been associated with decline and abandonment. In recent years, Somali communities have become concentrated in the area, leading to the flourishing of shops and cultural amenities and greater cohesion. In short, the debate on race and immigration must shift to a recognition of the value that migrants bring to a community rather than the problems they create.

The search for common identity may also be viewed as problematic. Increasing fragmentation pulls against an easily identifiable identity. In truth, established and new migrant communities have composite identities that provide a framework and reference point in day-to-day life. This will vary in different contexts and locations – at work, religious festivals, and cultural events. Trading ethnic identity for unclear notions of common identity leads to a zero sum scenario. Britons are defined by a number of different themes including ethnicity, class, region, city, and neighbourhood. Race relations legislation has encouraged the preservation of different groups and communities. Now government has to use equal opportunities legislation to manage societal change. It could be viewed as mediating a position between the cultural melting pot and the homogenous society. Growing prosperity and change in Britain means that neither will be a realistic policy objective that is worth pursuing. The third way should be predicated on promoting the economic and social benefit of immigration, addressing the damaging impact of racism and encouraging all Britons to buy into a new and modern multi-cultural society based on civic rights and responsibilities.

Conclusion

In this concluding chapter we have suggested that there has been a decline in the significance of race. This is the result of a complex mix of reasons relating to policy, organisational and institutional change. It could be argued that there has never been a more difficult time to formulate a new approach to race and housing. Community cohesion has led to a regressive agenda that is based on complex difference within a normative cultural framework. Black led housing associations seem to be in terminal decline in numbers, and without the FBHO there is no single or unified voice that advocates on their behalf. The Housing Corporation and its radical leadership on race is a distant memory embedded in the Thatcherite 1980s. To underscore the problem is the alarming economic forecast of reduced public investment for the next five years. In the midst of this deep foreboding, we are suggesting a new framework that may provide opportunities to conceptually move forward the race and housing agenda as well as creating space for new and reconfigured housing organisations. It questions some of the underlying assumptions of race and housing and the role of policies such as community cohesion. More than this, it suggests a dynamic and flexible response in theory, policy and practice that takes into account the reality of society rather than being limited by the past.

The real challenge is to conduct research that sharpens the issues and takes forward the debate. First, we need to reconfigure and redefine community cohesion. This means emphasising social justice and equality of opportunity as much as shared norms and values. Second, political leaders need to stress the value of diversity in the UK. This can be couched in terms of moving on from the old Britain of the World War II era and embracing a new Britain with creative industries, new technology and diversity. Third, we need to encourage modernity in thinking. Class remains important and is still a key factor, but we cannot, as President Obama noted during his campaign, ignore race and we must find ways to move beyond the deepening racial divides in the UK.

Appendix A

Public Service Futures

5 The future of identity and belonging

OPM®

Contents

Images

iStockphoto
Ankya
Galina Barskaya
Don Bayley
Rob Belknap
Steve Debenport
hammondovi
Marcin Kempski
Rene Mansi
Rapid Eye Media
Chris Schmidt
Eva Serrabassa
VasilikiVarvaki
spxChrome

Design

OPM Design & Editorial

Introduction

Public Service Futures is an ambitious programme sponsored by OPM, an independent public interest company, initiated as part of our commitment to improving social results. Through publications, events and interactive methods, Public Service Futures brings together visionary thinkers with decision-makers across sectors to decide how best to prepare for the future. In this latest briefing, we ask five experts what future they see for identity and belonging in Britain over the next two decades.

Who will we be in 2025? What will shape the way we feel about ourselves and our sense of belonging in society? Will the familiar differentiators like race and faith become more important in determining our sense of self? Can we look forward to a future where communities are better integrated and where individuals feel a greater sense of belonging, or will the benefits be unevenly distributed as some become more isolated and marginalised? And, in the context of all this, what will the implications be for public services? Our contributors tackle these and related questions from a variety of angles.

Former Lib Dem MP Mark Oaten looks at the changing nature of political identities and the 'consumerism of cause' that has the potential to unpick mainstream party politics in the years ahead. Julia Margo of think-tank Demos argues that gender will re-emerge as a key theme in identity, but where men, and not women, are the ones at risk of being the biggest losers. Reflecting on thirty years working with the criminal justice system, Leon Murray discusses the shifting significance of ethnicity and faith, and foresees an increasingly inclusive British identity where ancestral connections to other cultures inform, but no longer dominate, people's sense of who they are and how they belong. Professor Pat Thane focuses on age, exploring the way in which changing expectations about old age will alter the way we view older people, and how a new generation of strong, active elders will play a much greater role in society. Finally, Professor Harris Beider of Coventry University's Futures Institute looks at the differences between race and faith as aspects of identity and bonds that underpin belonging, before considering whether a smaller state will liberate us from restrictive, pigeon-holed identities or dismantle the very framework that has been so important in pushing cohesion up the agenda in recent years.

While each contributor takes a different focus, all pick up on the impact of income, status and mobility in informing the extent to which certain identities are likely to shape our experiences. Does being old seem all the more significant if you're old and poor? Is ethnicity more central to your sense of belonging if you live in close-knit, economically deprived neighbourhood than if you go to university and have friends from a range of backgrounds? No one is defined by or driven by a single characteristic. The question is whether certain aspects of our identity will rise or decline in our personal and collective consciousness as old challenges shift into new ones. Hopefully this short report will provide valuable food for thought for you, as public sector decision-makers and practitioners, as you consider the challenging times ahead.

... there is a growing phenomenon where people are quickly forming quite passionate (even ideological) stances over a variety of issues, but equally quickly are able to drop them. ... We're now seeing a 'consumerism of cause' where people rapidly consume issues just as they consume goods.

Identities and politics

*Mark Oaten, Former Liberal Democrat home affairs spokesman and MP for Winchester**

The way that people's identities are reflected in politics is changing. I think we're moving to a breakdown of the traditional political model in this country, and at the same time towards a more mainland European style of politics.

In Europe, they haven't had that same sense of a class system. In Britain, in spite of the social change we've witnessed since the war, class identity has continued to align closely with politics until relatively recently. The lower classes support Labour while the middle and upper classes support the Conservatives.

Up until the 1990s, this was the foundation of British politics and British political identity, but the more European outlook is signified in more fluid allegiances where class recedes into the background. In Germany, for example, it is not considered abnormal for someone to vote for one party in the local and federal elections, another in the national elections, and perhaps yet another in the European elections. They are used to a more flexible political system with a variety of parties in power, so why not have more flexible political loyalties to match?

In the same vein, I think smaller political parties in the UK will find themselves gaining influence with the break-up of the old British party system, especially if there is a proportional voting system that will enable more people to vote for a greater number of special interest parties. This could mean that the identities we have come to recognise as meaningful in our daily lives, relating to race, religion, geography and even age group, could find more tangible, focused outlets in the political system. We can see this in Europe where there are more diverse, smaller parties that can represent quite specific views and identities. For example, in Italy there is a strong pensioner's party and several active religious political groups.

There is also voting on the basis of regional identities, such as the Northern League in Italy. With the rise of smaller parties in the UK, could

* Mark was the MP for Winchester from 1997 until he stood down at the last election. He was a contributor to the 2004 publication, The Orange Book: Reclaiming Liberalism, a book written by several prominent Lib Dem politicians, and he stood for the leadership of the party in 2006. Before becoming an MP, Mark worked in public affairs as a lobbyist and was leader of the Social Democratic Party group in Watford Borough Council.

we see this emerge as trend here as well? It might not be something that happens everywhere, but I can certainly imagine the rise of a Cornish Party, for example. Many movements relating to the environment and sustainability are national, and even international, but are about emphasising the importance of the local, and organise themselves by locality. These can appeal to both those of the right and the left, and so again transcends those old political boundaries.

On the other hand, I think that any sort of politics wedded to specific places will come up against stiff competition from an emerging sort of politics that unites people on single issues and interests – and not just those that galvanise people along the familiar lines of identity like faith, race and age. Facilitated by the internet and social networking, people are now coming together on issues which, were they reliant on local activity, would never attract the weight of numbers to have an impact. This sort of approach also enables people to follow a range of causes in some detail, not through a single entry point of local party branch, trade union or church as once they would have done, but issues of all kinds with all sorts of different political (and non-political) associations.

Belonging: the fall or rise of localities?

There is, then, the potential for a strengthening of place and identity on the one hand, and its weakening on the other. More virtual networks (using mobile phones and the internet) link people and provide almost instant access to loved ones. 'Place' in this context is being able to access the people who matter to you. Rather than isolation coming from being geographically cut off from an area where you have a sense of belonging, it is being cut off from your network of friends, family and colleagues that is increasingly significant. With the continued development of mobile phone and social networking technology, and particularly its use by young people, this type of social interaction and structure of belonging is growing.

And yet, concepts like the Big Society imply a resurgence in identity, pride and activity associated with locality. There is perhaps a paradox that those driving this agenda are almost by definition the most transient: the sorts of people who do not live where they were born, were probably educated elsewhere and move around more than those for whom they want to deliver this agenda.

This new divide in society between the mobile and less mobile is an important one. In many areas, large sections of the young population

leave to pursue work or education elsewhere, leaving others behind. Are those who remain still there because they are more tied to their locality, more bonded with their community, or do they simply lack the 'get up and go' to leave with the rest? If it is the more entrepreneurial and ambitious members of a community who leave, then where will the impetus be to drive through changes and provide the services that these communities need?

This will be a challenge for policy-makers hoping to light the torch of volunteering and community action in localities across the country in the years ahead. Should people be encouraged to stay in their home towns and 'invest' in their communities – investing in rebuilding proud, local identities in depressed neighbourhoods and regions – or should we encourage more people to move around the country, uncoupling their sense of themselves and of belonging from their associations with places?

'A consumerism of cause'

People have always expressed a multitude of identities depending on the time and place – that isn't new – but it is more prolific as we become more geographically and culturally mobile. In times and places where people were less likely to move neighbourhoods or jobs, had smaller circles of friends and were more ethnically and religiously homogenous, the impetus for different identities was more limited. Today, that's different for many people, and in 2020 the shift will be greater still.

It seems that there is a growing phenomenon where people are quickly forming quite passionate (even ideological) stances over a variety of issues, but equally quickly are able to drop them. Their views are fluid and short-lived, and in sharp contrast to the long-term and embedded views – such as a firm belief in state ownership, or a rooted dislike of trade unionism – that people have historically held. It's not that people are apathetic about politics and political questions, but the questions they're asking are different ones, and the issues that once underpinned people's outlook of the world have been replaced a far more complicated and shifting landscape of ideas and loyalties.

This is linked with the growth of consumer culture in British society. We're now seeing a 'consumerism of cause' where people rapidly consume issues just as they consume goods. Of course for some people, a single cause or cogent set of causes will capture their attention and energy over a number of years. But that seems less commonplace than it was, with people often picking up an issue, trying it out, and then trying another. The MMR vaccine, salt levels in food, speed cameras, hospital parking charges, wind farms, tuition fees, sex education in schools – there's a long list of hot topics which rise and fall in the headlines, and on the letters pages and message boards.

These are issues that do not intersect naturally with political parties or wider ideologies, and offer people a 'pick and mix' of things to be concerned about. The way they might act to bring together normally detached and disparate groups of people may tell us something about the identities that really matter to people – as parents, as drivers, rural-dwellers, students and so on. The extent to which such impermanent, cross-cutting forms of identity come to replace the big, tangible communities of interest we know today, will be fascinating to see.

Impact on public services

The increasing uncoupling of people from one place, as they work farther from home and live to less routine schedules, is something that public services will need to get better at responding to. For example, we may need a more flexible attitude to how we access GPs, so that people can more easily drop in to see a doctor or a dentist anywhere in the country. At the moment health and social care services are too complicated and the local focus of how that's administered is increasingly unsuitable for people. I may break my hip anywhere, but my local NHS is still charged.

Public services will need to respond not only to a more transient population, but also to an ageing one. Society will be getting older in the decades ahead, and there is a desperate need to tackle the challenges that this ageing population will throw up.

Growing numbers of older people will want and expect (and indeed be expected) to live more active and independent lives until they are into their 80s and 90s, rather than just follow the route of entering a care home in their late 70s. This could mean a range of things for public services. For example, it points towards the need for more flexible provision of support for older people who are dealing with the effects of old age but do not need major interventions to 'look after' them. Access to simple medical equipment, to recreational activity and to volunteering opportunities that will help them stay active are examples. Services and equipment that have typically been available only through hospitals might be better located through supermarkets or online sources. An older population with a stronger, more positive identity will demand more from the services they use, and it will be the responsibility of a society that wants its elders to feel they belong to address those demands.

*Policy-makers
... don't want to
talk about gender
because women are
doing well, but this
misses the fact that
social trends have
already benefited
women and that
policy should now
be ensuring that
these trends do
not undermine
the status and
sense of belonging
experienced by men.*

Gender, identity and belonging

Julia Margo, Acting Director, Demos*

The two markers of identity that will dominate the next couple of decades in terms of belonging are not class and cultural background but gender and age. It's a young woman's society that we're moving towards.

In the 1950s and earlier, it was an older man's society, where middle-aged men owned it all. They had a strong sense of efficacy, belonging and empowerment, were able to accomplish things, and were able to change society in the way they wanted. That is how I would define a sense of belonging. But men and boys today often lack that assurance and are feeling increasingly disenfranchised.

The rise of women and the decline of men

Belonging and identity have a lot to do with people's lifestyles and life chances. What is expected of them? What do they feel enabled to do? What is their role in society and what can they achieve?

In terms of the way that people feel about themselves, gender is still very important in modern Britain, and will continue to be so in the future. We try and ignore gender in policy-making and say that it doesn't matter, but I would argue that it does, not because women still face discrimination or reach that glass ceiling, but because men are the ones increasingly unsure of themselves.

Girls are displaying greater levels of confidence and self-esteem than they did in the last decade. This is unsurprising because, across so many spheres of life, women are doing better. This change has had a serious feminist side to it but, in parallel with that, there has also been the less serious, 'girl power' side. Both represent the fact that females have benefited from social changes and commercial trends across the age spectrum and across social classes.

Boys, by contrast, have been undermined by those changes. There has been a feminisation of the labour market in the sense that women can do

* Prior to joining Demos, Julia was associate director and head of the strategic research team at the Institute for Public Policy Research (ippr). She was also editor of the leading politics and policy journal Public Policy Research (PPR). Her expertise is in social mobility, well-being and capabilities, education policy and antisocial behaviour – subjects on which she is a regular commentator in the national and international press.

any job. We haven't industrialised like the Finnish or Swedish economies where women tend to do the public service, part-time and service sector jobs. In the UK and America, women are turning up and doing all the jobs, so there's no area in which men are doing better.

People say the fact that women aren't getting to the very top in professions like law and the City is a sign of a gender bias, but that's nonsense. When you actually ask women, they often say they want to have a family and work, so they don't necessarily want to reach the very top. It's their choice. I think in future we'll find men continuing to do those very top jobs, at risk to their health and happiness, while women will be in relatively senior positions but also having the family life that they want, perhaps being a divorced single parent but being quite content with their lives. Divorced single men, on the other hand, will tend to deal with their situation less well.

And so we face a future where it is young women who feel the greatest sense of ownership of the society around them, who are empowered about their bodies, their capacity to succeed, and about the choices they have to balance their work and their families in the way they want. This is a new trend.

It used to be the man who decided when he was ready to have a wife. Then it was the man who decided when he was ready for his wife to give up her job and have a baby. The wife would acquiesce. I would say it's exactly the reverse of that now.

Today, men are typically more interested in the idea of marriage and do better psychologically by being married than women. Men who are divorced or unmarried are far more likely to suffer from depression than men who are married – a distinction not so evident among women.

So marriage is important to men's sense of belonging and their status; that is how they belong. It has never been so important for women's sense of belonging, even in the past. It was important for their material and social status, yes, but now it isn't even important from those perspectives, which is why there has been this rise in divorce rates and 'un-marriage' in recent decades – all of it driven by women.

The trouble with boys

Admittedly it seems strange to focus so much on gender, as it feels like an old-fashioned, outdated way of viewing the world. But I think it's one that holds water. Across all domains, we are seeing issues about boys emerging. Ten years ago in education we talked about gender. We talked about girls and worried about their achievement. Then suddenly, in the last few years, boys have started slipping behind very quickly.

Why has this happened? In part it's because we've changed how we educate in a way that benefits women and girls and the way their minds develop. In fact, lots of the changes that have happened in western society have been advantageous to girls, whose cognitive development is different from that of boys. Brain development is sparked by puberty and girls enter puberty earlier than boys. Girls are now entering puberty earlier they did 50 years ago, and with that they are developing self-esteem, understanding how to control their behaviour, and learning how to plan and complete tasks. Men, whose brains do not reach maturity until their mid-20s, are expected to be able to display the same skills from the age of 13. This is why City employers are running intensive courses for their 20-somethings who are finding that they are unable to work in a team and manage their workload effectively.

The suggestion is not that all men face uncertainty, falling self-esteem or a less happy life than they once did. Class still comes into it. If they are comfortably off, with the security of that financial or education cushion, then obviously men do very well and continue to succeed. If we think about crime and antisocial behaviour, for instance, it is rarely the married father of three with a job who's causing trouble, but it is males – males who have poorer social and emotional skills, who are unemployed and not in education, and who signify every element of disenfranchisement – and not their wives, sisters or girlfriends, whose social background may be the same. In the past we would never have dwelt on the fact that most criminals were men and boys, because so were most workers, most students, most everything in the public eye. But now in a society where women are so visible in all those other, positive spheres of activity, the fact that it remains men and boys who fill our prisons and youth offender institutions is something we cannot ignore.

And so, I believe, gender will continue to be a big defining theme unless we start to unpick some of the really huge, radical changes that have happened very quickly that are massively disempowering men and boys.

What does this mean for public services?

Policy-makers have been slow to respond. They don't want to talk about gender because women are doing well, but this misses the fact that social trends have already benefited women and that policy should now be ensuring that these trends do not undermine the status and sense of belonging experienced by men.

First, we need to radically reform the education system – as in Finland and Sweden – and take more of a Montessori approach where, until the age of six, you're essentially learning how to behave, how to manage your feelings, how to improve your mood and how to interact with other people. These are all things some politicians view as woolly and pointless, but which strongly underpin children's ability to gain technical cognition skills, and thus achieve in core subject areas like maths and English.

We need to break down the way we socialise gender differences. It's become OK to be dismissive and critical of boys and men in a way which you could never be with girls and women. You can see it very clearly with some young boys. They are acutely aware that it's expected – even tacitly encouraged – for them to be violent and naughty, and that to behave and act sweetly and considerately is feminine and pathetic. Girls, on the other hand, are given the message that for them, sweetness and consideration are positive traits.

On the health side, we need to find a way to boost the positive work of Surestart, health visitors and early years provision. Again, Finland sets an example. There, it is not a sensitive issue to support parents to raise their children. Here we still tend to see that as interference, as the 'nanny state'. But it's right that we should help parents who, because of cultural background or poverty or a challenging environment, are less well equipped to ensure their children are getting the right kind of stimulation to help develop those social and emotional skills. There are numerous examples in other countries where the state does not over-intervene in parenting, but does act to make sure children's well-being is being facilitated inside as well as outside the home. We need to learn from those examples.

It's important we act to address this issue of socio-emotional skills, not least because of its relationship to reduced social mobility. We now see a different skill-set being used to explain social mobility, with academic skills now less important than they were. This means that what happens to you at home in your early years, when those skills are first honed, is of greater relevance in determining the path your life takes later on. People born into families where there are low levels of affection, secure attachments or sensible discipline can struggle to provide these skills, so that even where there is intellectual and academic stimulation, some children do badly.

These trends can affect children of both sexes of course, but research suggests it's particularly the boys raised without fathers or without a

good relationship with their fathers, whose sense of self is undermined and who therefore bear the brunt of these changes.

The challenge in the decades ahead will be ensuring that boys and men are not left behind by a society that demands greater emotional sensitivity amongst its higher achievers, and which unwittingly places women at an advantage.

Like African-Americans and Irish-Americans, ... historic roots will give these emerging generations a sense of connection to other people and other places, but I think we'll find it has less resonance in how they actually see themselves day to day, or who they want to make friends with or live close to.

Feeling British

Leon Murray, CBE*

When people arrive in Britain as immigrants, their identity about where they come from matters a great deal. But now, the second and third generations of migrant families have evolved very different perspectives. Racial discrimination in jobs and housing has largely receded into the background, and is not experienced as overtly as it might have been by those parents and grandparents who arrived here in the last 60 years.

Many of these later generations now don't see themselves as Caribbean or African, for instance, but simply as British. They still recognise where their ancestors came from, and that can form an important part of their back story, but it's a back story in the wider context of them as young British people. This process will continue. Like African-Americans and Irish-Americans, those historic roots will give these emerging generations a sense of connection to other people and other places, but I think we'll find it has less resonance in how they actually see themselves day to day, or who they want to make friends with or live close to.

This is a good thing. It will help build cohesion in communities. If people are going to feel they belong in the communities they live in, if they're going to find enough in common to bind them to their neighbours – whatever their colour or faith – then they have to feel they belong to a wider, inclusive British society. You can't keep harking back to where your ancestors have come from if you're going to fully invest in the society in which you live. I think we're seeing this process among young black and minority ethnic (BME) people in Britain today, and I think it can only continue into the future. Certain groups may at present face disproportionate disadvantage, such as poor educational attainment, but these are issues about deprivation rather than race. It's the convergence of the two we need to deal with.

A lot of what shapes common identities is subtle and everyday, and those forces are bringing us closer together. I've noticed where I live, for

---

* Leon came to the UK from the West Indies in the early 1960s. For three decades he has been involved in the criminal justice system, working with the police on race relations and serving for 25 years as a magistrate. He was one of the first black JPs in the Midlands. In 2008 he was appointed to the National Probation Board by the Ministry of Justice. Leon was also the first black vice-president of British Methodism, and is now director of two charitable organisations, president of the YMCA for Shropshire, and chair of a local mental health charity.

instance, that over the last ten or fifteen years, the number of Asian families you see shopping at the main supermarkets has increased. We're shopping together; we're buying similar things. That may not be good for our small independent shops, but in terms of cohesion and integration it's a modest sign that modern life in Britain is increasingly similar for people of different backgrounds. Perhaps most importantly of all, the young people from all these different groups are being educated alongside each other in the same schools – they play together in the playground, they eat together at lunchtime – and that's where common ground is found and friendships develop.

Schools are places we should be immensely positive about in this respect. In my experience, whether state or privately-run, schools treat their children equally and, as far as possible, remove barriers to integration. This is where the real revolution is taking place, quietly. It isn't always an easy process, and in areas where communities remain physically segregated because of housing occupation patterns, schools end up being similarly segregated.

But even in these places, change is happening and the lines are becoming blurred, with young second and third generation BME families choosing to move out into other neighbourhoods away from the close-knit streets where their forebears first arrived. In the decades ahead we will see integration increasing in our local communities, and consequently our schools, where simple physical integration can blossom into social integration.

Does this paint too rosy a picture? It is not enough to say that people will naturally come together over time, because tensions caused by shocking events – local, national or international – can knock us off course, affecting how people from certain groups see themselves or are seen by others. There is no doubt some sections of the Muslim community, for instance, currently feel they are targeted by the criminal justice system, and there are sections of the white population who think they should be.

I've been working in that system for 25 years, and I genuinely don't think that such victimisation takes place for the most part, but there is a perception of injustice, and that creates resentment and reinforces a sense of difference. I believe there is sufficient goodwill within Britain's Muslim communities and hopefully with the rest of us too, that this is a storm we can weather and that, in 2020, we will be able to look back and see that the height of this resentment and distrust has passed. The onus is on all of us, and in particular politicians and the media, not to inflame tensions when they arise, and to always stand by the message that we are all unified as citizens of Britain and residents of our local neighbourhoods, and that these are connections that bind us regardless of faith and ethnicity.

Multicultural or integrated?

We need to emphasise what connects us and what gives us a shared identity. There will always be cultural differences between faiths and races because of what our different histories give us, but there are also many other things that create difference, such as whether you're from the north or south, or whether you are rich or poor. The important feature of a truly integrated society in the future will be that these differences are not constantly at the fore as characteristics that define us; they will inform our sense of self and they will make us interesting to one another, but they will not be our first refuge when anxiety or uncertainty strikes, either out of aggression or defensiveness, because they simply won't seem critical enough to serve that purpose.

Whatever Britain's flaws, we should not underestimate the fact that being British – whether born here or naturalised – does have the potential to give you a positive sense of identity and belonging, and that's a powerful starting point that we shouldn't dismiss. What it means to be British – what that label can encompass – has, I think, shifted significantly in the last 50 years. It still needs to shift some more, but one has to realise that this process of shifting to accommodate and include new people takes generations to achieve.

The role of public services

What does all this mean for government and public services? Legislation itself is not sufficient, and when community workers are employed directly as public servants, the work they do can suffer from bureaucracy. Sometimes it can feel like these people have been 'parachuted in'.

Things work better when local people take the lead themselves, and a lot of the most effective work is done by voluntary and community groups. The Equal Foundation in my own town of Wellington, for instance, is run by British-born Muslims and works to bring the whole local community together. It isn't about integration for its own sake, but offers practical help to people – in learning computer skills, for instance, or improving English language skills – and the police are involved as well. It has had a massive impact in what was quite a neglected neighbourhood.

This doesn't mean public services don't have a role, however. Their role must be to support and help sustain the sorts of groups and projects we're talking about – where people in the community have the idea and make it work, but where they need resources to keep it going. These organisations can't live on fresh air and water. Sometimes that external resourcing will be the only element a local council or government department needs to offer. But it's a big element, and without it many can't operate.

The other key role of public services is to ensure they're spending money in way that doesn't breed resentment and division. Among many white communities, there is still the perception that other groups get more help, more 'stuff' – whether it's housing, job opportunities, or leisure facilities. The evidence doesn't support that, but is a perception that the BNP and others exploit. It shows that if, as a council or other agency, you're going to spend money in a community, you need to spend it across the whole community and be seen to be doing that. I look forward to a future where those claims of unfairness are unable to take root because the evidence to the contrary will be so compelling, because residents from all backgrounds will be pooling their collective energies into making their area better, and because public services will be supporting them to do that with even-handedness, clear purpose and transparency.

A snapshot of 2020

So in 2020, what will be the key things that have happened? Education and skills will need to be at the heart of the change. Everyone will have – and will see they have – the opportunity for education and to advance themselves. Not all will succeed, but at least they will feel the power has been given to them to make the most of life, and it will not be their background that has held them back. This will enable people to have confidence in themselves and in their ability to shape their own destiny.

Society will not be 'equalised'. We will not all enjoy the same incomes, health outcomes, or quality of life. We can't pretend that society allows that: it simply has to be a manageable tension. The key thing is that everyone is given the tools to fulfil their potential, and that black and Asian people, for instance, will stand on every rung of the ladder, their race or faith an aspect of their identities but not a life-limiting factor in what they're able to achieve. The white majority will see people of other

colours and faiths all around them, in all walks of life, contributing not only to their own communities, but to their wider local and national community in which all benefit. Young people from BME backgrounds will respect their history and where they come from, as is healthy, but they will also mix and live and socialise in that wider, diverse British community of which they are a part.

Finally, I would confidently predict that British culture will ultimately prevail and unite us all. That phrase might concern some – it might suggest the sort of assimilation that wipes out all traces of cultural heritage and makes us tightly conform. But it doesn't have to mean that, because the British culture we share will be one we have all had a hand in building, and one to which – regardless of our multiple identities and our many back stories – we can all belong.

The new generation of fit, healthy, active older people will take an ever more prominent role in our local and national life. But that won't happen evenly across socio-economic groups. Increasing the retirement age, for instance, will not affect all older people in the same way.

The identity of age

Pat Thane, Emeritus Professor, King's College London*

Age as an equality strand is now well established, in a way that it wasn't ten years ago. For a long time, people were able to get away with jokes and assumptions about older people that would be unimaginable in other equality strands such as race or disability. Older people didn't make a fuss, or had mixed feelings themselves, so this behaviour was perpetuated. But this is changing, and will continue to change.

Age has a lot in common with the other equality strands. Society attaches various negative assumptions to old age just as it has to people of minority ethnicities, people who are gay and people who are disabled. To be old – as to be Muslim or gay or in a wheelchair – can unfairly affect the opportunities available to you. Moreover, like those other equality strands, old age can define someone in the eyes of society.

But there are also differences between age and the other equality strands that inform people's identities. Most notably, while being a woman, a black person or a gay person are generally pretty permanent states (and ones that some people will never experience) old age is something that's foreign to everyone at some stages in their lives yet which ultimately everyone experiences in the end, just by virtue of living long enough.

What does that mean for age as something that informs our sense of self? For one thing, it means that a lot of other things have come to define us before old age does, so it's one we acquire later than most of our other identities. It is also one that we arrive at later in life as national standards of living improve and life expectancy increases. And once you reach old age, the extent to which it shapes your experiences and how you're viewed by others will vary depending on how wealthy and how healthy you are.

* Before becoming emeritus professor at King's College London, Pat was professor of contemporary British history at the Institute of Historical Research, University of London, from 2001 to 2010. Her publications include: The Foundations of the Welfare State *(1982);* Old Age from Antiquity to Post-Modernity *(co-edited with Paul Johnson,1998);* Old Age in England – Past Experiences, Present Issues *(2000);* The Long History of Old Age, *(editor, 2005); and* Unequal Britain – Equalities in Britain since 1945, *(editor, 2010).*

Pat regularly speaks and writes on issues relating to the history of the welfare state, gender, old age and pensions. She is a convenor of History and Policy: www.historyandpolicy.org

Active, skilled and involved

The stage at which you 'become old' has risen, with many older people breaking the boundaries and defying the label of 'OAP' which kicks in when you hit 65. A lot of older people today are more positive about their lives and the opportunities available to them. People now in their 60s are from the 1960s generation, so more of them are better educated, better-off and better prepared to make a fuss about things they don't like. The medical evidence is clear: people in their 60s today are much fitter and not generally 'old' as most of us would define it, until they're in their 70s or even 80s.

The rest of society needs to catch up with this thinking. We talk a lot about the costs of an ageing society, but the benefits are that people are fending off the negative aspects of old age for longer, so those people in their 60s and 70s who years ago we might have viewed as having outlived their economic usefulness are now fitter, healthier, and providing a huge resource for society. Retired people are keeping the voluntary sector going, for instance, and in the decades ahead their role will increase. They have the skills and the time that's vital for voluntary and community groups. If you look at Voluntary Service Overseas (VSO), which used to be for school and university leavers, you see a lot of retired people signing up – social workers, doctors, nurses and so on – and they can add much more value than students can. For a government that's trying to build a 'Big Society' of community activists, these able, skilled and experienced older people are going to be incredibly important.

Age, work and retirement

The fact that all these older-but-active individuals are available for voluntary work is partly a result of our outdated retirement age, which sees perfectly healthy, able and engaged people compelled to leave work when they're basically middle aged. It's madness that we still have a retirement age set in the 1940s. The retirement age has got to go up, and it will in the next few years, but the government is terrified of the political effects of this because there's always such a furore when there's talk of this. The most sensible solution was a flexible retirement age, as proposed by Beveridge, and if it had been implemented then, we wouldn't have the issue that we have today.

People in their 40s and 50s resent the increase in retirement age because it means they'll be working for longer, and younger people resent it because they think it means older people clogging up the labour market and keeping them out of the best-paid jobs. But pensions cost a lot of money, and if people go on working for longer, they can contribute more in taxation, which is better for the public purse. It will save tax payers forking out for pensions and, with more older people remaining in work and thus socially integrated for longer, there are likely to be knock-on benefits in terms of health and well-being. Moreover, younger people have to appreciate that people don't get decrepit after 60, but have resources and skills that should be valued in the workplace.

As for the concern about clogging up the labour market, in the short-term at least there's no guarantee that older people will be replaced if they do leave work. Because of the recession, the barrier to younger people getting jobs and better-paid roles will be the state of the wider economy, rather than how many older people stay in work. This happened in the 1980s, when older people were retiring younger than ever, yet those vacated jobs were often not taken by younger colleagues, but simply disappeared with the incumbent.

Young people need to shift their expectations so that they do not anticipate such great career success so young. They need to start imagining longer working lives for themselves, because this is certainly going to happen. They should remember, too, that most people now in their 60s left school at 15 with no qualifications and less than four per cent of them went to university. Now 40 per cent do, and they don't start work until their 20s. Young people now expect to be chief executives, professors and senior politicians before they're 40, despite starting work later. It might be better for society if men and women could have more relaxed working lives in their 30s and 40s, when they are bringing up children, then work until later in life when the kids have left home, instead of combining maximum stress at work and at home in middle life as many do now.

Age and poverty

The new generation of fit, healthy, active older people will take an ever more prominent role in our local and national life. But that won't happen evenly across socio-economic groups. Increasing the retirement age, for instance, will not affect all older people in the same way. The wealthier people will be able to retire earlier, and give their time to those volunteering roles and active lifestyles. The very poor will be the ones who have to work 'till they drop'.

After the Second World War the income gap narrowed and now we're gradually going backwards. The really active, well-off older people will lead a good life and will never know what it means to be an isolated, poor, older woman in a tower block. The risk is that we go on having an enormous disparity between rich and poor, and one that gets worse. This is where the real division in society will be. The middle classes are used to being stroppy and know how to get what they want. If you're poor and old it's likely to be a much worse experience, especially if you're female. I think that's always been so, but the risk is that as more older people are able to defy that image of decrepitude, those still living at the sharp end of old age and poverty will recede into the background and become more and more invisible.

Responding to the fact that older people's needs are different, the Conservatives are talking about more means testing to restrict the help given to those older people who can look after themselves. But this is an inefficient way of going about it. If they think wealthier older people don't need the same level of support as others, they should tax them on the benefit they receive, not stop the benefit altogether, because means testing inevitably results in some of those who need the benefit slipping through the net. Only universal benefits ensure that those in need aren't missed. The problem with the pension credit, for instance, is that 20 per cent of eligible people don't apply, and they're likely to be the very people who need it most. Moreover, the cost of means testing is huge in terms of administration.

Defined by age: rich and poor

In future, then, we will see growing opportunities for better-off older people and stagnation or even worsening experiences for the poorest. So when it comes to belonging, contributing to society, being active and positive about yourself, better-off older people are likely to have the happier experience. In terms of identity, on the other hand, those who identify as 'old' and who feel more defined by their age will perhaps be those who are worse off and whose lives are more restricted in old age.

If you think about OAP lunch clubs, for instance, and other places and activities where age determines a person's involvement, it is more often economically poorer people who need and use those services most. It is the poor older people who have the greatest needs, and they are most likely to think of themselves as old and to have the problems associated with old age. The poorer you are the more you conform to the stereotype. Wealthier older people, meanwhile, might be better placed to enjoy less age-targeted, 'mainstream' leisure activities and social life, their lives seemingly less dominated by the fact they're not as young as they used to be. I would argue that the experience gap within the generation, based on income, is more important than the gap between different generations.

A cult of youth?

On the one hand, the fact that people look younger for longer reflects the better quality of life that many older people now enjoy, which is a positive. On the other hand, you could say that the pressure to look younger (e.g. through cosmetic surgery) suggests something more negative in society. Commentators talk about a 'cult of youth'. People have always wanted to look young for as long as possible, but in the past at least respect and wisdom were attached to age. I think young people appreciated this more, and had expectations to match. Professors and chief executives became such in their 50s, and didn't expect to reach such positions until that time.

In recent years, this norm has been eroded, with organisations increasingly believing that the experience of age is trumped by the dynamism and fresh ideas of youth. In the 1990s, Barclays Bank was not alone in getting rid of their older managers and installing younger replacements – before realising this was a mistake and reversing the policy.

Age and gender

More disturbingly, this cult of youth is something that disproportionately affects women. There is a tradition of respecting the grey-haired older man. The tradition is not there for grey-haired women, and in that sense we're just seeing the continuation of a gender inequality we've had for centuries. Think about leading men in films or male television presenters: there aren't many female equivalents of Harrison Ford or Bruce Forsythe who continue to take centre stage alongside a younger male co-star into their sixties and beyond.

And again, income is a significant factor. Those people best placed to avoid the negative effects of ageing are those with the healthier lifestyles and incomes associated with affluence. The poorer you are, the less likely you are to be able to fend off ageing so successfully. My hope would be that in 2025, healthier lifestyles will mean that more older people are able to 'feel younger' for longer, choosing to remain in paid or voluntary work for longer and able to enjoy an active social life. What I hope we don't see, however, is a society in which youthfulness itself has become the thing we value most.

So does wealth
mean you can
'buy your way'
out of ethnic or
faith identities?
Will increasing
prosperity amongst
Britain's BME
communities
necessarily coincide
with declining
attachment to
ethnic and faith-
based associations
and identities?

Identities: fluid and fixed

Harris Beider, Professor, Futures Institute, Coventry University*

The boundaries that we draw around certain identities are much less rigid than they were in the past. The mainstream view of people in Britain about the characteristics that make someone British, for instance, are more permeable than they were forty or fifty years ago. There is also arguably more fluidity in the way that people self-identify, with ethnic and faith identities overlaid onto nationality in a way that was much less common in a more homogeneously white, Christian Britain.

But while this is the picture of progress within the broad 'middle' of society, there has been some retrenchment and a fixing of negative or 'embattled' identities at the margins. White working class communities, for instance, often feel they're being ignored and their identities challenged. This is partly the impact of immigration, but also has a lot to do with changes that have occurred in the economy and wider society, which in turn play out in the decline of a whole range of institutions and amenities important in working class culture – from pubs to trade unions to public sector housing – and also in a greater disengagement from politics. The result is that their identity and sense of belonging is being squeezed. As other elements of society move forward – including other ethnic groups – white working class communities have found it difficult to do the same. They become resistant to progressive change.

At the other end of the retrenchment/separation spectrum, we have seen the remaking of Muslim identity, a process that has been both self-imposed and imposed from outside. On the part of wider society, we have a 'suspect community' perspective, fuelled by narratives about terrorism and extremism. On the part of some British Muslims themselves, this remaking has been about using Islam as a form of cultural resistance, a way of standing back from a society because it seems unfriendly or

---

* Harris Beider has been a professor at the Futures Institute, Coventry University, since April 2010. He was appointed professor in community cohesion at the Institute of Community Cohesion, also at Coventry University, in September 2007. Previously Harris was senior fellow at the Centre for Urban and Regional Studies at the University of Birmingham.

  Prior to his academic career, Harris was executive director of the Federation of Black Housing Organisations and founding director of People for Action. He has written extensively on race, cohesion, community and housing and spoken about these and related subjects both nationally and internationally.

undesirable or both. Among the mass of people in the 'mainstream', identity is more fluid and its relevance in forging aggressive or defensive stances against others is, thankfully, diminishing.

Faith and identity

Religion can be seen as a hero and as a villain in debates on community cohesion. It can provide a focal point – culturally and physically – for new communities, helping them to develop strong social networks and self-confidence.

Hindu temples, Muslim mosques and African churches in Britain are hugely important in this respect. Faith can also serve to bring together people from different socio-economic or ethnic backgrounds, and through interfaith initiatives it is evident that religious organisations can in fact be a conduit through which people of different cultural backgrounds are encouraged to interact.

And yet, the rise of faith as the primary determinant of identity can pose challenges to community cohesion, particularly where there are concerns about the juxtaposition of the values and practices of some faith groups with what we might perceive as British values. Some, such as the practice of female genital mutilation, clearly clash with legislation and principles, and most people in Britain agree that these should be condemned whatever the cultural or religious motivations. Others, such as the Muslin women wearing veils, inspire much more divided opinion about what should and shouldn't be tolerated, accepted or encouraged by the rest of society.

This all serves to illustrate that the basis for identity conflicts has shifted over time. It could be argued that conflict on phenotype – being categorised as black or white – is being replaced by a more nuanced, visceral conflict on faith.

Muslims are placed at the frontline of that redrawn map of identity conflict. In part, that has been able to happen because a range of domestic issues about deprivation, low attainment and housing segregation allow them to be singled out, but it's also complicated by international politics.

While domestic and social challenges alone are difficult to address, they are at least within the remit of the state to deal with. The international element, however, means there are some key levers completely out of the state's control, and thus it will always be difficult for the government to fully address the tensions we are currently seeing. This being so, the extent to which that faith-based division grows or narrows in the next two decades is difficult to call.

The reductionism we see in debates about faith identities in Britain is, then, problematic, and the risk in the next two decades is that the emphasis on faith as a way to identify oneself and others becomes a fertile ground for a new generation of prejudice and tension.

Race and belonging: 'recycled racism'

There has been a deconstruction of the concept of 'race' related to the changing nature of immigration and minority groups present in the UK. The binary definition of 'race', of 'black and white', is no longer appropriate for the society that we live in now. Where race and immigration have been synonymous in the past, we are entering a period where the two issues start to part company, with settled BME communities – already at least sixty years old in many areas – no longer viewed so interchangeably with more recent waves of immigration.

In fact it is interesting that some of the most hostile attitudes towards those newer migrant communities, for example, from the Horn of Africa and parts of Asia, are expressed by members of earlier immigrant communities. It is often these more settled BME communities who are sharing their neighbourhoods with the newcomers, who are perceived to be competing for the social housing, healthcare, jobs and neighbourhood 'turf' in these areas.

So, the sharp end of the conflict is no longer necessarily between white and black communities but between established minority communities and newly arrived migrants. This is a form of 'recycled racism' where established minority communities use the same racist narratives that they were subjected to in the 1950s and 1960s from white people. Established minority communities are reproducing these racist perspectives to make sense of the migration and changing neighbourhoods they are part of. Essentially, the key narrative being communicated is that of trying to keep people out, to ensure protection of jobs, housing and political representation. This prejudice against new arrivals hints at new kinds of cohesion challenges in the decades ahead in some of our more deprived communities.

Income is an important factor in how much integration can appear to be a problem, whether with new or old communities. I did some research in a suburb of Newcastle-upon-Tyne, which showed that people of South Asian origin, particularly British Indians, generally feel there is no problem

with integration in their area. This seems to be because they are as wealthy as their white British counterparts, so those issues of inter-community competition for housing, jobs, education, and healthcare are absent, since everyone in this neighbourhood can afford and choose their home, job, school, GP and so on. Faith and ethnicity do not appear to adversely affect the quality of these people's life experiences, and so their sense of identity and belonging is not being forged by a sense of disadvantage or grievance based on those characteristics. In a poorer area, for both white working class and BME residents, that is not so often the case.

Faith, race and economic status

So does wealth mean you can 'buy your way' out of ethnic or faith identities? Will increasing prosperity amongst Britain's BME communities necessarily coincide with declining attachment to ethnic and faith-based associations and identities?

The fact that faith is apparently more important among immigrant communities and in more deprived areas is not a coincidence, and the fact that, as is visible in New York's Catholic churches for instance, those ties to faith diminish as communities disperse, become more geographically and socially mobile and 'marry out'. For these people who lose touch with their families' faith communities, the social and cultural need for maintaining the connection – often so important to minority groups in their early years – clearly peters out.

In the long term, we may see that same process in Britain among future generations of what were immigrant communities. That said, it is not necessarily the case that rising income and opportunity means a flight from ethnic and faith identities or forms of belonging. We currently see, for example, how faith remains an important cultural marker of identity that transcends place and class to give people a sense of common ground and belonging with others. You witness this among Muslim communities in Birmingham, as in other UK cities, where families have moved up the social ladder and moved out of the inner-city neighbourhoods to more middle class suburbs, but regularly return to those original neighbourhoods to visit the shops and the mosque and so on. While enjoying the economic, social and educational benefits associated with a 'nicer' neighbourhood, therefore, these people also maintain a strong sense of belonging to something different through their faith and family ties – an example of how we like to have multiple identities and how one sense of ourselves does not necessarily need to crowd out another.

White working class identities

It seems that unlike faith, it is difficult for race and class to remain important cultural factors through changes in space, time and politics. Class in particular has shifted significantly as a determinant of identity, and it will be interesting to see how that develops in the next twenty years.

Recently, we have also seen greater appreciation for the white working class as an identity group. Both from left and right, the broadsheet press and middle class establishment have been able to moralise, caricature and ridicule this social group in a way that would no longer be acceptable in relation to ethnic or faith groups, at least not as blatantly. White working class communities have been lumped together as one group with a checklist of negative characteristics, but they are as diverse as any other community. They haven't been given a space to articulate their ideas and speak for themselves. I think we're now aware that, in the decades ahead, we are going to have to pay more attention to how these poorer white neighbour-hoods are being affected by social, economic and technological change.

It isn't just immigration that has undermined their self-confidence and ability to 'feel in control' of their lives and their neighbourhoods, although that might often be the most tangible change they can identify. Economic restructuring has led to the decline of cultural markers of belonging that have traditionally brought together white working class communities and helped galvanise a positive identity and strong sense of belonging. So, during the time when immigrant communities have been bonding very effectively and growing in voice and in confidence, these neighbouring white communities – no longer coalescing around the church or the pit or the factory, their shops and pubs disappearing – are perhaps less well con-nected to each other, less engaged and less self-supporting than they once were. They can find not only their positive sense of identity severely dented as the rest of society tells them they're idle, obese and ignorant, but also their sense of belonging is undermined by social and economic changes.

Implications for public services

I'm in two minds about the role of the state in integration, and therefore what the implications of a more 'hands-off' state will be. While the public sphere has been relatively good at seeking to be inclusive and improving equality through necessary legislation, it has also been guilty of telling people what to do, and that has perhaps stifled an 'organic' process of integration.

At present, I see both local and national government as being out of step with the shifts that are taking place with identity. Their responses to challenges in this arena have often been clunky and misjudged, such as this love of 'myth busting' leaflets as a means of fending off the messages of the far right, or blithely declaring that we should 'celebrate diversity' and believing that this will be enough to convince people of the merits of immigration and its impacts.

When society needed politicians to have open and frank discussions, they weren't there to have them. More widely, government has tended to expect community organisations and local authorities to translate its top-down messages into everyday solutions, but this is a back-to-front, paternalistic way of doing things, and on the whole it hasn't worked.

In the years ahead, I think the personalisation agenda will be an important factor in moving the state away from that rigid view of ethnic and faith identities that can stifle empowerment and cohesion. The more you build services in a way that can respond to individuals, the less easy it becomes to maintain those fixed assumptions about certain communities' identities and needs – and the less you enable cultures of dependency to emerge.

But does a rolling back of the state and encouragement for us to 'take the initiative' risk opening the door to widening inequality between groups within local areas? There are concerns about plans to enable communities to set up their own schools and lead on delivering other public services, but I believe that the outcome could actually be better integrated local communities where people from different ethnic and faith backgrounds are drawn together in the creation and maintenance of those quality services they all want.

For the politicians' part, we need leaders who buy into a progressive 'brand' of identity in Britain, which can unite people on common hopes and concerns without having to pin down some grand narrative about what 'Britishness' means.

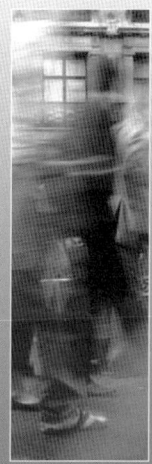

About OPM

OPM is an employee-owned, not-for-profit research and
consultancy organisation. Since 1989, we have worked
alongside public service organisations to help them
improve outcomes for stakeholders, service users and
communities. A major part of our work is in the area of
strategic futures: using analysis, scenario planning and
interactive processes to help organisations develop
policies, strategies and services that are 'future proofed'.

For more information please visit:
www.opm.co.uk

OPM

252B Gray's Inn Road
London WC1X 8XG
t: 0845 055 3900
f: 0845 055 1700
e: office@opm.co.uk

Appendix B

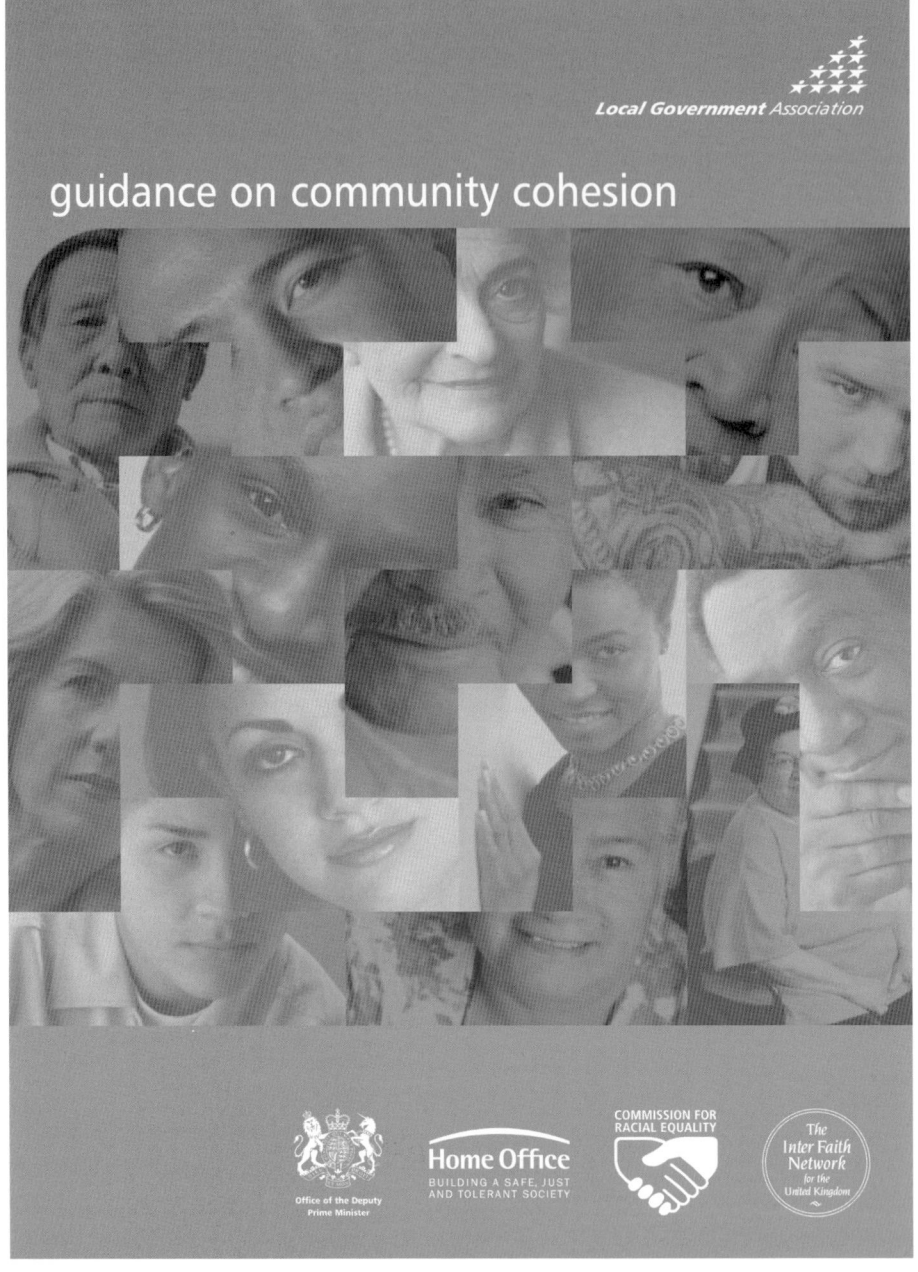

Published by LGA Publications
Local Government Association,
Local Government House,
Smith Square, London SW1P 3HZ
Tel 020 7664 3000
Fax 020 7664 3030

LGA Code F/EQ005
ISBN 1 84049 313 5

Acknowledgements

This guidance is the product of extensive consultation and discussion across central/local government and beyond. In addition to the bodies that have formally agreed and 'badged' this document, the following deserve acknowledgement for their work in assisting in the drafting of various sections of the guidance:

- Association of Police Authorities (www.apa.police.uk)
- Department for Education and Skills (www.dfes.gov.uk)
- Employers' Organisation for local government (www.lg-employers.gov.uk)
- National Youth Agency (www.nya.org.uk)

Note – future intentions

This guidance is designed to assist all local authorities (from the largest counties to the smallest districts) and their partners in strengthening and building community cohesion. Further joint guidance is being developed to assist authorities and local strategic partnerships to assess (and measure) cohesion. In addition, examples of existing and emerging good practice in policy development and service provision will be posted on the LGA and community cohesion websites: www.lga.gov.uk and www.communitycohesion.gov.uk

As part of the Neighbourhood Renewal Unit's skills and knowledge programme, which aims to promote better skills and access to best practice for all involved in delivering neighbourhood renewal, there is also www.renewal.net, an all-in-one place website providing access to what works. This includes practical advice and case studies on community cohesion.

This document is initial guidance, following the consultation draft issued in May 2002. Further advice will be provided in early 2003 on ways to measure community cohesion. This guidance will be updated in 12–18 months time to account for new learning from initiatives such as the Community Cohesion Pathfinder Programme and the work of the Community Cohesion Practitioner Groups. The learning derived from these and other initiatives will significantly contribute towards future guidance.

Linked to these future intentions and the broad cross-cutting nature of community cohesion, we see this as an area in which practice (both that which works well and that which does not) together with new ideas, should be shared and disseminated to as wide an audience as possible. We encourage people to email the LGA direct or to post examples onto the community cohesion website.

Contents

Foreword

The United Kingdom is a changing society. Socio-economic changes are reflected in our growing ethnic and cultural diversity. These changes bring many gains but sometimes there are tensions and divisions that may lead to fracturing within and across local areas and local communities. Against this background, the enormous importance of working for social cohesion becomes evident.

The nature of these tensions and divisions may differ from one area to another – in some along racial lines, in others faith; there may be tensions and mistrust between urban and rural dwellers or between incomers and longer term residents, in others the key conflicts may be inter-generational. Whatever the nature of community divisions, however, the basis of the solutions is often the same; raising awareness and understanding to break down barriers, developing shared values and mutual respect and trust.

None of us can be complacent about community cohesion. Community cohesion, and the factors that can help build or undermine it, is an issue that we believe all authorities need to address. Cohesive communities are stronger and safer communities and they are better able to address issues affecting the social and economic well-being of all their residents.

We need strong local leadership from all sections of the community. We see local authorities as key drivers of change, promoting and facilitating the development of harmonious communities but working hand in hand with their partners at local level. This guidance sets out some practical steps that authorities and their partner organisations can take to build the promotion of community cohesion into their policies and delivery of services.

We are under no illusion that there are any quick fixes or simple answers but we do have to start the process in earnest now.

Sir Jeremy Beecham
Chairman, Local Government Association

The Rt Hon Beverley Hughes MP
Minister of State for Immigration, Citizenship and Community Cohesion, Home Office

The Rt Hon Nick Raynsford MP
Minister of State for Local Government, the Regions and Fire, Office of the Deputy Prime Minister

Beverley Bernard
Acting Chair, Commission for Racial Equality

Rt. Rev Dr Tom Butler
Mrs Rosalind Preston OBE
Co-Chairs of the Inter Faith Network for the UK

Introduction

Building cohesion is not an approach that government – central or local – can impose. Like most aspects of community life, cohesion is something which people themselves generate but which government and its partners can facilitate. Indeed, many authorities have been working to avoid fractured communities or to respond to specific incidents but have not necessarily described this work in community cohesion terms. Local authorities do, along with other local agencies, continually adapt to the rapid changes within their economy, environment and social mix, these all impact on communities and community cohesion. It is the combined, joined up and sustained efforts that build a cohesive society.

The challenge facing us all, since the publication of the Cantle and other reports, has been to translate our understanding of the issues raised into practical action to improve the situation on the ground. This action needs to tackle the causes that can lead to conflict and to guard against circumstances that could lead to the fracturing of communities. Local authorities have a key role to play in driving this agenda forward for their area – working closely with other local players through local strategic partnerships, community safety and crime and disorder reduction partnerships. However, each area's economic and social make-up is unique and the circumstances and events, which result in cohesion in one area, may not always do so everywhere.

The publication of this guidance provides advice on ways to review existing policies and practices so that they help to build more cohesive communities. It suggests actions that local authorities and their partners can take which are highlighted in the text boxes at the end of each chapter.

There is a wealth of existing guidance that complements this, particularly in respect of community strategies, community leadership and local strategic partnerships and race equality schemes. Such guidance is not repeated here but is given key references and should be revisited where appropriate.

What is community cohesion?

Community cohesion incorporates and goes beyond the concept of race equality and social inclusion.

The broad working definition is that a **cohesive community** is one where:

- there is a common vision and a sense of belonging for all communities;
- the diversity of people's different backgrounds and circumstances are appreciated and positively valued;
- those from different backgrounds have similar life opportunities; and
- strong and positive relationships are being developed between people from different backgrounds in the workplace, in schools and within neighbourhoods.

Strategies and plans

Community cohesion lies at the heart of what makes a safe and strong community and is, therefore, a key outcome for both local and central government to work towards. Indeed, it is one of the key priorities drawn up in the statement of shared priorities between the Local Government Association (LGA) and central government. Work across central government is brought together through the Inter-Departmental Ministerial Group chaired by Home Office Minister, Beverley Hughes.

A key first step for any local authority will be to conduct a baseline assessment of how effectively current policies and programmes promote-community cohesion for communities and neighbourhoods throughout their area. Some will conclude that their existing arrangements are satisfactory. They will have been developed through the community planning systems that are already in place – notably the community strategy, the race equality scheme, crime and communit safety strategy and local neighbourhood renewal strategies – and may address all the issues relevant to community cohesion within and across their communities.

Many other authorities will conclude that they need to amend some policies to better build community cohesion. A small number of areas may need to go further by developing a specifically focussed action plan, which complements the community strategy.

Regardless of whether an individual local authority decides to develop a specific action plan or not, community cohesion is an issue all local authorities need to consider and ensure that their specific policy actions promote. This guidance gives a steer about how to identify and address this issue.

The duty to promote race equality

The Office of the Deputy Prime Minister (ODPM) guidance, *Preparing Community Strategies: Government Guidance to Local Authorities (December 2000)*, addresses how community strategies should fit with other plans and strategies, specifically Best Value performance plans, local public service agreements (PSAs) and development plans. Since this guidance was produced, however, local authorities have a further responsibility that should be a crucial element of any authority's work on community cohesion.

The Race Relations (Amendment) Act 2000 introduced a new positive duty to promote race equality. This requires authorities to have 'due regard to the need', in everything they do, to:

- tackle racial discrimination;
- promote equality of opportunity; and
- promote good relations between people from different racial groups.

The third of these prongs will be central to the work that local authorities do on community cohesion. In particular, local authorities can work in different ways to promote good race relations.

This can be achieved by:

- creating opportunities for people from different communities to connect, meet openly and honestly to discuss issues and concerns that affect them all. It could be that different groups have different priorities and concerns; and
- consulting with all groups, including ethnic minority communities, to involve them in service planning and policy development as part of the requirement to involve people in shaping local services, particularly through partnership working and community development.

It is important for local authorities to view the Race Relations (Amendment) Act (RR[A]A) as a positive management tool. The specific duties within the RR[A]A, at the most basic level, require public authorities to consult, listen, review and monitor functions, policies and employment practices as well as assess their impact. Local authorities already do this under other processes such as Best Value. What the Act makes clear is the need to ensure race equality is at the heart of all planning and delivery of services.

See Commission for Racial Equality (CRE) *Statutory Code of Practice on the Duty to Promote Race Equality* and accompanying guidance for public authorities, for schools and on ethnic monitoring.

What is the role for central government?

While building community cohesion is primarily about proactive action at the local level, it is clear that central government has a role to play. An inter-ministerial group, chaired by Home Office Minister, Beverley Hughes, meets regularly to oversee and co-ordinate the government's role. This group is supported by a cross-government unit, the Community Cohesion Unit (CCU), based in the Home Office. This unit works with departments across Whitehall, and government offices for the regions in developing and implementing the government's strategy.

There are two strands to the government's approach, based on a commitment to making community cohesion a goal of all government policy. Firstly, working with government departments, to review national policy in ensuring that it promotes community cohesion at the local level.

This review of government policy is being assisted by the Community Cohesion Panel and its practitioner groups, comprising people independent of government, whose practical knowledge of specific policy areas and local issues is used to analyse policy and make proposals that are considered by the ministerial group.

Of specific importance is the Office of the Deputy Prime Minister's plan to publish its *Communities Plan* in 2003. This will aim to create thriving and sustainable communities in all regions, providing local people with opportunities to make local decisions about local needs. This will play an important part in helping to improve community cohesion, in providing high-quality affordable housing, a faster and fairer planning system, regenerating declining communities, tackling social exclusion and homelessness, designing and maintaining attractive, clean and safe towns, cities and public spaces and improved community leadership.

Community facilitation and conflict resolution work stream

As part of its response to the independent report on community cohesion, the government outlined a community facilitation programme led by the Neighbourhood Renewal Unit. This involves government, operating primarily through the regional government offices, working in close partnership with a number of local authorities and others to provide community facilitators. This will help local areas develop a longer-term strategic approach to capacity building and conflict resolution. The emphasis is on developing skills and knowledge and putting in place processes at local level so that communities themselves are better equipped to resolve conflict.

Youth activities

To date, government has provided funding in a number of specific areas to run a range of activities for young people aiming to reduce crime, meet their developmental needs and specifically help to develop cross-cultural activities as a means of breaking down barriers between young people of different groups. To build on the positive impact of these activities and to achieve greater synergy with other government funding programmes, a more streamlined process is being developed in time for summer 2003.

The second strand of the government's approach involves putting in place mechanisms to encourage and assist local authorities and other agencies. Key to this is getting community cohesion effectively recognised as an issue to be addressed and integrate it into mainstream processes and procedures. In achieving this, the government is mindful of working within the spirit of the Local Government Bill now before parliament and the shared priorities agreed between government and the LGA.

The key themes of this second strand include:

1 providing advice and guidance;
2 acting to disseminate good practice; and
3 encouraging and facilitating new learning through pathfinder programmes.

1 Providing advice and guidance
Government, primarily through the Community Cohesion Unit, has broadened its knowledge base of community cohesion issues and has been working with a wide range of local authorities. Its national perspective is being shared with partners through the organisation of, and participation in, national conferences, seminars and other events.

2 Acting as a source of and disseminator of good practice

The government's aim is to integrate thinking of community cohesion in all authorities and organisations at all levels of society. The intention is that community cohesion should be formalised into planning and delivery mechanisms, rather than requiring specialised or dedicated resources or structures.

This will involve central government having a clear understanding of what is actually taking place in local areas in order to transmit good practice across the country. The Community Cohesion Unit and the LGA have already collated a range of good practice examples covering a variety of community cohesion issues. These are hosted on both LGA's website and at www.communitycohesion.gov.uk, which will be added to on an ongoing basis.

Of specific note is the inclusion of community cohesion as a theme for the fourth round of the Beacon Council scheme with successful applicants to be announced in April 2003. These successful applicants will be engaged in a dissemination programme during 2003/04 – organised through and with the Office of the Deputy Prime Minister. Details of all community cohesion beacon councilswill be included on the Community Cohesion Unit's website with relevant links as appropriate.

3 Encouraging and facilitating new learning through the community cohesion pathfinder programme

A lot can be learnt from the effective dissemination of existing good practice. However, the changing nature of community cohesion is such that local authorities and other agencies could also benefit and learn from developing new processes and methods by which community cohesion can be integrated across planning and service delivery. To encourage and assist in this learning process government announced, in October 2002, a community cohesion pathfinder programme that will involve 15 local areas (with resources to be provided for the local authorities, the community and voluntary sector) over a two-year period. The programme aims to build real life examples of local areas that are getting community cohesion right – by developing approaches to integrating community cohesion into forward planning and long term sustainability. The key issue, from a local authority perspective, will be the mainstreaming of community cohesion – not treating it as an add-on activity that sits apart from core service delivery functions. Interim findings and final guidance on lessons learnt will be actively disseminated (to other authorities and agencies) both during and at the end of the programme. As part of a package of support that the Community Cohesion Unit and the Neighbourhood Renewal Unit will be offering to pathfinder areas, there will be access to face to face advice and support in developing and implementing their plans.

Ownership of the community cohesion agenda

Why is ownership important?

It is essential that the local approach to community cohesion is developed and owned by all local agencies and organisations. They should work in partnership, and integrate the issues within the community strategy and service planning systems in order to sustain progress and achieve the positive benefits. Local strategic partnerships (LSPs) are one means of developing community and neighbourhood renewal strategies. They are multi-layered structures that seek to facilitate joint working across and consultation with the public, private and voluntary sectors. (See *Local Strategic Partnership: Government Guidance, March 2001*).

In areas where LSPs do not exist, other strategic partnership bodies can fulfil the function of securing ownership.

Effective partnership working

- Ensure that all partners (public, voluntary, community and private) are involved and understand the agenda.
- Ensure the work dovetails with the impact on relations between government and the voluntary and community sector. Refer to the HM Treasury's cross-cutting review, *The Role of the Voluntary and Community Sector in Service Delivery*.
- Involvement of different sections of the community is essential. Real cohesion and real change will only happen if this occurs.
- Recognise, value and use the diversity of knowledge and skills available in the voluntary and community sectors.
- Be prepared to be flexible in order to respond and adapt to circumstances and issues as they arise.
- Make use of the joint CRE/ODPM guidance on partnerships under the Race Relations (Amendment) Act, to be issued in March 2003.

Community and political leadership

Why is this an important factor?

Local authorities' community leadership role, enshrined by the Local Government Act 2000, is fundamental to local government's role in building cohesive communities. It provides a legislative basis for local authorities to promote the social, economic and environmental well being of their areas. The LGA guidance document, *Community leadership: What is it? (March 2001)*, provides a range of good practice examples of the way in which different authorities have been exercising their community leadership role.

Community leadership was a central theme of the local government white paper, *Strong Local Leadership-Quality Public Services (December 2001)*. There is a real opportunity for local authorities, through effective local democracy and strong accountable political leadership, to consolidate their role as leaders of their local communities.

Community strategies: political leaders roles

Local authorities have a duty to develop a community strategy. This requires them to bring together local stakeholders to agree a 'vision' for the local area and an action plan to achieve it. *Preparing Community Strategies: Government Guidance to Local Authorities (ODPM December 2000)*, sets out how a community strategy should be developed via strategic partnerships and in consultation with the wider community. The guidance has been in place for two years and many authorities have made good use of it in developing their community strategies. It provides detailed guidance on partnership working, community involvement and the role of elected members. (Note numerous reports and toolkits on community strategies can be accessed from Improvement & Development Agency's (IDeA) knowledge at www.idea.gov.uk/knowledge).

The role of local councillors

Local councillors have a key role to play in building cohesive communities at ward level. Local forums that bring together different community interests can be convened by councillors as a mechanism not only to feed into the council's decision-making process but also to address conflicts or misunderstandings between different groups within a local community. Under new political management structures, non-executive council members may find they have more capacity in building links with broad cross sections of constituents.

Wards in rural areas may contain multiple small villages. In these cases councillors will need to work with local structures such as parish councils to promote community cohesion and tackling conflicts.

Community representatives

There are differing views when gauging the role of 'community leaders.' There is often a need to rely on the views of 'community representatives' when there is neither the time, nor the resource, for broader consultation. Local authorities should seek to work closely with community representatives who are themselves democratically elected, ie in parish and town councils, and with those who are less formally elected such as, residents' and community associations, neighbourhood watch groups and resident panels. This work should dovetail with an area's community strategy, which should also seek to develop the knowledge base and capacity of community representatives.

The independent review report and others, emphasised the importance of ensuring the active involvement of young people, who were not always most effectively represented by existing community leaders. This can be achieved in a number of ways, including involving UK youth parliament representatives, the local youth council or pupil parliaments. Engaging young people through youth projects or outreach projects is also important.

Care should be taken to make every effort to ensure that these representatives have the backing and support of the majority of any group that they may be seen to represent. There is the tendency to rely on the loudest voices or rely on the most vocal representative or organisation, particularly when consulting on major initiatives.

Parish and town councils are encouraged to consult widely and to ensure the breadth of views of all their residents are addressed. Rural areas have a long history of community planning through parish plans that generate wide participation as well as contributing to building local social capital. These also serve to promote mutual understanding of the widely differing needs and aspirations of residents. Parish plans are valuable vehicles for encouraging community cohesion.

Provide a clear lead

- Establish an unequivocal sign-up by all principal agencies, including themainstream political parties, based on an acceptance of the value of diversity and to ensure that there is a common 'zero tolerance' of racism and discrimination.
- Develop a communications strategy to communicate the community strategy on an ongoing basis across the entire community and to ensure that there is the widest possible support.
- Encourage and value the work of existing representative structures in undertaking effective local community planning activity.
- Get a commitment from each agency to carry out actions for their own services, which underpin the strategic objectives.
- Encourage all sections of the local community (majority and minority groups) to establish community leaders who are also committed to the strategic objectives and to ensure that they actually do listen to the views of their community, represent them fairly *and* collaborate with other communities. Involve young people particularly in this process. Build capacity amongst communities that are not often heard.
- Build cross-cultural networks and inter faith structures.
- Ensure that there is a leadership capacity to facilitate the level of change required and to bring in external support as required.
- Encourage all councillors to represent the needs of their electorate as a whole and not a narrow constituency.
- Elect a member champion to lead on community cohesion work. Appoint a senior officer (and possibly a small team) to work with him or her.
- Set up a programme of introductory talks or seminars about community cohesion.
- Involve key local agencies and networks from the voluntary, community, private and public sectors.

Vision and values

Why is this issue important?

Political leaders need to develop a vision of the type of place that their constituents want their locality to be and the work needed to make that vision a reality as part of its community strategy. People moving towards a commonly agreed goal are more likely to interact, understand and value differences positively. This approach builds cohesive communities and can also reduce anti-social behavior.

Developing a shared vision

A shared vision should be challenging, inspirational and inclusive, grounded in respect for our common humanity and recognition of our shared responsibility for the future of our society. It should stem from an open discussion involving the whole community and give local communities a clear sense of direction. Unity in diversity should be the theme – the message must be that cultural pluralism and integration are not incompatible. Values, principles and standards from a public authority's race equality, disability discrimination and gender equality schemes will also be relevant.

Through open discussion, each community should look to explore and discuss some of the following issues:

- developing a sense of ownership and pride in the local community;
- pride in the local physical environment;
- a desire to engage in relationships and partnerships with other local communities;
- working together to address common concerns;
- welcoming newcomers by offering support and induction that embraces the whole community;
- the need to combat discrimination on the basis of race, religion and belief, gender, sexual orientation, disability and age;
- a desire to promote cross-cultural interaction but to celebrate and value differences;

- asking what each community can do for others as well as what others can do for them; and
- tackling serious deprivation and disaffection in ways that do not alienate other parts of the community.

Exploration of these issues should be based on an open and honest dialogue and consultation involving all sections of, and organisations involved with, the community (public, voluntary, community and private). Special efforts should be made to involve young people, especially those who are not usually engaged in issues of this sort and feel disengaged from the life of their community.

Turning the vision into action

From this discussion, a work programme should be drawn up that outlines what needs to be done to make the shared vision a reality. This could include:

- the development of conflict resolution strategies;
- a programme of 'myth busting' to counter traditional stereotypes;
- an ongoing series of events and programmes to foster openness and cross-cultural contact; and
- developing festivals and celebrations that involve all communities.

The benefits of an agreed vision

The vision and strategic objectives agreed should be directed towards achieving the following outcomes:

- an improvement in community cohesion for the local area;
- a reduction in racial and inter-religious tension and conflict;
- a reduction in perceived or actual inequalities for all sections of the local community;
- creating value from the diversity of the local community;
- adding to the quality of life and sense of well-being; and
- greater participation and involvement in civic life from all sectors of the community.

Developing a vision: getting started

- Make connections with all local community and neighbourhood planning activity, including thoseinitiated by other organisations or programmes not led by the local authority.
- Consult widely among all communities (majority and minority) to encourage involvement and participation of different ethnic, gender, cultural, faith, disabled, young people and older peoples groups. Encourage these groups to explore together their mutual aspirations.
- Work with Trade Unions and the business community, encouraging them to also participate in building the vision.
- Ensure full involvement of all elected members and the local strategic partnership (LSP), where they exist, so that they own the work; making community cohesion a regular item at cabinet and all partnership meetings.

Making a statement of intent

- Make a public commitment, supported by all other agencies, to building good community relations and to tackling problems where they exist.
- Invite the leaders of all communities and faiths, both majority and minority, to launch the process and ask for their ideas and support. Involve them closely in the development of a work programme.
- Make it clear that the diversity in your area is valued and supported and that a modern multi-racial and multi-faith society, based on mutual respect, understanding and tolerance is the aim.
- Confront those that spread hate and division.
- Closely involve local press and media from the beginning of the process: they are key in shaping local opinion.

Building support

- Get people talking and facilitate an open and honest discussion.
- Set up a local website, develop questionnaires, host meetings, get schools involved, get out on to the estates, etc.
- Focus on values – respect cultural differences and foster those basic commonly-held civic values.
- Ask, don't tell – give people a chance to have their say.
- Set out the shared values for your area as the debate unfolds. These should include both rights and responsibilities.
- Ask the local press and media to help (see section on *press and media*).
- Use existing channels like the youth service, parish and town council networks and voluntary bodies.
- Use the LGA/Inter Faith Network for the UK/DTLR/HO report *Faith and community: a good practice guide for local authorities, (February 2002)*, on how to capture the resources of faith communities for promoting cohesion.

Local context, baseline assessment and monitoring progress

All local agencies, not just local authorities, need a detailed understanding of the nature of the communities they serve to assess how equipped they are in building community cohesion. An up-to-date assessment of the local context will enable improved delivery of services and monitoring of trends. Local authorities are encouraged to map and share information about such issues as ethnicity, age, culture and faith by area and by social and economic characteristics.

Developing baseline assessments

As part of this assessment, each local authority should consider how it performs against the various themes of community cohesion, which are covered through the rest of this guidance. In particular, local areas should ask themselves questions such as:

- Are we clear about the regeneration needs and aspirations of all sections of our community?
- Do we really listen to people who truly represent all sections of our community?
- Do youth activities help to build understanding and tolerance between different groups?
- Do we have effective mechanisms to listen to the views of young people? Do we respond to those views?
- Do school pupils develop a tolerance and respect for the different cultures that make up the UK?
- Do some groups achieve much lower levels of educational attainment than others?
- What impact does the housing situation have on community cohesion? Do people get real choices about where they live?
- Are particular sections of the community disadvantaged in the labour market? What can be done to address these differences?
- Is racist crime or other hate crime a feature of the local area? What measures are being taken to address it?
- Is there evidence of religious discrimination?
- Are local authorities, the police and other partners sensitive to the needs of different sections of the community?

The assessment should also seek to establish any particular characteristics of each group which might provide further information about their values and identity, for example, familial links in the local area, other parts of the country and within other countries; use of first and second languages; intra and inter cultural marriages; press and media usage, etc. This should not, of course, be limited to the minority communities and should compare and contrast the experience of all identifiable communities. The outcome should be a much clearer understanding of the nature of different communities – and how they relate to each other.

In spring 2003, the 2001 Census data will be published as a major source of data about local communities. The data will be available through the Office for National Statistics at below ward level.

Both the results from the 2001 Census, and the increase in data being made available at local areas through neighbourhood statistics, will provide invaluable local information for local people, local authorities, voluntary and community groups. These, and others should feed into processes measuring the impact of initiatives working to build community cohesion. In turn, this will help to identify the extent of residential segregation in local communities, where this is an issue, in order to feed into long term planning.

The perceptions and attitudes of different groups can be recorded through survey data and monitored over a period of time. The extent and nature of cross-cultural contact can also be plotted, again with a view to monitoring over time.

Evaluating community cohesion

Local authorities need to decide how they will measure improvements in community cohesion. Working with the Audit Commission, the CCU has captured the essential qualitative element of community cohesion in a survey question that has been included in Quality of Life indicators. The headline indicator of community cohesion is number 25 and the indicator is 'percentage of people surveyed who feel that their local area is a place where people from different backgrounds and communities can live together harmoniously'. While this can be regarded as a headline indicator, we emphasise the need to develop a basket of measures that can be used to monitor more effectively the starting point and progress over time. The government intends to produce a booklet providing detailed advice on how to measure community cohesion. Aimed primarily at LSPs it is envisaged that the booklet will be published in early 2003.

This booklet will outline how existing data, primarily performance indicators, which relate to a wide range of organisations could be collated and together with new survey data help to build a 'picture' of community cohesion for a local area. It would not be prescriptive but suggest themes, with 'indicative' performance indicators, to assist local authorities and their partners to own the community cohesion agenda, to understand more clearly the gaps, and to monitor progress.

Work out where you are, get the facts and measure

- Make sure that you understand all your communities – where they are, who they are, how old they are, and how they live their lives.
- Do a baseline assessment, asking yourself questions like 'what impact does the housing situation have on community cohesion?'
- Decide through consultation what issues need to be addressed and act on them.
- Identify and develop both qualitative and quantitative measures of community cohesion to help monitor progress.

The value of local strategic partnerships

The key tasks of local strategic partnerships are to:

- help the local authority with the preparation and implementation of the community strategy for the area;
- bring together local plans, partnerships and initiatives to provide a forum through which mainstream public service providers work effectively to meet local needs and priorities, and;
- work with local authorities who are developing local public service agreements to help devise and then meet suitable targets.

LSPs can also be key vehicles for developing composite strategies, including crime and disorder reduction strategies and health improvement and modernisation programmes. LSPs can assist in joining up local housing strategies by bringing together the housing authority with registered social landlords, social care providers and the private sector in developing local neighbourhood renewal strategies.

Police authorities are responsible for publishing policing strategies and plans that reflect the views of local communities about their priorities for policing, including the policing contribution to the community safety agenda. They are also responsible for ensuring an ongoing dialogue with all parts of the community. They are, therefore, the strategic body with which LSPs must work closely to ensure joining up of the policing and broader community cohesion agenda.

An inclusive LSP is very well placed to pull all of these various strategies together, and to look at how they are complementing each other in building cohesive communities or where they are pulling in different directions, perhaps contributing to breakdowns in community relations.

Guidance on community strategies provides advice on developing strategies, working with central government and local agencies. These include regional bodies, business, community and voluntary groups. It also offers advice on ensuring that the strategy is developed across the whole of the community to gain the widest possible sense of ownership.

There are a great many opportunities for these public bodies (local authorities, police authorities and forces, health trusts, government departments and agencies and education and learning provision including schools) to work together at both the political and technical level, sharing best practice and building consensus.

It is essential that each organisation also works closely with their own stakeholders and service users. This should again help to build a wider-community ownership of all aspects of community cohesion.

Community and voluntary organisations

Why is the role of the community and voluntary sector important?

The voluntary and community sector covers an enormous spectrum, with organisations being key partners working to build community cohesion. However, their skills are sometimes not fully utilised by the statutory agencies.

The Compact on relations between government and the voluntary and community sector in England (1998), provides a framework to build closer working between the sector and local and central government. It recognises the importance of voluntary and community organisations as active partners bringing experience and expertise to initiatives.

The subsequent cross-cutting review completed by HM Treasury in September 2002, provides further reinforcement of the value and the importance played by the sector in the reform of public services and invigoration of civic life. This review, now being implemented, will have far reaching consequences for service delivery in achieving its aim of providing more efficient services in a more caring and cohesive society.

What makes up the sector?

Voluntary and community organisations vary in size and capacity, from highly professionalised, national bodies to small, informal associations at neighbourhood level. National organisations have the capacity to act as a strategic resource. The National Council for Voluntary Organisations (NCVO) for example, is one of the sector's main umbrella organisations. Its activities include co-ordination of the sector's views for the purposes of consultation, as well as dissemination of information, advice and good practice. Other organisations have both a national and local infrastructure, such as the National Association of Councils for Voluntary Service and its network of local councils. Another example is Age Concern and the National Neighbourhood Watch Association. Both organisations have local and regional structures (with Neighbourhood Watch groups often formed down to street and ward level) supported by a national body. Local statutory agencies will often already have a working relationship with such umbrella organisations. This relationship may need only a relatively small amount of development to release its potential for contributing to community cohesion.

The regional voluntary sector networks and the related regional black and minority ethnic networks represent additional infrastructure. Though relatively new, these networks are a valuable route to engagement with the sector. Part of their purpose is to build the capacity of the sector for more effective involvement in society.

How can they help?

Smaller community organisations at the local level play an integral part in community development. One of their great strengths can be sensitivity to local issues and culture. Many such organisations live a precarious, hand-to-mouth existence because of scarcity of funding. Despite this they will often have accumulated extensive expertise and knowledge of their specific areas. In some cases an organisation working at the neighbourhood level can offer unrivalled insight into the perceptions of local people about their community. They are generally well placed, given the right support and encouragement, to foster cross-cultural links.

Engagement with these groups will support a 'bottom up' approach to building community cohesion. The Standing Conference for Community Development's *Strategic Framework*, published in 2001, offers a good starting point for local partnership building and engaging the sector at a strategic level.

Where a local 'Compact' exists, there is already a sound basis on which to engage the sector's resources for community cohesion. The process of establishing a local Compact will enable all partners to address community cohesion issues more effectively. The national Compact and its associated codes also contain material relevant at a local level.

Make best use of voluntary and community networks

- Adopt a 'Compact' between local authority and the voluntary and community sector and adapt the new framework to suit your relationship with the sector.
- Use the networks of statutory and voluntary agencies to develop cross-cultural contact at all levels.
- Review and influence the funding of voluntary and community organisations (including that of national and regional agencies) to provide incentives to promote community cohesion and cross-cultural contact and understanding.
- Recognise that voluntary and community organisations providing culturally or religiously sensitive services continue to have an important role to play in many communities.
- Develop joint training between the local authority and those involved in the sector, particularly those representing Hard to Reach Groups. Courses on the workings of government (local and central) and how they differ from the sector are useful.
- Reappraise your policy-making processes. Ensure it is flexible enough to allow for the more dynamic contribution the sector can bring – dispel myths of 'red tape' barriers.
- Allow enough time for meaningful consultation.
- Gather best practice examples and evaluate your own experiences, feeding back learning.
- Ensure you have the right people around the table and be open to contributions and suggestions.

Faith communities

Why is addressing faith issues important?

Faith can be a powerful factor in personal and community identity. The diversity of British society cannot be fully described if faith is left out of the picture. Policies for the promotion of diversity are incomplete if they fail to recognise that multi-cultural communities are also often multi-faith communities. Equality statements now routinely deal with the need to tackle discrimination on the grounds of religion or belief. The place of faith communities in the public life of communities has been increasingly understood and acknowledged in recent years.

At community level it is important to foster understanding and respect between different faith traditions as well as between different cultural and ethnic groups. All major faiths promote equality and respect for others as a fundamental value. In most cases, at a personal and community level, this translates into good community relations and integrity in public life. Such values can be a real resource in the practical implementation of community cohesion strategies.

The school curriculum (including the early education element) is important in establishing this understanding and respect from an early age. Opinions differ about the role and value of faith schools in developing positive images of others. But this does not detract from the basic commitment of even those who hold opposing views on this subject to the importance of education in resisting negative stereotypes of different identities.

Stereotypes based on religion can be stubborn and pernicious, as in the cases of anti-semitism and Islamophobia. Such attitudes must be addressed within cohesion strategies if people of all faiths are to feel an equal sense of belonging and enjoy equal security in society.

Faith communities often provide significant forms of association at the local level and can offer a wide range of services from their place of worship. This can be a particularly important method of delivering mainstream services in a culturally sensitive way. Or in more informal ways it can represent a valuable form of community self-help, through work with the young, older people, lunch clubs or drop-in and advice centres. Resources and support need to be given wherever possible to increase their involvement.

When a celebration can incorporate contributions from different local faith communities, as a public witness to their shared values, this can be a practical source of community pride and cohesion.

The development of effective local inter faith structures, bringing together representatives of different faith communities in a local authority area, can provide a valuable framework both for promoting mutual understanding and co-operation between them and as a mechanism for consultation by the local authority and other public bodies. Local authorities can provide valuable encouragement and support for the launching of initiatives of this kind in areas where they have yet to be established and also in helping to sustain existing local inter faith structures.

Working with faith communities

- Recognise faith communities in public life as a distinctive part of the voluntary and community sector and involve their representatives in partnerships.
- Support faith communities by promoting this role in relations with the local voluntary and community sector infrastructure.
- Explore local potential for a forum of faiths.
- Seek opportunities to support the public celebration of festivals.
- Challenge religious stereotypes, particularly in media reporting.
- Use available resources to establish good practice in working with faith communities:

  1. *The Local Inter Faith Guide, (1999),* The Inter Faith Network for the UK in association with the Inner Cities Religious Council
  2. *Faith and Community, (2002),* Local Government Association in association with Inner Cities Religious Council, Active Community Unit, Home Office, and the Inter Faith Network for the UK (available on the LGA's website at: www.lga.gov.uk/documents/publication/ faith.pdf)
  3. *Religions in the UK, Directory 2001–03, (2001),* The Multi-Faith Centre at the University of Derby and the Inter Faith Network for the UK
  4. *Shap calendar of religious festivals, (2002),* Shap Working Party on World Religions in Education
  5. Inner Cities Religious Council
  6. Local Government National Training Organisation's *Cultural Competence framework* (see www.lgnto.gov.uk/culture/index.htm)

- Seek advice from existing local and national organisations:

  1. Inter Faith Network for the UK, 5–7 Tavistock Place, London WC1H 9SN, Tel: 020 7388 0008, Fax: 020 7388 7124, e-mail: ifnet@interfaith.org.uk, Website: www.interfaith.org.uk
  2. Inner Cities Religious Council, Urban Policy Unit, Office of the Deputy Prime Minister, 4/J10 Eland House, Bressenden Place, London SW1E 5DU, Tel: 020 7944 3704, Fax: 020 7944 3729, e-mail: icrc@odpm.gov.uk, Webpages: www.urban.odpm.gov.uk/ community/faith/index.htm

- Promote use of local places of worship by schools and youth organisations as a resource in teaching the values of diversity.
- Establish and sustain a strong local inter faith structure for inter faith co-operation and mechanism for consultation with faith communities by the local authority and other local public bodies.

Young people

Why is engaging with children and young people important?

Children and young people are a core group that must be centrally involved in helping to build and sustain strong local cohesive communities. By all local partners and institutions involving children and young people locally and taking responsibility for doing so, the local community can benefit enormously in bringing segregated communities together.

Failure to recognise this has a detrimental impact on society in many ways: lack of involvement of children and young people now affects communities negatively in the present and future. The social capital to be gained by communities through involving young people fully is large. It supplements the benefits from avoiding negative impacts on communities (such as offending in drugs and crime) that may surface when children and young people are disenfranchised and excluded from processes.

The disengagement of young people from local democratic processes is clear to see from local election turnouts and the age profile of those involved in local politics.

Young people are our future leaders and involving them in the decision-making process can therefore be regarded as a long-term approach to capacity building and community development. The LGA's report *Representing the People: Democracy and Diversity (July 2001),* examined the reasons behind the lack of diversity in our council chambers, and made a series of recommendations for addressing this in the medium and longer term.

A sense of belonging is critical to children and young people taking ownership and responsibility for their community and their local area. Children and young people in modern Britain are more diverse than ever – they have a large variety of experiences and cultures. Young people living within close proximity can have very different experiences. The young are not a homogeneous group and a variety of activities and methods will be required to ensure they are able to contribute fully to the shared local vision. Different approaches may be required depending on age, disability, gender, ethnicity or geographical location. It is of paramount importance that work on shared values takes account of the diversity of young people's experiences and opinions. The Children and Young People's Unit (CYPU) *'Colour Blind'* video can help stimulate debate with young people on what it means to be British and our shared values (available from mailbox@cypu.gov.uk).

Children and young people need to be involved at a strategic as well as delivery level in public services, particularly those that directly affect them. In some cases this may require opportunities to build their capacity in order to involve them. Giving responsibility to children and young people needs appropriate management that caters for local needs, but is essential. The capacity for staff and institutions to connect with children and young people in relation to community cohesion should also be enhanced in staff training and in service planning. This will allow better and more appropriate interaction and engagement with children and young people.

Why are the youth service and Connexions important?

The role of the local youth service, voluntary and community sectors in provision of local facilities and activities, and the benefits to the local community, cannot be underestimated. The quality and quantity of youth service provision is an important component in building community cohesion.

Youth services should work in partnership with key local stakeholders – private and public. Innovative methods of involving private partners such as local football clubs or arts and culture bodies should be sought. In particular local voluntary and community organisations should be used where shared expertise can improve the delivery of youth provision.

This includes effective engagement with existing and developing Connexions partnerships, Children's Fund programmes and other initiatives underway to support young people. In this way, holistic and flexible approaches can be ensured.

Connexions is a crucial partner. By providing tailored support to young people, Connexions partnerships will help to ensure that young people receive the necessary advice and support to make a smooth transition to adulthood. For many young people, especially those who may become disaffected, Connexions will be an important source of support. Linking with Connexions partnerships – both to make sure that its work is fully responsive to community cohesion issues, and to take on the views of young people – is crucial.

Tools available to encourage engagement and better youth provision

Young people are key members of any community, however, there is evidence of widespread disengagement of young people. A variety of tools are available to help reverse this trend within local democratic processes. These include the LGA/National Youth Agency report, *Hear by right: setting standards for the active involvement of young people in democracy (July 2001),* which sets out key principles in engaging young people and highlights good practice examples. The report establishes standards for engaging young people, which the LGA encourages all member authorities to adopt.

The 'Hear by right' initiative is complemented centrally by the government's *Learning to Listen: Core Principles for the Involvement of Children and Young People, (November 2001),* in the planning, delivery and evaluation of government policies and services. These can be found on the CYPU website www.cypu.gov.uk

The Youth Service, in accordance with the government's Transforming Youth Work agenda, can provide the corporate lead for the engagement of young people across the community.

The Youth Justice Board, through schemes such as youth inclusion programmes, has been engaging young people – particularly those who are disaffected and disengaged – in various prevention and pre-court processes and activities. www.youth-justice-board.gov.uk

The *Transforming Youth Work* consultation document and the Com*mon Planning Framework (Sept 2001)* provides clear guidance on what youth services should do to promote community cohesion. Also the *Resourcing Excellent Youth Services Adequacy and Sufficiency Document (Dec 2002)* details what should be expected from a modern youth service. www.dfes.gov.uk

Youth workers have a crucial role to play in helping to build trust and respect across communities. Having sufficient youth provision is clearly essential. It also needs to be accessible and accessed by people from different backgrounds. Youth services should monitor the extent to which take up varies by socio-economic or ethnic group.

In some parts of the country, youth provision can become segregated – with local youth clubs staffed by a particular ethnic group servicing the needs of that particular ethnic group.

Assisted by the greater emphasis on detached youth work, there is a significant potential for youth workers to help break down such divisions – by tailoring provision so that it helps people from different backgrounds interact. The staffing of youth services is also of crucial importance – in particular, local authorities may need to put in place specific development programmes which identify, train and mentor youth workers from groups which are under-represented. For example, one local authority has been working with the local race equality council to recruit and develop youth workers by setting up a special programme, which brings together people from different ethnic groups for youth activities. This programme has helped to build community cohesion in the locality – whilst also training a new cohort of youth workers.

Give young people a chance

- Use the provision of statutory and voluntary agencies to develop cross-cultural contact at all levels.
- Ensure there is a cross-cutting/joined up approach to children and young people that recognises the benefits to other sectors – not just the youth services/Connexions and education.
- Engage with disaffected young people, using 'what works' programmes – for example, using peers and positive role models.
- Develop a 'youth voices' programme which young people recognise as their own and is designed to a national standard to facilitate the development of their input into political processes, ensuring that programmes are connected to actual political processes in a meaningful manner.
- Ensure that service design and delivery is truly responsive to the points raised by young people.

Youth services should:

- ensure integrated service provision that is flexible and holistic, to meet the needs of young people;
- develop youth provision which can achieve national or statutory standards (standards to be agreed between local authorities and other agencies);

- provide community cohesion training and support for staff involved in youth provision;
- ensure a diverse workforce is recruited and represented within youth services;
- ensure youth workers from a diverse range of backgrounds are employed in youth services to help build bridges between communities;
- train and use teams of workers from different backgrounds to deliver programmes, particularly in mono-cultural areas;
- provide opportunities for young people to engage and interact with other young people from different backgrounds;
- encourage initiatives that develop the leadership potential of children and young people that also work to empower them. Provide routes for them into mainstream decision-making processes and structures, and
- promote values of tolerance and respect between communities.

Asylum seekers, refugee and travelling communities

Why is this an important issue?

The dispersal of asylum seekers can result in rapid changes to the ethnic or cultural 'mix' of a geographic community. If communities are unprepared, they can feel threatened by new arrivals, giving rise to tensions that may lead to incidents of public disorder. Central government is taking practical steps to ensure that community cohesion concerns are taken into account when dispersing asylum seekers and refugees. However, local authorities have a vital role to play in working with asylum seekers and the wider community to help reduce tension.

Local authorities have a role in providing adequate services to new and existing communities. As well as providing services, local authorities and local agencies need to have a joined up strategy in place to 'prepare the ground' for the arrival of asylum seekers and refugees. Where communities are educated about the cultures and backgrounds of newly arrived asylum seekers or refugees they tend to be more understanding and accepting of differences and better able to empathise with the plight of their new neighbours. The process of raising awareness of incoming communities can and should involve local schools, youth clubs and community centres. Local press and media can also be an important means of communicating the experiences of new arrivals and explaining their circumstances.

Local authorities, working with local partners, also have an important role to play in seeking to facilitate the integration of newly arrived communities. Again, this may best be achieved through information sharing – by publicising the community and leisure activities that can be accessed locally. Many new arrivals may have particular skills that may be of benefit to the local community if put to use in voluntary work, for example. There are problems with encouraging asylum seekers to volunteer. Police checks will often be difficult for those who want to work with children. Voluntary organisations' insurance policies may often not cover those with a poor grasp of the English language. But the benefits are great. Volunteering can help develop social skills and self-esteem. Such initiatives can be helpful not only as a means of helping asylum seekers and refugees feel at home in unfamiliar communities but also as a means of demonstrating to the 'host' community the benefits that new arrivals can bring.

The benefits of this approach

These initiatives will help to achieve the following outcomes:

- a reduction in tension on the ground in dispersal areas;
- an increase in the contribution to the community from asylum seekers;
- a sense of well-being for asylum seekers in their new communities; and
- local communities feeling informed and involved in the settlement process.

The first national strategy for the integration of refugees, Full and Equal Citizens, was published in November 2000. The strategy seeks to identify what constitutes good practice in integration, building where possible on examples, which already exist in many areas of the country and elsewhere.

How you can help

- Locate and communicate with local voluntary organisations and refugee self-help organisations in identifying the needs of asylum seekers that could be catered for by local authorities.
- Work with local police to ensure that systems are in place to monitor community tension.
- Appoint local personnel with the appropriate skills to mediate in cases of conflict.
- Get the local police force to explain their role to asylum seekers as soon as possible after their arrival.
- Produce leaflets explaining the backgrounds and cultures of asylum seekers that can be placed in public areas such as libraries, GP surgeries and churches. The leaflets could include a 'mythbusting' section.
- Include a section on the local authority website offering information about the local area to asylum seekers and information on the cultures and backgrounds of asylum seekers.

- Engage the local population in the induction process; such as organising sports competitions that encourage integrated teams of asylum seekers and local residents, or encouraging asylum seekers to talk of their experiences at community meetings.
- Allocate clear responsibility for promoting positive coverage of asylum seekers and refugees in the local media.
- Draw up a programme of awareness raising in schools, residents associations, libraries and other such organisations.
- Introduce a programme of volunteering for asylum seekers, matching their skills to those shortages in the local areas, where possible. Produce leaflets for asylum seekers, outlining the benefits of volunteering, and the local organisations that can help them obtain a volunteering post.
- Communicate with local self-help organisations and other local authorities in recognising and building on examples of good practice.

Travellers

Travelling communities – both settled and nomadic – are often isolated from non-travelling communities and may be viewed with suspicion by areas where they choose to set up sites. Local authorities can play a key role in partnership with other agencies to facilitate communication and interaction between settled and travelling communities. Schools, youth clubs and community centres might invite travellers' representatives to talk to pupils about their background, experiences and ways of life. Authorities should also seek to ensure that travellers are appropriately advised and informed as to involvement in local community life.

Central government is reviewing its current policies on gypsy and traveller site management, which will include the publication of a good practice guidance for local authorities, police services and both the settled and traveller communities. Government strategies already in place include the extension of the 2003/04 round of the Gypsy Sites Refurbishment Grant, which currently upgrades the existing network of 234 local authority authorised sites. This round will now include funding for new temporary and emergency stopping places.

Regeneration

Why is addressing regeneration and neighbourhood renewal issues important?

Historically, the competitive nature of some regeneration funding has been a focus for inter-community and inter-neighbourhood tension. Some regeneration schemes had the effect of pitting neighbourhoods against each other in competing for resources. They relied on one-off regeneration expenditure, which made it difficult for local authorities and other local agencies to develop and deliver a long-term comprehensive approach to addressing poverty and deprivation within their locality. Furthermore, in many cases regeneration funding failed to meet the needs of ethnic minority populations and ethnic minority groups were significantly under-represented amongst those running regeneration projects.

These factors have generated resentment and suspicion across communities in some areas – a feeling that 'other' areas were being favoured in the allocation of resources. This seems to be exacerbated in parts of the country where ethnic minority communities live in different areas to white communities. These affect perceptions that one community is being favoured by the local authority and others who provide central funding. People in these areas do not understand why they too do not receive similar levels of funding. The reports from the local and regional roundtable meetings, convened by LGA member authorities in October and November 2001, highlighted some of these problems.

Recognition of other partners and agencies involved in regeneration activity also needs to be made. It is recognised that decisions on allocating regeneration funding do not solely rest with local authorities and local residents. Regional and sub regional partnerships also have a role. For example in London economic development, skills and training (including post 16 and adult learning) and business competitiveness issues are split between the London Development Agency, Learning and Skills Council and Business Link for London. Their priorities are set regionally and sub regionally. In order to ensure community cohesion issues are adequately reflected, more input from local communities is encouraged.

Local authorities are encouraged to establish liaison and partnership arrangements with neighbouring boroughs and together appraise new ways to build and further enhance cohesion within their communities.

A suggested approach

The National Strategy for Neighbourhood Renewal is designed to address many of these issues. Resources will always need to be targeted at those areas and communities suffering the worst deprivation but the new approach puts the onus on local agencies, though the local strategic partnership, to prioritise and target expenditure. The Neighbourhood Renewal Fund provides unhypothecated additional funding to the most deprived local authorities to help start delivering real improvements on the ground. Further work is planned through the regeneration practitioner group established by the independent Community Cohesion Panel.

The process of defining need is confusing and can lead to perceptions of unfairness if not handled appropriately. Local authorities need to ensure that the process is open and transparent. Communicating the defining process should involve not only the target community but also those in the neighbouring areas.

Use the voluntary and community representative on the LSP as part of your communication strategy and ensure that positive aspects of the regeneration programme are highlighted to the local media.

In areas where relations between communities are already under strain, however, delivering these new programmes and dealing with the wind down of old regeneration programmes will be an exceptionally challenging task. Local strategic partnerships, where they are established, need to consider how:

- conflict and suspicion between communities in their area can be addressed to enable everyone to participate effectively in the renewal of their neighbourhoods;
- to involve local communities in the development and decision-making of Local Neighbourhood Renewal Strategies so that the reasons behind priorities are understood;
- to ensure that their understanding of the conditions in local neighbourhoods is kept up to date to reflect changing needs and to take account of the new data from Census 2001;
- they promote their approach to regeneration so that perceptions of unfairness are countered;
- they can ensure that the lessons and benefits of more targeted regeneration programmes are spread and shared amongst other parts of the community; and
- segregated communities are encouraged to work together on projects of mutual benefit.

Regeneration in rural areas

Building community cohesion is equally important within suburban and rural areas. Incidents have occurred in less populated areas that could have escalated. In some local authorities the issue of balancing the needs and interests of urban and rural areas within their own boundaries will be an important one. The more mixed the community in socio-economic terms, the wider the diversity of individual aspirations for the very local neighbourhood. The conflicting pressures that this can bring needs resolution in agreeing a shared vision for the community and building cohesion within it.

Provide a fair deal

- Ensure all authorities, at district, county, unitary and regional level are involved.
- Identify the most disadvantaged and disaffected sections of the community and devise programmes that tackle their needs.
- Develop programmes that promote community cohesion as an end in itself, through cross cultural contact, understanding and respect for diversity.
- Work to develop a long-term agreement between all local agencies and funding partners in central and regional bodies, which establishes priorities for all sections of the community that is transparent and equitable.
- Develop and deliver a local neighbourhood renewal strategy to secure more jobs, better education, improved health, reduced crime, and better housing, narrowing the gap between deprived neighbourhoods and others and contributing to national targets to tackle deprivation.
- Develop clear links with regional and sub regional partnerships in planning regeneration programmes and in jointly working to build and enhance cohesion.
- Ensure that each partnership has representation from the community it serves – both majority and minority communities and, moreover, a full understanding of the dynamics of community cohesion and a programme to promote it.

- Promote greater transparency and understanding of investment priorities, in the context of a long-term strategy.
- Develop a communications strategy to counter false perceptions about resource distribution.
- Ensure that the local strategic partnership's local action on learning plan, which will support delivery of the outcomes of the local neighbourhood renewal strategy, includes the learning needed by all sections of the community to participate fully in the regeneration of their neighbourhood.

Sports and cultural services

Why are sports and cultural services important?

Art, sport and leisure services can be a powerful tool to engage all sections of the community and to break down barriers that exist between them. People take part in leisure and cultural activities through choice and marginalised groups are often more willing to engage with such activities than other locally/nationally government funded activities.

It can provide personal and community development through different avenues and the personal space to express and share experiences. The sector is also one of the fastest growing areas of the economy and therefore provides job opportunities.

Sport and cultural activities also provide an opportunity for 'joined up working' with other public and voluntary agencies seeking to address social issues, which contribute to community cohesion. For example, the sector can be used as a means of tackling crime and anti-social behaviour, encouraging investment and as an avenue to lead people into formal training, education and employment. Arts, sport, libraries, museums, parks and tourism can all impact on social issues.

How to address the issue

The Department for Culture, Media and Sports has published guidance on *Local Cultural Strategies (December 2000),* in partnership with the Local Government Association, the Chief Cultural and Leisure Officers' Association and a steering group of professional associations and non-government agencies. The cultural strategy should link other area strategies and make a key contribution to the overarching community strategy.

However, as a discretionary service the potential of sport and cultural activities to address community cohesion will only be sustainable and maximised if:

- a clear strategy is established which reflects the needs of all sections of the local community; and
- this strategy is reflected within the overall corporate strategy for the local authority.

Integrating the role of these services with the community strategy and Compacts with the voluntary and community sector will help to maximise and sustain the valued inputs cultural and leisure services can bring to building a cohesive community.

The power of sport and culture to break down barriers

- Undertake user surveys to gauge the range of services accessed and identify gaps in provision.
- Ensure incentives for cross community sport and cultural activities, eg by use of an appropriate funding and inspection regime.
- Establish what barriers there are to accessing facilities and activities for particular groups. These could be proximity related, cost related, perception related or related to times that facilities are open/activities take place. And then identify actions that can be taken.
- Involve all sections of the community in planning, delivering and evaluating. Consider how this can be done in innovative ways, eg using video or theatre.
- Develop realistic targets for sport and cultural activities.
- Empower and encourage schools to open up schools as a resource.
- Introduce safeguards to ensure that PFI arrangements do not adversely impact on the ability of a school to be a community school.
- Organise inter-school sports and cultural events.
- Organise cultural events to promote inter-cultural and inter-faith understanding and respect.
- Mainstreaming summer activities for children and young people into all year round activities, eg by providing supported entry and exit routes.
- Consider thematic approaches to problems such as drug use, literacy and communication skills using leisure and cultural activities to engage people from across communities/ethnic groups rather than area-based initiatives.
- Ensure an effective information/communications plan is in place so that all sections of the community know what is available.

Education

Why are education issues important?

One of the most frequently made observations in assessing polarised or fragmented communities is the need for communities to develop common values and a common identity. Education is often cited as the best way to introduce positive values, because the opinions formed by young people will often be those they carry with them into adulthood. Education, including pre-school activities, should bring with it enlightenment, knowledge, tolerance, understanding and appreciation of others. All forms of education provision – including schools and pre-school activities – have a vital role to play in promoting community cohesion. Schools, and educational institutions generally, are well placed to tackle social exclusion and make communities more cohesive. By raising attainment levels, and promoting the participation in education and training of all those who under achieve, educational institutions can improve opportunities for finding employment and therefore enhancing people's life chances.

Initiatives underway to assist local authorities

The government has taken a number of steps to close the achievement gap between pupils of different ethnic origins by introducing key policies such as:

- The Race Relations (Amendment) Act 2000 which, from May 2002, placed a duty on schools to promote race equality, to have in place a written race equality policy, to introduce measures to assess the impact of their policies and to monitor the impact on pupils, staff and parents;
- The *Pupil Level Annual Schools Census* published in January 2003 will contain greatly improved data on pupil ethnic background. This data can be matched against achievement and socio-economic data. This will enable the tracking of individuals' progress so that value added data can be obtained;
- The teaching of citizenship in all primary schools and as a statutory subject in secondary schools. Citizenship education within the National

Curriculum will develop and encourage pupils' understanding and mutual respect of each other's differences; and

• The Learning and Skills Council has a statutory duty to promote race equality and diversity within post-16 education.

The education white paper 2001 set out the government's wish to welcome more faith schools, ie schools with a religious character, into the maintained sector where there is clear local agreement. There are currently 7,000 existing maintained schools with a religious character such as Church of England, Roman Catholic and, in smaller numbers, Muslim and other religious schools. However, as the Cantle report pointed out, a more significant issue is that of mono-cultural schools, which include many non-faith schools.

The impact of schools on the wider community

Schools also often reflect the segregation within housing and the wider community and, therefore, cross agency work between housing and education should be promoted. Many local Learning Partnerships are well placed to co-ordinate cross agency work in support of lifelong learning and community cohesion.

As the Cantle report also highlights, the use of inter-school activities, particularly in areas of segregated schooling, can go a long way to help raise awareness of other people's cultures, break down barriers and promote shared values. Schools contain the leaders of the future, and have a huge potential to demonstrate the benefits of community cohesion and bring together groups within the community. Citizenship education as introduced in both primary and secondary schools will encourage all pupils to respect and understand all forms of diversity and help them to develop skills and confidence to combat all forms of prejudice in becoming responsible citizens.

Using education to promote community cohesion

- Ensure that all schools, colleges and other educational providers take action to develop and promote understanding and respect for the diverse range of cultures and faiths within the local area and in the UK as a whole.
- Ensure they take effective measures to address racial harassment and bullying. Anti-bullying guidance for schools already gives advice on the tracking and prevention of racist bullying. It is currently being updated in light of the Race Relations (Amendment) Act.
- Ensure that all formal education utilises a curriculum that recognises the contribution of the diverse cultures and faiths to the development of the UK.
- Ensure that local syllabuses on religious education promote awareness of the importance of good inter faith relationships and, in this respect, make a contribution to citizenship education.
- Ensure that schools for which the LEA is the admission authority attract an intake that reflects their community. Encourage other schools and education providers to do so.
- Ensure schools promote cross-cultural contact within their own parental network.
- Ensure that the disparities in educational attainment are being addressed (in terms of teaching and by use of role modelling and mentoring programmes).
- Obtain 'value added' data on the educational attainment levels of the various groups (and by gender) in the community.
- Encourage all schools to develop school twinning and exchanges, to include teaching and learning projects, with schools with different intakes to promote cross cultural contact, respect and understanding.
- Further encourage schools to develop curriculum and extra-curriculum cross cultural programmes and activities, eg for arts and sport, parental schemes, travel to school arrangements and seating plans.
- Actively involve parents from different communities in pre school activities and out of school childcare. Existing programmes such as Sure Start have made a significant contribution to promoting community cohesion through a range of childcare and early education increasingly alongside family and health services.

- Ensure every effort is made to reach out to parents, whose help is needed in creating tolerant home environments and supporting the values taught in schools.
- Review supplementary education programmes to focus on basic education and cross-cultural contact.
- Assist the review of further education and higher education provision at a local level to ensure that it provides equal opportunities.
- Consider setting up extended schools, which provide additional facilities from the school site, to help engage local communities. (See DfES guidance on extended schools, October 2002).
- Use Adult and Community Learning to encourage greater awareness, understanding and participation amongst 'mature' learners.

Housing and planning

Why are housing and planning issues important?

It is generally accepted that people should, wherever possible, be able to exercise meaningful choice over housing options, including the area in which they live. Choice may contribute to the concentration of people from one ethnic background in particular localities. This is not in itself a problem, and there are many examples of successful communities in the UK and overseas that have high concentrations of residents from one ethnic background. There is clear evidence, however, that concentrations of people from one ethnic background in certain areas of housing, and their separation from other groups living in adjacent areas has contributed significantly to inter-community tensions and conflict. Further evidence shows that in some towns, Asian communities are concentrated in poor quality private rented housing and impoverished members of the white community on social housing estates. In other towns Bangladeshi households are less likely to be owner occupiers than Indian or Pakistani households, and black Caribbean households are significantly over-represented in social housing. The role of local authority housing departments, housing associations (also known as RSLs) and private sector housing is crucial in reversing these trends and building cohesive communities.

The effects of segregation

The lack of interaction, as a result of segregation, may lead to fear and mistrust. This can be passed on through generations as segregated housing leads to segregated schooling and leisure activities. Resentment can build up as area-based regeneration programmes are perceived to have unfairly favoured other groups. Equal opportunities in employment and education may be limited by the physical distance of some groups from these opportunities. The more entrenched the segregation, the harder it is to break out of it and ensure true equality of opportunity for all groups. Housing, therefore, has an important role to play alongside other factors such as low incomes, poor health, lack of education and employment opportunities and options and limited skills.

The impact of housing policies

The causes of housing segregation are extremely complex. Historical, cultural preferences, nearness to sources of work and cultural facilities, willingness and ability to travel, lack of experience in accessing social housing or fear of harassment are all factors. It is not straightforward to assess whether segregation is 'voluntary' or 'enforced'. Neither is it straightforward to reverse. Unless there is a comprehensive understanding of the reasons for segregation, and the aspirations of different groups, attempts to reverse segregation are likely to fail.

It is critical that policies are informed by sound information on the issues facing each group in the locality. As part of this, any barriers (perceived or otherwise) by black and minority ethnic (BME) groups in terms of their access to different housing tenures need to be clearly understood. Choice-based lettings approaches can be used to help break down barriers that exist for some BME groups in relation to certain tenures, eg social housing.

How local authorities and housing associations can play a part

Not all of the causes of segregation are within the control of the local authority but there is still much they can do. Local authority housing departments must ask whether their current policies have helped to build integrated and mixed communities, or whether they have exacerbated social, racial and faith divisions within them. Where policies are found to have failed in this respect, action must be taken. *A Framework for Partnership* produced by LGA/National Housing Federation/Housing Corporation, suggests that local authorities and housing associations can work together on research and service delivery that helps them understand housing need and supply in their area in addition to sharing knowledge on community participation.

The need for further advice and guidance has been identified by the Housing Practitioner Group established by the Community Cohesion Panel and the Community Cohesion Unit.

Long term strategic approaches through housing investment

The financing of housing programmes is still largely tenure driven and interaction between this and segregation based on tenure needs to be addressed at national, regional and local level. Some communities have been perceived as 'winning' or 'losing' over the years according to the pattern of investment in different tenures. In the 1970s, for example, urban based renewal programmes were perceived as benefiting private rented households in inner city areas.

The 2000 housing green paper sought to tackle years of under-investment in council housing by pledging to bring all social housing to a decent standard by 2010.

The Spending Review 2002 announced that this target would be extended to cover private housing occupied by 'vulnerable households'. An ambitious target for improving the quality of rundown private sector homes occupied by low income families could help address some of the underlying causes of the disturbances in 2001 and address the imbalance caused by the previous focus on investment in social housing.

The government's intention to take forward nine sub-regional, low demand pathfinder projects to tackle those areas in the North and Midlands most acutely affected by low demand and abandonment has been welcomed. The key to the project's success lies in stakeholders working together to a unified and comprehensive agenda – one that will deliver housing market renewal and alongside that the economic and social regeneration of the areas. As part of this, the pathfinder projects will play an important role in helping to improve community cohesion in these areas.

The importance of spatial planning

The green paper *Planning: delivering a fundamental change* and the deputy prime minister's 18th July Statement *Sustainable Communities: Delivering through planning*, put forward an agenda for the reform of the planning system. The ODPM's concept of how land-use planning must operate in the future is labelled 'spatial planning'.

The reforms put forward in the green paper and the 18th July Statement propose the abolition of county structure plans and unitary development plans and their replacement with regional spatial strategies (RSS) and local development frameworks (LDF) the characteristic of these new generation of development plans is that they are spatial development strategies, as oppose to strictly land-use plans.

The ODPM perceives planning as a strategic broad ranging activity, taking a spatial (geographical), evidence based approach when formulating development plans and planning policies. Planning policy in the future will be rooted in 'a sense of place', the villages, towns, suburbs and neighbourhoods in which individuals, families and communities identify with. The RSSs and LDFs will provide the land-use element informing other partners' and stakeholders' strategies. The reformed planning system will be able to build upon its tradition of working in partnership with stakeholders to provide its partners with a positive tool to inform the delivery of environmental, regeneration and social policy objectives in any given geographical area.

The production of LDFs and the assessment of major development applications will be informed by the creation of the statements of community involvement regime. Effective community involvement in the preparation and review of development plans is crucial for achieving legitimacy for, and local ownership of, those plans that are critical to the determination of planning applications under the plan-led system.

A major aim of the planning reform agenda is to see local development planning founded in the aspirations of the community and to bring community participation higher up the agenda for local planning authorities.

Review housing policy

- Ensure that housing agencies, including housing associations, jointly review existing and proposed housing provision, to consider its impact upon cross cultural contact and community cohesion. Such reviews need to be informed by sound information on the make-up of the local community and issues and barriers they face.
- Review, with other services such as health, leisure and education, the impact of housing policies on access to those services. Ensure the requirements of 'supporting people' address community cohesion in providing appropriate support to marginalised, vulnerable and disengaged people within communities.
- Consult different communities about their housing preferences, and what they consider are the barriers to achieving them. Work to overcome the barriers.
- Encourage and facilitate inter-community contact, ensuring that methods of engagement are wide enough to reach all communities. In particular, identify the needs of under-represented groups and young people particularly in relation to housing.
- Work with private landlords, developers and estate agents, to challenge potentially discriminatory practices in lettings and property sales. They can also help through their procurement role, in developing new and positive approaches to the promotion of community cohesion and equal opportunities.

- Make sure that housing authorities improve awareness of, and access to, social housing for groups which are currently under-represented in social housing. Choice-based lettings approaches can be used to good effect here. Make use of the report *Breaking Down the Barriers,* Chartered Institute of Housing (CIH), to open up access to housing, particularly objectives 1 to 4 of the report's action plan.
- Ensure that housing authorities provide accessible advice and information appropriate to the needs of different communities in the locality. There needs to be appropriate advice and assistance to help people apply for social housing. Housing authorities should evaluate, in liaison with different groups in the locality, the effectiveness of current advice.
- Build race equality and community cohesion issues into local authorities' consideration of the transfer of ownership or management responsibility of their stock to, for example, arms length management organisations. Consider housing strategies in relation to the *Race Equality Code of Practice for Housing Associations* which arose from the Race and Housing Inquiry Challenge Report. Resources should be made available not just for the physical aspects of housing improvement, but also for regenerating the wider environment and the community that lives within it – see CIH's report *Beyond Bricks and Mortar: Bringing Regeneration into Stock Transfer.*
- Implement existing good practice guidance on race and housing, equalities and diversity issues:

Addressing the needs of Black and Minority Ethnic People: a DTLR (Housing Directorate) Action Plan (2001)
Joint DTLR/Housing Corporation *Code of Practice for Social Landlords on Tackling Racial Harassment,* DTLR 2001
Black and Minority Ethnic Housing Strategies – A Good Practice Guide by Blackaby and Chahal (CIH, FBHO, Housing Corporation, 2000)
Tackling Racial Harassment:
ODPM/CRE/HO/ HC National Assembly for Wales 2001
Race Equality Toolkit – De Montfort University – H.C 2002
www.raceactionnet.co.uk

Review housing management

- Establish reappraisal systems to monitor allocations policies.
- Ensure formal and informal mechanisms for resident involvement are proportionate, representative and focused. Regular review of engagement structures need to be in place and linked to other service provision.
- Work with bodies such as the Housing Corporation and National Federation of Housing Associations in implementing race and diversity action plans and sharing good practice.
- Make available translated materials or provide access to community language speakers.
- Act promptly to address anti social behaviour (ASB) but ensure preventative approaches are in place to minimise the need for expensive or protracted legal procedures. Maximise the range of approaches to tackling ASB – ranging from mediation and Acceptable Behaviour contracts to injunctions and possession orders.
- Establish support from statutory agencies (for example police/social services) and local community groups for new households (such as asylum seekers, refugees, travellers or emerging communities) moving onto estates, particularly where those families may be at risk of hostile receptions. Ensure a planned and co-ordinated approach linked to clear and unambiguous media messages.
- Aim to ensure that when under-represented groups are exposed to social housing it is as positive an experience as possible (eg review procedures for viewing empty properties).

Review planning procedures

- Reform the planning system to enable local authorities to be more directive in specifying the mix of property types, sizes and tenure required for particular sites.
- Ensure community cohesion is recognised as a legitimate objective for planning authorities within the planning guidance so that new development encourages greater mixing of ethnic groups, incomes and family types.

Employment and economy

Why are these issues important?

The issue of employment is broad ranging, and affects every member of every community. Discrepancies in opportunity can affect people from a wide range of groups. We must consider age, gender, ethnicity, disability and locality as issues. All these factors, and any others that are relevant, should be tackled to ensure holistic solutions are developed and sustained.

Poor employment opportunities have an adverse impact in many areas in building cohesion. In particular, wide variation in the unemployment level within relatively small areas can breed significant resentment between communities.

One aspect of this is the research conducted recently by the Performance and Innovation Unit in the Cabinet Office into ethnic minorities and the labour market, *Ethnic Minorities and the Labour Market – the Interim Analytical Response, (Feb 2002)*. This presents evidence that, despite a generally improving trend for specific ethnic minority groups, there remain significant differentials between black and minority ethnic groups and their white counterparts in terms of unemployment, earnings levels and access to promotion.

We also know that some sections of the white community are also severely disadvantaged. In particular, there are indications that some employers may operate 'postcode discrimination'.

How to address these issues

Suitable and affordable childcare provision for all age groups can play a crucial role in maximising employment opportunities for parents. This is also important when parents are training, or retraining, and studying for employment.

Local authorities should work with public and private employers and other agencies to address poor employment opportunities through the appropriate framework for regional employment and skills action. Local authorities also need to work with local higher education institutions, further education and other forms of post-16 learning provision to address training in direct relation to employment. They should also continue with and expand on their work with regional development agencies, business representative groups, large private sector firms and other agencies with an interest in economic regeneration. In partnership they can encourage the growth of local economic clusters, which can benefit all local businesses, through for example, supply chain development.

Local authorities could also consider how the growth of corporate social responsibility can be harnessed to the greater benefit of the whole community.

Integrating workforce skills building and addressing skills mismatching (as experienced in areas of old and declining industries to be replaced by more technological industries) should be addressed through reservation programmes, work of Business Links and Learning and Skills Councils.

Bridging the employment gap

- Review employment opportunities for all sections of the community, to establish the barriers to equal opportunities and to develop a programme of remediation (delivered on a cross cultural basis).
- Take action to raise the expectations and, where possible, facilitate the progression of under achieving groups, through for example participation in the Entry to Employment programme currently being introduced; and challenging of views about stereotypical occupations.
- Encourage programmes that ensure equal access to all public sector agencies and subsequent advancement.
- Develop compacts with all local employers to develop equal access to the full range of employment opportunities.
- Develop special assistance in areas of greatest disadvantage, through regional and national aid programmes, to tackle the problems of de-population and low demand housing.
- Ensure proper and effective representation from the business sector on the LSP.
- Monitor recruitment, uptake and retention of work-based learning routes for evidence of unrepresentative recruitment (eg numbers of young people in work with training – such as Modern Apprenticeship – and those without training, by ethnic origin).

Local government as an employer and as a purchaser of services

Authorities should consider their own role as major employers especially under their specific duty on employment made as a result of the Race Relations (Amendment) Act 2000. In particular, it is important that the workforce of local authorities is seen to be representative of those who live in the local areas. Unfortunately, in many areas that have populations that are ethnically diverse, the local authority workforce is much less diverse, particularly at senior levels. Addressing this is a key issue – if the authority is to maintain credibility, then it will need to develop a strategy to address this and to meet the requirements in forthcoming UK legislation to give effect to the European Directive on discrimination in the employment field.

Local authorities now purchase a significant volume of services from the private and voluntary sector. Proactive use of the new powers to take workforce matters into account in contracting could contribute to the development of, and improvement in, jobs by contractors. There are some legal constraints arising from European public procurement rules, but there is more scope than most authorities are aware of and use.

In relation to the Race Relations (Amendment) Act and the public duty, the CRE will be publishing a guide to Race Equality and Procurement in March 2003.

Set an example as an employer

- Public authorities need to ensure they are compliant with the specific duty on employment introduced by the Race Relations (Amendment) Act 2000.
- Conduct detailed ethnic monitoring to establish the composition of your workforce.
- Develop an action plan, where the workforce is unrepresentative, for addressing the issues including targets for representation from different sections of the community and by gender, utilising positive action schemes where possible.
- Consider mentoring programmes for ethnic minority staff, outreach into local communities, participation in schemes such as Common Purpose using head-hunters and secondments for senior vacancies.

Community safety and policing

The role of crime and disorder reduction partnerships

The Crime and Disorder Act 1998 establishes local crime and disorder reduction partnerships (CDRPs) led by local authorities and police. They are required to conduct a full audit of crime and disorder issues in their areas and then develop and implement a strategy for dealing with the main problems identified. CDRPs are required to consult with a wide range of local public, private, voluntary and community groups to formulate and implement their crime and disorder strategies.

The measures in the Police Reform Act 2002 reflect the increasing contribution that crime and disorder and its impact has on the health, well-being and economic welfare of neighbourhoods. The 1998 Act and the amendments made by the Police Reform Act recognise that tackling crime and disorder is not a matter for the police alone but should engage the community. Working in partnership means adopting a cross-cutting approach which not only identifies more effective interventions to tackle crime and disorder, but also delivering solutions which help create safer neighbourhoods which contribute to healthier, more productive communities.

The need to build trust and confidence

Gaining the trust and confidence of all sections of the community through the elimination of discriminatory practices and the development of appropriate policing methods remains crucial to the delivery of effective policing.

The Stephen Lawrence Inquiry report highlighted the importance of the use of stop and search powers in the context of policing and community relations. A draft PACE Code A contains new provisions. These aim to significantly increase both the confidence of the public and officers using the powers. These include:

- a new obligation on forces to involve police authorities in the monitoring and supervision of stop and search records by communities;
- an officer who has carried out a search must now give a copy of the record made immediately to the person searched; and
- the Code gives a clearer definition of what constitutes 'reasonable grounds for suspicion' in the exercise of stop and search powers.

The Lawrence Steering Group has agreed a work programme to look at five key issues that were central to the Lawrence Inquiry Report. These are: racist incidents; stop and search; recruitment, retention, and progression of minority ethnic officers; community and race relations training; and trust and confidence of minority ethnic communities in the wider Criminal Justice System. In particular, the work will assess the current situation, evaluating the impact of the relevant recommendations and making proposals for the future. Monitoring progress in these areas will figure in the work of Her Majesty's Inspectorate of Constabulary and the Police Standards Unit.

Ongoing work at central, force and basic command unit level

The Community Cohesion Practitioner Group on policing and crime is developing a definition of what community cohesion means in the context of policing. There is also a range of work underway embedding and mainstreaming community cohesion within the police reform programme. This includes:

- the first 'National Policing Plan' reflects the importance of community cohesion, and this is critical as it will determine the national policing agenda;
- the Police Performance Assessment Framework will include indicators to measure forces' performance in building cohesive communities;
- the government, together with Association of Chief Police Officers (ACPO) and practitioners, is currently developing and sharing good practice so that forces are able to systematically identify priority areas where social tension is high or rising and why, and to commit resources necessary to achieve long-term change. These include: NCF guidance on policing community disorder, ACPO operational guidance on the management of inter-ethnic conflict, and further ACPO work on effective community involvement and the development of tactical policing options to support community cohesion;
- the full establishment of the National Centre for Policing Excellence in April 2003 will be an important part of developing knowledge and expertise in community cohesion, and disseminating good practice;
- continue the work to establish a service, which reflects the community it serves and which progresses minority ethnic officers at the same rate

as white colleagues. This will be monitored through the Lawrence Steering Group sub-group on recruitment, retention and progression; and

- for the revised PACE Code A, Centrex, formerly National Police Training (NPT), have prepared a full training package. This includes four packages to cover probationers, substantive constables, supervisors and strategic managers.

The promotion of community cohesion and community safety should be central to the work of the police, and policing strategies and tactics should be consistent with approaches that support the achievement of those objectives. The reasons why communities fragment can be varied, but disproportionate vulnerability, high crime levels and the alienation of young people can all play a part. It is critical that forces are able to systematically identify 'priority areas' where social tension is high or rising, identify the causes and commit the resources necessary to sustain long-term change. In this context, the ability of forces to support neighbourhood renewal initiatives in partnership with local authorities and other agencies will be of particular importance to crime reduction.

The government, together with ACPO, and the policing and crime practitioner group, is currently developing best practice and guidance for this work and forces should look to embed it into 'mainstream policing'.

What local authorities can do

Local authorities have a statutory requirement to work with police and others on crime and disorder. They are also required to consider the impact of crime and disorder on the exercise of all their functions. These requirements are in place to reflect the seriousness of the impact of crime and disorder on individuals and the effects on community cohesion. Delivery of local authority services must be reviewed against their contribution to reducing crime and disorder and raising community safety. Some local authorities have raised their commitment to CDRPs by creating multi-disciplinary teams to support service delivery. This provides senior level input into the partnerships, resource allocation, leadership and a strong sense of ownership.

For example working in partnership on issues such as removing provocative graffiti and raising awareness across communities, contributes to maintaining civic pride, increasing local ownership and securing collective responsibility for neighbourhoods.

The role of police authorities

It is the job of police authorities to make sure that there is an efficient and effective local police force, which gives best value to the whole local community. Police authorities set the strategic direction for the force through three-year strategic and annual policing plans, and hold the chief constables' to account on behalf of the local community for the policing service delivered through consultation and dialogue. Police authorities are increasingly building strong links between individual members of the police authority and divisional commanders at Basic Command Unit (BCU) level and the performance assessment framework being developed for policing will increasingly focus attention on monitoring at BCU level.

The relevant police authority member can therefore act as a powerful bridge between discussions between partners at BCU level, and the strategic considerations of the police authority and chief constable of the force.

Crack down on crime

- Ensure CDRP's have effective stakeholder representation (including a housing association (or RSL) nominated representative) on the partnership body in addition to active involvement in task groups addressing key objective areas.
- Establish targets and actions with the crime and disorder strategy, ensuring that these are reviewed and measured.
- Ensure that there are good relations between police authorities and forces and the local authority with regular meetings to ensure close working.
- Review with the police authority and force the incidence of crime and anti-social behaviour generally and at the local and neighbourhood community level; take account of existing and developing strategic policing plans in drawing up local strategies through the CDRPs; and, work with the police authority and force to ensure that police, local authority and other community safety resources are appropriately targeted.

- Review and assess local authorities' contribution to crime reduction and safer more cohesive communities across the full range of their service and strategic responsibilities and to work constructively with the police including the sharing of information.
- Work with the police authorities, forces and other partners to ensure that strong links are developed with all sections of the community through recognisable patch responsibilities, with clear and rapid communication channels, especially with local young people, and the ability to respond to and manage rumours.
- Work with police authorities, forces and other partners to ensure consistent high standards of diversity/community and race relations training in public agencies.
- Encourage effective multi-agency arrangements for addressing racist incidents and where possible set in place third party reporting arrangements. Use these arrangements for monitoring particular hotspots such as badly run pubs that may act as a focal point for racist activities.
- Ensure wide consultation on the crime and disorder reduction partnerships involving all sections of the community. Ensure that the consultative mechanisms used actually reach and actively involve all communities, in particular 'Hard to Reach' groups.
- Discuss with the police authority a strategy to ensure that the police respond to all racist and provocative incidents with vigour on the basis of pre-established routines.
- Develop a contingency plan for any future disturbances and to identify and respond to triggers which may increase community tensions or potential social disorder.

Press and media

Their role and impact

The independent review report, led by Ted Cantle, highlighted the positive and negative roles that the media can play (particularly local and regional media), in framing the perceptions of local people. Many local authorities are all too aware of the power that local and regional press can wield in this respect. There are examples of authorities developing close relations with local papers and other media to promote more positive reporting of events in the community and to promote better liaison between the media and community representatives. This is something that could be essential in helping to dispel rumours and to project clear messages to the whole community. Local authorities should use their own media such as newsletters to promote community cohesion (eg advertise shared activities and successes and bust myths). Positive media relations prove productive in not only building community cohesion, but also in allaying other concerns such as the fear of crime and downturns in local economies.

Sefton Metropolitan Borough Council has worked with the local press to ensure sensitive and balanced reporting of the introduction of asylum seekers and refugees to the area. This is thought to have been a key factor in the welcome that local people have extended to their new neighbours.

Leicester City Council services a community forum chaired by the editor of the Leicester Mercury. This allows a direct channel of communication between community representatives and the local media that is of benefit to all parties.

The Independent Broadcasting Commission is keen that its constituent members develop positive relations with the communities they serve. Offering positions to media representatives on regeneration partnership, the LSPs or community planning forums can help to build positive relations between communities and the media.

A practitioner group focussing on press and media issues will be established working to the independent Community Cohesion Panel and the government's Community Cohesion Unit. Working with the LGA, this group will also look at larger regional and national media, often owned by national conglomerates.

Make sure the press and media hear and see the picture

- Ensure that the press and media are keeping pace with improving community relations and reporting on positive developments as well as setbacks.
- Invite the press and media to discuss a protocol between themselves and other agencies to ensure extremist views do not predominate, nor do such views get reported in ways in which they prey upon fears and prejudice.
- Encourage press and media participation in strategic and delivery partnerships.
- Encourage the press and media to promote a positive view of diversity, dispel ignorance and promote understanding – again covered by a local protocol.
- Consider whether the press and media have fair representation from all sections of the community amongst their staff and offer training in local diversity issues.
- Provide press with information relating to community cohesion activities and achievements.
- Use the local press and media more generally to promote an honest and open dialogue about attitudes, behaviour and culture – again within the protocol.

References

This document refers to many existing guidance notes that are relevant. For ease of reference the key documents are listed below.

Preparing Community Strategies: Government Guidance to Local Authorities
(ODPM, December 2000)

Community Leadership: What is it?
(LGA, March 2001)

The Duty to Promote Race Equality: The statutory code of practice and non-statutory guides for public authorities
(CRE, May 2002)

Faith and Community
(Local Government Association in association with Inner Cities Religious Council, Active Community Unit, Home Office, and the Inter Faith Network for the UK, 2002)

Local Strategic Partnerships: Government Guidance
(ODPM, March 2001)

Representing the People: Democracy and Diversity
(LGA, July 2001)

Hear By Right: Setting Standards for the Active Involvement of Young People in Democracy
(LGA/National Youth Agency, July 2001)

Learning to Listen: Core Principles for the Involvement of Children and Young People
(Children and Young Peoples Unit, November 2001)

Resourcing Excellent Youth Services: Adequacy and Sufficiency Document
(DfES, Dec 2002)

Full and Equal Citizens
(Home Office, November 2000)

Local Cultural Strategies
(DCMS/LGA, December 2000)

A Framework for Partnership
(LGA/National Housing Federation/Housing Corporation, September 2001)

There are further references to more specific guidance on particular issues within the relevant sections of the main body of this document. Full details about LGA publictions can be found on the LGA's website at www.lga.gov.uk

For further information, please contact
the Local Government Association at:

Local Government House,
Smith Square, London SW1P 3HZ
Telephone 020 7664 3000
Fax 020 7664 3030
Email info@lga.gov.uk
Website www.lga.gov.uk

or telephone our information
centre on 020 7664 3131

LGA Code F/EQ005
ISBN 1 84049 313 5

Printed by The Chameleon Press

Appendix C

Three Definitions of Community Cohesion

LGA

'A cohesive community is one where:

There is common vision and a sense of belonging for all communities;
The diversity of people's different backgrounds and circumstances are appreciated and positively valued;
Those from different backgrounds have similar life opportunities; and
Strong and positive relationships are being developed between people from different backgrounds in the workplace, in schools and within neighbourhoods.' LGA (2002)

CIC

'The commission's new definition of an integrated and cohesive community is that it has:

- a defined and widely shared sense of the contribution of different individuals and groups to a future local or national vision
- a strong sense of an individual's local rights and responsibilities
- a strong sense that people with different backgrounds should experience similar life opportunities and access to services and treatment
- a strong sense of trust in institutions locally, and trust that they will act fairly when arbitrating between different interests and be subject to public scrutiny
- a strong recognition of the contribution of the newly arrived, and of those who have deep attachments to a particular place – focusing on what people have in common
- Positive relationships between people from different backgrounds in the workplace, schools and other institutions.' CIC (2007)

CLG

Community Cohesion is what must happen in all communities to enable different groups of people to get on well together. A key contributor to community cohesion is integration which is what must happen to enable new residents and existing residents to adjust to one another.

Our vision of an integrated and cohesive community is based on three foundations:

- People from different backgrounds having similar life opportunities
- People knowing their rights and responsibilities
- People trusting one another and trusting local institutions to act fairly

And three ways of living together:

- A shared future and sense of belonging
- A focus on what new and existing communities have in common, alongside a recognition of the value of diversity
- Strong and positive relationships between people from different backgrounds.'

(CLG, 2008)

References

Audit Commission (2007) *Crossing Borders: Responding to the Local Challenges of Migrant Workers.* London, Audit Commission.

Bachrach, P. and Baratz, M. (1970) *Power and Poverty: Theory and Practice.* Oxford University Press, New York.

Back, L. and Solomos, J. (2000) *Theories of Race and Racism. A Reader.* Routledge, London.

Ballard, R. and Ballard, C. (1977) The Sikhs: The Development of South Asian Settlements in Britain. In: *Between Two Cultures: Migrants and Minorities in Britain,* (ed. J. Watson). Blackwell, Oxford.

Banton, M. (1955) *The Coloured Quarter: Negro Immigrants in an English City.* Jonathan Cape, London.

Banton, M. (1967) *Race Relations.* Tavistock, London.

Banton, M. (1997) *Ethnic and Racial Consciousness.* Longman, London.

BBC News (2006) *Rise of UK's 'inter-ethnic conflicts'.* Available at http://news.bbc.co.uk/1/hi/uk/4989202.stm [accessed 8 August 2011]. British Broadcasting Corporation, London.

BBC News (2010) *BNP vote increases, but fails to win a seat.* Available at http://news.bbc.co.uk/1/hi/uk_politics/election_2010/8667231.stm [accessed 5 August 2011]. British Broadcasting Corporation, London.

Beider, H. (2005) *Housing, Social Capital and Integration.* Paper presented to *ENHR Conference Reykjavik,* 29 June–3 July 2005.

Beider, H. (2006) *Race, Housing and Representation: Towards new approaches for inclusion and empowerment.* Paper presented to *ENHR Conference,* Ljubljana 30 June – 5 July 2006.

Beider, H. (2007a) The Rise and Fall (and Rise) of Community Development Corporations and Black and Minority Ethnic Housing Associations. In: *Housing Markets and Neighbourhood Renewal: Community Engagement in the US and UK.* (ed. H. Beider) Blackwell, Oxford.

Beider, H. (2007b) Towards a New Policy Agenda. In: *Housing Markets and Neighbourhood Renewal: Community Engagement in the US and UK.* (ed. H. Beider), Blackwell, Oxford.

Beider, H. (2011) *Community Cohesion: A White Perspective.* Joseph Rowntree Foundation, York.

Benyon, J. and Solomos, J. (eds.) (1987) *The Roots of Urban Unrest.* Pergamon Press, Oxford.

Bibby, P. (2005) *Report on Change in BME Population 1991–2000: Shared Evidence Base Report West Midlands Regional Housing Strategy.*Government Office West Midlands, Birmingham.

Black Housing (1998) *The 100th Issue.* Federation of Black Housing Organisations, London.

Black Radley (2006) *Community Relations in Lozells: An Outline of Good Practice.,* Black Radley, Birmingham.

Blackaby, B. and Chahal, K. (2000) *Black and Minority Ethnic Housing Strategies: A Good Practice Guide.* Chartered Institute of Housing, Federation of Black Housing Organisations and the Housing Corporation, Coventry.

Race, Housing & Community: Perspectives on Policy & Practice, First Edition.
Harris Beider.
© 2012 Harris Beider. Published 2012 by Blackwell Publishing Ltd.

Bourdieu, P. (1986) The Forms of Capital. In: *Handbook of Theory and Research for the Sociology of Education* (ed. J. Richardson), Macmillan, New York.

Bourne, J. and Sivanandan, A. (1980) Cheerleaders and ombudsmen: the sociology of race relations in Britain. *Race and Class*, **21**, 331–352.

Burnett, J. (2004) Community Cohesion and the State. *Race and Class*, **45**(3), 1–18.

Burney, E. (1967) *Housing on Trial: A Study of Immigrants and Local Government.*, Oxford University Press, London.

Cameron, D. (2011) *Speech at Munich Security Conference*. February 5, 2011. Available at http://www.number10.gov.uk/news/speeches-and-transcripts/2011/02/pms-speech-at-munich-security-conference-60293. [accessed 06/02/2011].

Cantle, T. (2008) *Community Cohesion: A New Framework for Race and Diversity*. Palgrave. London.

CARF (2001) Burying Macpherson. *CARF*, **59**, December 2000/January 2001.

Carter, B., Harris, C. and Joshi, S. (1987) The 1951–55 Conservative government and the racialisation of black immigration. *Policy Papers in Ethnic Relations No.11*, University of Warwick, CRER, Warwick.

Castles, S. and Kosack, G. (1973) *Immigrant Workers and the Class Structure in Western Europe*. Oxford University Press, London.

Centre for Contemporary Cultural Studies (CCCS) (1982) *The Empire Strikes Back*. Hutchinson, London.

CEP (2010) *Immigration and the UK Labour Market: The Evidence from Economic Research*. CEP, London.

Chahal, K. and Julienne, L. (1999) *We Can't All Be White: Racist Victimisation in the UK*. Joseph Rowntree Foundation, York.

Chartered Institute of Housing (CIH) (2005) Non-Standard Mortgages for Purchasing Social Dwellings. *Response to the ODPM consultation on helping tenants in social housing buy their home using Islamic and other non-standard finance products*. CIH, London.

CIH (2005) *The Future of BME Housing Associations*. CIH, Coventry.

Commission on Integration and Cohesion (CIC) (2007) *Our Shared Future*. DCLG, London.

Commission for Racial Equality (CRE) (1984a) *Race and Council Housing in Hackney*. CRE, London.

Commission for Racial Equality (CRE) (1984b) *Race and Housing in Liverpool. A Research Report*. CRE, London.

Communities and Local Government (CLG) (2008) *National Indicators for Local Authorities and Local Authority Partnerships: Handbook of Definitions*. DCLG, London.

Crenson, M. (1971) *The Un-Politics of Air Pollution: A Study of Non-Decision Making in the Cities*. Johns Hopkins Press, Baltimore.

Daniel, W. (1968) *Racial Disadvantage in England*. Penguin, Harmondsworth.

Dayha, B. (1974) The nature of Pakistani ethnicity in industrial cities in Britain. In: *Urban Ethnicity*, (ed. A. Cohen). Tavistock, London.

Dench, G., Gavron, K. and Young, M. (2006) *The New East End: Kinship, Race and Conflict*. Profile Books, London.

Denham, J. (2009) *Connecting Communities*. Speech by Communities Secretary John Denham at the Institute for Community Cohesion on Connecting Communities. 14 October 2009.

Department of Work and Pensions (DWP) (2007) Persistent Employment Disadvantage. DWP, London.

Dyer, R. (1988) White, *Screen*, **29**(4) 44–45.

Eatwell, R. and Goodwin, M. (eds.) (2009) *The New Extremism in 21ˢᵗ Century Britain*. Routledge, London.

Equality and Human Rights Commission (EHRC) (2010) *How Fair is Britain? The First Triennial Review*. EHRC, Manchester.

Fanshawe, S. and Sriskandarajah, D. (2010) *You Can't Put Me In A Box: Super-Diversity and the End of Identity Politics in Britain*. London, Institute for Public Policy Research.

FBHO (2000) *FBHO Annual Report 1999/2000*. Federation of Black Housing Organisations, London.

Fenton, A., Tyler, P., Markkanen, S., Clarke, A. and Whitehead, C. (2010) *Why do Neighbourhoods Stay Poor? People, Place and Deprivation in Birmingham*. Barrow Cadbury Trust.

Ferrari, E. and Lee, P. (2007) A United Kingdom? Changing Spatial, Ethnic and Tenure Patterns in England. In: *Housing Markets and Neighbourhood Renewal: Community Engagement in the US and UK*. (ed. H. Beider) Blackwell, Oxford.

Flett, H. (1979) Dispersal policies in council housing: arguments and evidence. *New Community*, **7**, 184–194.

Flint, J. and Robinson, D. (2008) *Community Cohesion in Crisis?* Policy Press, Bristol.

Forrest, R. and Murie, A. (1983) Residualisation and council housing: aspects of the changing social relations of housing tenure. *Journal of Social Policy*, **12**, 453–468.

Fryer, P. (1984) *Staying Power. The History of Black People in Britain*. Pluto Press, London.

Future Shape of the Sector Commission (2006) *Working Brief*. London and Quadrant Group, London.

Garner, S. (2006) The uses of whiteness: what sociologists working on Europe can draw from US work on whiteness. *Sociology*, **40**(2) 257–275.

Garner, S. (2009) Home Truths: The White Working Class and the Racialisation of Housing in Contemporary Britain. In: *Perspectives: Who Cares About the White Working Class?* (ed. K. Sveinsson), Runnymede Trust, London.

Giddens, A. (1976) *New Rules of Sociological Method*. Hutchinson, London.

Gilroy, P. (1987) *There Ain't No Black in the Union Jack*. Hutchinson, London.

Glass, R. (1960) *Newcomers: West Indians in London*. Allen and Unwin, London.

Goodhart, D. (2004) Too Diverse? In: *Prospect*, February 2004.

Goodson, L. and Beider, H. (2005) *BME Communities in the Eastern Corridor: Aspirations, Neighbourhood 'Choice' and Tenure*. Birmingham City Council, Birmingham.

Goodwin, M. (2009) In Search of the Winning Formula: Nick Griffin and the 'Modernisation' of the British National Party. In: *The New Extremism in 21ˢᵗ Century Britain*. (eds. R. Eatwell and M. Goodwin) Routledge, London.

Goulbourne, H. (ed.) (1990) *Black Politics in Britain*. Avebury, Aldershot.

Greater London Authority (GLA) (2005) *London's Changing Population, Diversity of a World City in the 21st Century. Data Management and Analysis Group Briefing 2005/39*. Greater London Authority, London.

Gryszel-Fieldsned, T. and Reeve, K. (2007) *The Housing Pathways of Polish New Immigrants in Sheffield*. CRESR: Sheffield Hallam, Sheffield.

The Guardian (2008) Q&A: Ujima Housing Association, *The Guardian*, 16 January 2008.

Hall, S. (1980) Cultural Studies: Two Paradigms, *Media, Culture & Society*, **2**(1), 57–72.

Hamnett, C. and Butler, T. (2010) The Changing Ethnic Structure of Housing Tenures in London, 1991–2001 *Urban Studies*, **47**(1), 55–74.

Hann, C. and Bowes, E. (2004) *The Housing Corporation's BME Housing Policy: Assessing its Impact*. The Housing Corporation, London.

Harris, G. (2010) The Politics of the Far Right in London: Challenges to Diversity. Presentation delivered at the iCoCo/Manchester University, *ESRC Seminar Community Cohesion and the Politics of the Far Right*, University of Manchester, 25 March 2010.

Harrison, M. (1995) *Housing, 'Race', Social Policy and Empowerment*. Avebury, Aldershot.

Harrison, M. and Davis, C. (2001) *Housing, Social Policy and Difference: Disability, Gender, Ethnicity and Housing*. Policy Press, Bristol.

Harrison, M., Karmani, A., Law, I., Phillips, D. and Ravetz, A. (1996) *Black and Minority Ethnic Housing Associations: An Evaluation of the Housing Corporation's Black and Minority Ethnic Housing Association Strategies*, Source Research 16. The Housing Corporation, London.

Harrison, M. and Phillips, D. (2003) *Housing and Black and Minority Ethnic Communities. Review of the Evidence Base.* Office of the Deputy Prime Minister, London.

Harrison, M. Phillips, D., Chahal, K. Hunt, L. and Perry, J. (2005) *Housing, 'Race' and Community Cohesion.* CIH. Coventry.

Haylett, C. (2000) 'This is about Us, This is Our Film!' Personal and Popular Discourses of 'Underclass'. In:, *Cultural Studies and the Working Class: Subject to Change*, (ed. S. Munt), 69–84. Routledge, London.

Henderson, J. and Karn, V. (1987) *Race, Class and State Housing. Inequality in the Allocation of Public Housing in Britain.* Gower, Aldershot.

Hoggett, P. (1992) A place for experience: a psychoanalytic perspective on boundary, identity and culture, *Environment and Planning D: Society and Space*, **10**, 345–356.

Home Office (1999) *The Stephen Lawrence Inquiry: Report of an Inquiry by Sir William Macpherson of Cluny*, Cm 4262–1. HMSO, London.

Home Office (2001) *Community Cohesion: A Report of the Independent Reviewing Team.* HMSO, London.

Home Office (2007) *Accession Monitoring Report A8 Countries May 2004–March 2007.* HMSO, London.

Homes and Communities Agency (HCA) (2009) *Our Single Equality Scheme: Diverse Interventions.* HCA, London.

Housing Corporation (1992) *An Independent Future: Black and Minority Ethnic Housing Association Strategy 1992–1996.* Housing Corporation, London.

Housing Corporation (1998) *Black and Minority Ethnic Housing Policy.* Housing Corporation, London.

Housing Corporation (2002) *Regulatory Code Good Practice Note.* Housing Corporation, London.

Housing Corporation (2003) *Equality & Diversity. Policy & Strategies.* Housing Corporation, London.

Housing Corporation (2004a) *BME Association Rent Restructuring Grant Announced.* The Housing Corporation, London.

Housing Corporation (2004b) *Regulatory Code Good Practice Note.* Housing Corporation, London.

Housing Corporation (2008) *Report of the Ujima Inquiry.* The Housing Corporation, London.

Inside Housing (2001) *FBHO Slams Cohesion Chair's Comments.* 2 December 2001.

Inside Housing (2007) *Cameron Blames Division on Multicultural Approach.* 1 February 2007.

Inside Housing (2008) *Ujima: why didn't anyone step in?* 6 June 2008.

Inside Housing (2009) *Mixed Messages.* 20 March 2009.

Inside Housing (2010) *Gypsy Sites Budget Cut After £15m Underspend.* 20 August 2010.

Jacobs, M. (1988) Margaret Thatcher and the Inner Cities, *Economic and Political Weekly,* **23**(38), 17 September 1988.

Jenkins, R. (1967) Address by the Home Secretary to the Institute, *Race and Class,* **8**, 215–221.

Joyce, P. (1995) *The Oxford Reader on Class.* Oxford University Press, Oxford.

Katz, B. (2004) *Neighbourhoods of Choice and Connection: The Evolution of American Neighbourhood Policy and What It Means for the United Kingdom.* Brookings Institution, Washington DC.

Katznelson, I. (1973) *Black Men, White Cities: Race, Politics & Migration in the United States 1900–30 & Britain 1948–68.* Oxford University Press, Oxford.

Koscielak, M. (2007) *Migrant Worker Network Development Project Report.* CVS, Exeter.

Kudnani, A. (2002) The Death of Multiculturalism, *Race and Class,* **43**.

Kyambi, S. (2005) *New Immigrant Communities: New Integration Challenges?* Institute for Public Policy Research, London.

Lawrence, E. (1982) Just Plain Common Sense: The 'Roots' of Racism. In: *The Empire Strikes Back: Race and Racism in 70s Britain,* (ed. Centre for Contemporary Cultural Studies). Hutchinson, London.

Layton-Henry, Z. (1984) *The Politics of Race in Britain.* Allen and Unwin, London.

Lee, T. (1977) *Race and Residence. The Concentration and Dispersal of Immigrants in London.* Clarendon Press, Oxford.

Levitas, R. (1998) *The Inclusive Society? Social Exclusion and New Labour.* Macmillan, Basingstoke.

LGA (2004) *Community Cohesion: An Action Guide.* LGA, London.

Little, K. (1947) *Negroes in Britain: A Study of Race Relations in English Society.* Routledge and Kegan Paul, London.

Lupton, M. and Perry, J. (2004) *The Future of BME Housing Associations.* Chartered Institute of Housing, Coventry.

Madood, T., Berthoud, R., Lakey, J., Nazroo, J., Smith, P., Virdee, S. and Beishon, S. (1997) *Ethnic Minorities in Britain: Diversity and Disadvantage.* Policy Studies Institute, London,

Malpass, P. (2008) Housing and the New Welfare State: wobbly pillar or cornerstone? *Housing Studies,* **23**(1), 1–19.

Malpass, P. and Murie, A. (1994) *Housing Policy and Practice.* 4th Edition. Macmillan, London.

Markkanen, S. (2009) *Looking to the Future: Changing Black and Minority Ethnic Housing Needs and Aspirations.* Race Equality Foundation, London.

MDA (2004) *Evaluation of the Housing Corporation's BME Housing Policy.* Managing Diversity Associates, London.

Miles, R. (1982) *Racism and Migrant Labour.* Routledge and Kegan Paul, London.

Miles, R. (1995) *Racism.* Routledge, London.

Miles, R. and Phizacklea, A. (1984) *White Man's Country.* Pluto Press, London.

Mullins, D. and Goodson, L., Phillimore, J., Beider, H. and Jones, P. (2007) *Final Report Accommodate Project.* HACT, London.

Mullins, D., Beider, H. and Rowlands, R. (2004) *Empowering Communities, Improving Housing: Involving Black and Minority Ethnic Tenants and Communities.* ODPM, London.

Murray, C. (1996) The Emerging British Underclass. In: *Charles Murray and the Underclass: The Developing Debate* (ed. R. Lister). IEH, London.

National Community Forum (2009) *Sources of Resentment and Perceptions of Ethnic Minorities Among Poor White People in England.* NCF/CLG, London.

National Equality Panel (2010) *An Anatomy of Economic Inequality in the UK: Report of the National Equality Panel (Jan 2010).* Government Equalities Office, London.

National Housing Federation (2001) *Race and Housing Inquiry Challenge Report.* NHF, London.

Nayak, A. (2009) Beyond the Pale: Chavs, Youth and Social Class. In: *Perspectives: Who Cares About the White Working Class?* (ed. K. Sveinsson). Runnymede Trust, London.

Netto, G. and Beider, H. (2011) Minority Ethnic Communities and Housing: Access, Experiences and Participation. In: *Understanding 'Race' and 'Ethnicity',* (ed. G. Craig). Policy Press, Bristol.

Newman, P. (2007) 'Back the bid': the 2012 summer Olympics and the governance of London, *Journal of Urban Affairs.* **29**(3), 255–267.

Newton, K. (1976) *Second City Politics.* Clarendon Press, Oxford.

Niner, P. (2006) Accommodating Nomadism? An examination of accommodation options for Gypsies and Travellers in England, *Housing Studies,* **19**(2), 141–159.

Notting Hill Housing Trust (2008) *Rethinking BME Housing.* Notting Hill Housing Trust, London.

Office of the Deputy Prime Minister (ODPM)/Social Exclusion Unit (2004) *The Drivers of Social Exclusion: a Review of the Literature – Summary.* ODPM, London.

Office for National Statistics (ONS) (2005) *Total International Migration (TIM) estimates.* ONS, London.

Office for National Statistics (ONS) (2009) *Migration Statistics.* ONS, London.

Patterson, S. (1963) *Dark Strangers.* Harmondsworth Press, London.Pawson, H. and Mullins, D. (2010) *After Council Housing, Britain's New Social Landlords.* Palgrave Macmillan, Basingstoke.

Peach, C. (1968) *West Indian Migration to Britain: A Social Geography.* University Press, Oxford.

Phillimore, J. (2010) Refugees, Acculturation Strategies, Stress and Integration. *Journal of Social Policy,* **40**(3), 575–593.

Phillimore, J. and Goodson, L. (2006) Problem or Opportunity? Asylum Seekers, Refugees, Employment and Social Exclusion in Deprived Urban Areas, *Urban Studies,* **43**(10), 1–22.

Phillimore, J. and Goodson, L. (2008) Making a Place in the Global City-The Relevance of Indicators of Integration, *Journal of Refugee Studies,* **21**, 305–325.

Phillips, D. (1998) Black minority ethnic concentration, segregation and dispersal in Britain, *Urban Studies,* **35**, 1681–1702.

Phillips, D. (2006) Black minority ethnic concentration, segregation and dispersal in Britain. *Urban Studies,* **35**(1), 1681–1702.

Phillips, D. and Harrison, M. (2010) Constructing an integrated society: historical lessons for tackling black and minority ethnic housing segregation in Britain. *Housing Studies,* **25**(2), 221–237.

Phillips, T. (2005) *After 7/7: Sleeping Walking to Segregation.* Speech given to Manchester Council for Community Relations, 22 September 2005.

Pollard, N., Latorre, M. and Sriskandarajah, D. (2008) *Floodgates or Turnstiles? Post-EU Enlargement Migration Flows to (and from) the UK. London.* IPPR. 21.

Putnam, R. (2000) *Bowling Alone. The Collapse and Revival of Community in America.* Simon Schuster, New York.

Putnam, R. (2007) *E Pluribus Unum*: Diversity and Community in the Twenty-first Century: The 2006 Johan Skytte Prize Lecture, *Scandinavian Political Studies*, **30**(2), 137–174.

Raisborough, J. and Adams, M. (2008) Mockery and Morality in Popular Cultural Representations of the White, Working Class, *Sociological Research Online*, 13(6), 2.

Ratcliffe, P. (1981) *Racism and Reaction: A Profile of Handsworth*, Routledge and. Kegan Paul, London.

Ratcliffe, P. (1996) Social geography and ethnicity: a theoretical, conceptual and substantive overview. In: *Social Geography and Ethnicity in Britain: Geographical Spread, Spatial Concentration and Internal Migration. (Ethnicity in the 1991 Census, Volume 3).* (ed. P. Ratcliffe). HMSO, London.

Ratcliffe, P. (2000) "Race", Ethnicity and Housing Decisions: rational choice theory and the choice-constraint debate. In: *Rational Choice Theory: Resisting Colonisation* (ed. M. Archer and J. Tritter). Routledge, London.

Ratcliffe, P. (2009) Re-evaluating the links between race and residence. In: *Rethinking Race and Residence* (ed. H. Beider), Special Issue of *Housing Studies*.

Ratcliffe, P. Harrison, M., Hogg, R., Line, B., Phillips, D. and Tomlins, R. (2001) *Breaking Down Barriers – Improving Asian Access to Social Rented Housing.* CIH, London.

Rex, J. (1983) *Race Relations in Sociological Theory*, 2nd Edition. Routledge and Kegan Paul, London.

Rex, J. and Moore, R. (1967) *Race, Community and Conflict.* Oxford University Press, London.

Rex, J. and Tomlinson, S. (1979) *Colonial Immigrants in a British City.* Routledge and Kegan Paul, London.

Richmond, A. (1954) *Colour Prejudice in Britain. A Study of West Indian Workers in Liverpool, 1942–51.* Routledge and Kegan Paul, London.

Roberts, K. (2001) *Class in Modern Britain.* Palgrave, Basingstoke.

Robinson, D. (2007) Living Parallel Lives? Housing, Residential Segregation and Community Cohesion in England. In: *Housing Markets and Neighbourhood Renewal: Community Engagement in the US and UK* (ed. H. Beider). Blackwell, Oxford.

Robinson, D. and Reeve, K. (2006) *Neighbourhood Experiences of New Immigration: Reflections from the Evidence Base.* Joseph Rowntree Foundation, York.

Robinson, V. (1986) *Transients, Settlers, and Refugees: Asians in Britain.* Clarendon Press, Oxford.

Royce, C. (1996) *Financing Black and Minority Ethnic Housing Associations.* Joseph Rowntree Foundation, York.

Rutter, J. and Latorre, M. (2009) *Social Housing Allocation and Immigrant Communities.* Equalities and Human Rights Commission, Manchester.

Salt, J. (2004) *International Migration and the United Kingdom: Report of the United Kingdom*, SOPEMI Correspondent to the OECD, 2004: Migration Research Unit, University College London, London.

Sarre, P., Phillips, D. and Skellington, R. (1989) *Ethnic Minority Housing: Explanations and Policies.* Avebury, Aldershot.

Saunders, P. (1990) *A Nation of Homeowners.* Unwin, London.

Scarman, L. (1981) *The Scarman Report: The Brixton Disorders 10–12 April 1981/Report of an Inquiry by the Right Honourable the Lord Scarman*, Presented to Parliament by the Secretary of State for the Home Department. HMSO, London.

Shelter (2000) *Immigration and Housing Fact Sheet*. Shelter, London.

Simpson, A. (1981) Stacking the Decks. A Study of Race, Inequality and Council Housing in Nottingham. Nottingham Community Relations Council Nottingham.

Sivanandan, A. (1982) *A Different Hunger. Writings on Black Resistance*. Pluto Press, London.

Sivanandan, A. (2000) Speech given at the *Reclaiming the Struggle Conference*, 19 February, London.

Skeggs, B. (2005) The Making of Class and Gender through Visualizing Moral Subject Formation, *Sociology*, **39**(5), 965–982.

Skeggs, B. (2009) Haunted by the Spectre of Judgement: Respectability, Value and Affect in Class Relations. In: *Perspectives: Who Cares About the White Working Class?* (ed. K. Sveinsson). Runnymede Trust, London.

Smith, S. (1989) *The Politics of 'Race' and Residence*. Polity Press, London.

Social Exclusion Unit (2000) *Minority Ethnic Issues in Social Exclusion and Neighbourhood Renewal*. HMSO, London.

Solomos, J. (1986) Trends in the political analysis of racism, *Political Studies*, **XXXIV**(2), 313–324.

Solomos, J. (1993) *Race and Racism in Britain*. 2nd Edition. Macmillan, London.

Solomos, J. and Back, L. (1995) *Race, Politics and Social Change*. Routledge, London.

Somerville, P. and Steele, A. (2002) *'Race', Housing and Social Exclusion*. Jessica Kingsley, London.

Somerville, W., Sriskandarajah, D. and Latorre, M. (2010) *United Kingdom: A Reluctant Country of Immigration*. MPI, London.

Spencer, S., Ruhs, M., Anderson, B. & Rogaly, B. (2007) *Migrant Lives Beyond the Workplace: The Experiences of Centre and East Europeans in the UK*. Joseph Rowntree Foundation, York.

Staniewicz, T. (2007) *A Critical Evaluation of Factors Inhibiting A8 Polish Migrants' Full Participation in Civil Society*. Centre for Rights, Equality and Diversity, London.

Stewart, J. (2006) A Banana Republic? The Investigation into Electoral Fraud by the Birmingham Election Court, *Parliamentary Affairs*, **59**(4), 654–667.

Sveinsson, K. (ed.) (2009) *Perspectives: Who Cares About the White Working Class?* Runnymede Trust, London.

Venkatesh, S. (2000) *American Project: The Rise and Fall of the Modern Ghetto*. Harvard University Press, Cambridge MA.

Vertovec, S. (2007) *New Complexities of Cohesion in Britain: Super-Diversity, Transnationalism and Civil-Integration*. CIC, London.

Weber, M. (1976) *The Protestant Ethic and the Spirit of Capitalism*, (trans. T. Parsons). Allen and Unwin, London.

Whitehead, C., Marshall, D., Royce, C., Saw, P. and Woodrow, J. (1998) *A Level Playing Field? Rents, Viability and Value in BME Housing Associations*. Joseph Rowntree Foundation, York.

Worley, C. (2005) 'It's not about race. It's about the community': New Labour and 'community cohesion', *Critical Social Policy*, **25**(4), 483–496.

Young, M. and Willmott, P. (1957) *Family and Kinship in East London*. Routledge and Kegan Paul, London.

Index

Race, Housing & Community: Perspectives on Policy & Practice, First Edition.
Harris Beider.
© 2012 Harris Beider. Published 2012 by Blackwell Publishing Ltd.